T0295704

CHANGE OF CHINA'S RURAL COMMUNITY
A Case Study of
Zhejiang's Jianshanxia Village

WSPC-ZJUP Series on China's Regional Development

Print ISSN: 2661-3883
Online ISSN: 2661-3891

Series Editor
SHI Jinchuan *(School of Economics, Zhejiang University, China)*

Advisory Board Members
GU Yikang *(China Academy for Rural Development, Zhejiang University, China)*
MAO Dan *(School of Public Affairs, Zhejiang University, China)*
LU Lijun *(Zhejiang Institute of Administration, China)*
CHEN Lixu *(Zhejiang Institute of Administration, China)*
CHEN Shengyong *(School of Public Administration, Zhejiang Gongshang University, China)*

Since China's reform and opening-up in 1978, the world's most populous country has enjoyed rapid economic development. This book series sheds new light on China's phenomenal success by examining its regional development and disparity. The series starts from first few volumes focusing on Zhejiang province, one of the country's forerunners in economic, social and political transformation. These volumes analyse Zhejiang's local governance innovation, regional economic development, and social and cultural changes over the past few decades.

Published:

WSPC-ZJUP Series on China's Regional Development – Vol. 3

CHANGE OF CHINA'S RURAL COMMUNITY
A Case Study of Zhejiang's Jianshanxia Village

MAO Dan

Zhejiang University, China

ZHEJIANG UNIVERSITY PRESS
浙江大学出版社

World Scientific

NEW JERSEY · LONDON · SINGAPORE · BEIJING · SHANGHAI · HONG KONG · TAIPEI · CHENNAI · TOKYO

Published by

World Scientific Publishing Co. Pte. Ltd.
5 Toh Tuck Link, Singapore 596224
USA office: 27 Warren Street, Suite 401-402, Hackensack, NJ 07601
UK office: 57 Shelton Street, Covent Garden, London WC2H 9HE

and

Zhejiang University Press
No. 148, Tianmushan Road
Xixi Campus of Zhejiang University
Hangzhou 310028, China

Library of Congress Cataloging-in-Publication Data
Names: Mao, Dan, author. | World Scientific Publishing Co.
Title: Change of China's rural community : a case study of Zhejiang's Jianshanxia Village /
      Mao Dan, Zhejiang University, China.
Description: Hackensack, New Jersey : World Scientific Publishing Co. Pte. Ltd. |
      Zhejiang University Press, 2019. | Series: WSPC-ZJUP Series on China's regional
      development ; volume 3 | Includes bibliographical references.
Identifiers: LCCN 2019031074| ISBN 9789813279551 (Hardcover)
Subjects: LCSH: Rural industries--China--Zhejiang Sheng. |
      Industrialization--China--Zhejiang Sheng.
Classification: LCC HC428.Z454 M36 2019 | DDC 354.5095124/2--dc23
LC record available at https://lccn.loc.gov/2019031074

British Library Cataloguing-in-Publication Data
A catalogue record for this book is available from the British Library.

This edition is jointly published by World Scientific Publishing Co. Pte. Ltd. and Zhejiang University
Press. This edition is distributed outside the Chinese mainland by WorldScientific Publishing Co. Pte. Ltd.

For any available supplementary material, please visit
https://www.worldscientific.com/worldscibooks/10.1142/11252#t=suppl

Desk Editors: Anthony Alexander/Lixi Dong

Typeset by Stallion Press
Email: enquiries@stallionpress.com

Preface

This book focuses on the observation and interpretation of the industrialization of a mountain village in Zhejiang Province in the 1980s and 1990s, and its corresponding organizational changes. The field work I did for this book was completed between 1995 and 1997. The manuscript was roughly completed in 1998 and was first published in 2000 in Xuelin Press.

I observed that as a small mountain village far from the city, Jianshanxia Village used the only, contingent funds and years of accumulated village collective organizational framework in the 1980s and 1990s, boldly ran the rural industry, cracked open the market gap as the township enterprise and made efforts to change the villagers' life and the village appearance. According to their own understanding of the happy life of the city dwellers, the unit was positioned as the organization mode for common prosperity and betterment of society, and the path of industrialization and unitization was adopted, namely, to run a factory or a unit like a city dweller. In this way, the village quickly held a large share of the domestic electric mosquito repellent market during this period. Villagers' income, village appearance, village collective's economic strength have all been greatly improved, contributing to the success of the popular model village in Xiaoshan of Zhejiang. Looking back today, we still have to say that the village was a miracle and a typical example of the emergence of township enterprises.

Change of China's Rural Community:
A Case Study of Zhejiang's Jianshanxia Village

As one of the first studies of Chinese villages since the reform and opening-up, this book has had an impact in the field of Chinese sociological research and rural sociology since its publication. Some overseas colleges and universities include it under designated reference books on China's rural industrialization. The concept of unit village put forward in this book has been given importance by some colleagues and also cited to generalize and analyze the phenomenon and process of collective industry run by village cooperatives in other areas. Of course, this concept or term has been ridiculed to the effect that the unit and the system of unit form a phenomenon of the state's adjustment and control of the urban society and is not suitable for discussion in the context of countryside. In fact, there is a clear understanding and discussion about units in the introduction to this book. The so-called unit in this book refers to the villagers trying to run a village like city dwellers in the process of learning how to run a factory like a city dweller; it includes the farmers' understanding and expectation of the life in the city, contains the complex organizational resources accumulated by the rural collectivization and the People's Commune system as the unit variation and also includes the changes to the village society caused by running the unit. This is an observed fact or phenomenon, not a deliberate fiction, and it shows the effects, illusions and even shadows of urban units as urban–rural dualization and the marked signs of inequality to the countryside for many years.

Generally speaking, of course, it was regarded as socialism and as a guaranteed way of production and life that deserved to be pursued by rural residents as the beautiful dreams of the peasants. Typical units are run by the state, and resources are always supplied by the state. Villages do not have the national resources to establish and maintain units. Let's not discuss whether the unitization is good or not. Was the unit village ever really in a condition to run a unit? Back in the 1990s, as in units, they were under market pressure, villages often lacked human resources, capital and organizational management mechanisms. After 1995, the unitization path for the village started becoming increasingly

narrower, and various setbacks were encountered. Of course, the most direct setback was that the business decisions in the village were too advanced, which directly affected the operation of the village industry and shrunk until the interpretation of the capital maintenance capacity of the village unit. In 1995, the village introduced the most advanced paper diaper production line from Italy, which cost nearly 10 million yuan. The product category, quality and price were all ahead of the domestic market for more than 10 years, and each piece cost 7 or 8 yuan. Prices were wish at the time, and two days of production would have to be sold for a full year. When this production line was open, on the one hand, the need to guide market consumption, solve the capital supply capacity and so on obviously exceeded the upper limit of the management control of the village at that time, increasing the financial chain burden on the village industrial production. On the other hand, around 1997, the state and local loans to township enterprises became increasingly tighter, until the rejection of loans, the village was in deep capital chain crisis. In order to solve the production dilemma and solve the debt problem, both the town and village levels chose the property right reform in the strategy, transformed the factory system into the shareholding system, made the main operator raise funds as the controlling large shareholder, at the same time, keeping the agreed amount of return on financial support to the village collective. However, in hindsight, the result of the transformation was only the settlement of the village's debts and the maintenance of the villagers' employment opportunities in the factory. However, the crisis of the enterprise operation itself and the village unit development mode behind it could obviously not be solved through the reform of the property right system advocated by the government.

My observations ended on the day of the 1997 village restructuring convention. On the last two pages of the book, I couldn't help but write a little obscure comment expressing my worries: "all those who have gone through the process of transformation feel that some of the most important things in the village have obviously changed: look at the city, the city people's units were suddenly out of fashion; look at the village, the village no longer has the strength to learn people from the city units. Suddenly, people don't seem to think it's a satisfactory way to end. More importantly, it seems that no one can really predict the way in which the villages will go after the disintegration of the unit system. Uncertainty about the future can sometimes be confusing!" This is probably the only part in the book that expresses one's mind. I also clearly remember that when I finished writing this paragraph in the office of Ouyang Chunmei Building, Yuquan Campus, Zhejiang University, I was moved to tears. In the end, I had to laugh at the observer's due objective yardstick, which was finally not observed, and reluctantly calmed down. The village situation was later more serious than I prejudged at the time. After restructuring, the situation of production and operation was not reversed quickly; staff and workers under the stock system were not used to the new management system. Most crucially, when the financial crisis hit in 1998, the local government completely stopped lending to the village industrial group. The restructured enterprise still close to the village collective was finally unable to carry the debt, declared bankruptcy and was transferred. The production brand has since been withdrawn from the market. Although the new owner of the business continued to produce mosquito repellent, and still hired villagers as much as possible, the relationship with the village collective had been loosened. There was at least a complete end to the path of the unitization of the village, and the economic ability of the village collective organization of the village affairs was almost exhausted.

In November 2017, I made a brief return visit to the Jianshanxia Village in order to understand the general situation of the village after 1997 for the purpose of the translation of the book. I ran into some of the villagers, especially those who went out from the factory after 1998 to set up their own businesses successfully, who lamented that several batches of operators had been trained in the village-run enterprise. They called the leader of Jianshanxia Village the Principal of Huangpu

Military Academy in Jianshanxia Village and also calculated their respective periods. When I visited the Principal, I deliberately changed my sentence and asked him what regrets he had, to the following effect: If you were to go back to work that year, what would you not do? After a little bit of meditation, the principal said that the production line was put into production too early and took up the money. If the factory was able to carry on for 10 years after introducing this production line, it would be the time for similar products to open the market on a large scale in the country in the next 10 years. That would be completely different. Second, electric mosquito-repellent incense tablets occupied most of the national market for a few years. In the mode of management, because of the system and the quality of the management, it was obvious that he and the management of the village could not control the loopholes in the operation and management. The trouble with some of the city's state-run units was particularly evident in the factories, especially the distributors, and the salesmen dispatched by the factory were beyond control. They took the goods from the factory and actually sold them, but they claimed that they didn't sell them until the next year at discount. Some money was returned to the factory. In this way, they earned the difference, resulting in years of production loss and difficulty in capital withdrawal. The factory did everything possible to solve the problem, but instead of making money, it turned into a loss. The hole was getting even bigger, and the factory was destroyed. By the time of the 1998 financial crisis, there was no way out. I asked the following: in 1997, did the prescription of restructuring with special effect as a solution to the production and debt crisis count as a wrong prescription by misdiagnosis? At least, at the time, it was thought that solving the restructuring would be a case of catching the bull's nose and simplifying the complicated problem. The "Principal" approved completely, and I was deeply impressed by his reflection.

During my return visit, I learned that since 2000, the village has made every effort to change its decline. However, just as the complete conditions of the unit were not really available, the process of the post-unit village was not smooth. The ability to mobilize the village collective was difficult to recover for a long time. After the factory went bankrupt, the town and village changed the team of the two committees (village committee and village party branch committee) many times, rearranging the relationship between the village and the enterprise and so on. For a time, the "Principal" was asked to return to serve as party branch secretary again. The "Principal", on the other hand, liaised with all kinds of social relations and made great efforts to make use of the geographical environment around the village, especially the 120-million-year-old volcanic eruption site Zainiu Mountain near the village and the folk cultural resources of the "Horse Lantern" festival, which has been circulating in the village for more than 300 years, so as to develop mountain tourism economy, but, after several twists and turns, the results were fruitless. Since then, the village leadership had been shifted several times, but did not reverse the situation. On the contrary, in a decade or so, the interpersonal contradictions, business practices and objective resource inferiority accumulated in the earlier unit process of the village had a lagged outburst phenomenon. In 2014, the village was even designated as a weak and lax village by the local government. This was the bottom of the village development process.

After 2015, the Jianshanxia Village ushered in a new opportunity. In addition to the new competent village committee leaders, more importantly, the surrounding environment had undergone great changes. The trend of other areas in Zhejiang Province to organize the rural environment and develop rural tourism experience, homestay economy and rural tourism economy finally affected the south of Xiaoshan area where the village is located. The government and the villages have been very active. It is understood that the local government and Hangzhou Intime Group signed an agreement with an investment of 20 billion yuan for overall development of an economic zone of homestay facilities in Daicun Town; the government of Daicun Town has received about 4 billion yuan of land consolidation benefits, and has invested 550 million yuan in cooperation with the UK in the establishment of Yawei Public

School in Daicun Town; construction of the national hiking trail and forest road in Xiaoshan has already begun; the high-quality "Fengqing Avenue" from Hangzhou will be extended to Daicun Town by the end of 2017; construction of Hangzhou–Huangshan high-speed railway has begun and passes Daicun Town with a station set. Both the local government and the village have noted the opportunity, found it necessary to cooperate and use the above conditions to improve the village environment and to move toward the development of the tourism economy and the homestay economy. On June 16, 2016, Jianshanxia Village invested 5 million yuan to renovate the village hall as a cultural auditorium and reach the standard of "four-star cultural hall" in Hangzhou. In May 2017, Daicun Town completed acceptance inspection of the upgrading project of the housing demonstration site, which includes one village and one scene (Shiling Park), parking lot, eco-friendly public toilet, guardrails along the road and along the stream, etc., with the total estimated project investment of 6 million yuan. In my view, the construction of the homestay demonstration village, which shows more than half of the progress, is quite impressive. The various designs to be completed in the blueprints look very good. There are 10 new houses in the village with complete certificates, and one demonstration site at the Xiaoshan district level. City dwellers come to the village for holidays every weekend. In the new cultural auditorium, two phrases were written under the sign "livable Jianshanxia". One line is "official language" from the Party and government organizations: "Cultural auditorium, spiritual home", it expresses the guiding will of the party and government departments. The second line in the villagers' own words, "horse lantern and 100-million-year-old volcano gorge in Jianshanxia", expresses that the villagers regard the unique mountain village resources as the golden name card, and are unwilling to fall behind in terms of the homestay economy and rural experience economy.

Looking back 20 years later, the Jianshanxia Village represented a large part of the aborted experiments on rural industrialization, could even be regarded as the aborted rural road to spontaneous industrialization, and of course, could also be regarded as the aborted unitization of the village in the 1980s and 1990s. The basic reason may be that global agricultural products and rural commodity pricing systems forced farmers to turn to industry whenever they had the opportunity, while farmers and rural areas generally did not have the advantages of capital, organization, market, etc. Therefore, the process of rural industrialization, especially the spontaneous promotion of rural industrialization, would always be full of grief, and would inevitably come to an untimely end. However, in general, agriculture is still meaningful even in societies where industry is dominant, and countryside or rural areas are generally meaningful. It is not necessary to blindly embrace the new dogma of "the way out for agriculture, farmer and rural area is beyond them", and simply stick to the old road of farmers' residentialization and rural industrialization. Rural areas and farmers need to find a more viable new path. From the experience of rural restoration in developed countries and the experience of rural change in eastern China in the last 10 years, the better prospect of a village is likely to be in post-production. That is, agricultural modernization cannot be simply expected to improve agricultural production to transform the countryside. This type of rural development path usually leads to overproduction of agricultural products and consequently a large number of rural social problems. Of course, rural industrialization should not be expected to eliminate rural areas. With the support of policies and capital, the proper exploitation of resources in rural areas can be turned around to provide housing function, consumption function, cultural function and environmental protection function so as to form a benign urban and rural organic connection on the basis of new economic and social types. This new type of country is technically known as the post-production country, which is the so-called pastoral community in everyday sense. However, it is necessary to have a conversion condition for the lucid waters and lush mountains to turn into invaluable assets. The successful transformation from a productive country to a rural area depends on a set of conditions. In terms of villages, post-production villages need to be transformed into rural communities, and villagers need to become post-smallholder farmers. This requires the village and the villagers to make a lot of effort to change. In terms of external resource support, what the new village wants to do clearly requires external supply of personnel, money, policies and systems. Taking the work already done in the village as an example, the first major project was to build a four-star cultural auditorium (one of the only two in Xiaoshan) with an investment of 5 million yuan. The town, district and municipal governments supported only about 6 or 700,000 yuan. The village basically exhausted the land transfer funds accumulated by the village collective for this project. The second major project, namely, the construction of the 6 million yuan homestay demonstration village, has been invested with only 3 million yuan and the follow-up funds will mainly rely on the village staff to raise from the government departments. In my view, this is neither a long-term solution nor a real demonstration for other villages. So, I really hope that as regards working together to develop the post-production villages, the villagers, the village organizations and the local government can think alike with concentrated efforts. It is hoped that national and local governments will come up with an integrated approach as soon as possible.

Before the end of the return visit, I stood in the village committee and looked at the slogan on the wall, "horse lantern and 100-million-year-old volcano gorge in Jianshanxia", and once again, the objective observer's position, which has always been deliberately maintained, crossed my mind, and I quietly wished the village of Jianshanxia to move forward well and smoothly complete the transformation to the post-productive village.

About the Author

Mao Dan is Qiushi Distinguished Professor of Zhejiang University. He is a member of the Sociology Review Panel of the National Social Science Fund of China, member of the Expert Consultation Committee of the Ministry of Civil Affairs of the People's Republic of China. Mao's research focuses on grassroots social and political studies in contemporary China, community social management, and social work and community development, among others. He has written numerous academic papers and his latest monograph is titled *Research on the Citizenization of Peasants in Suburbs*. Mao also serves as an editorial board member of many periodicals, such as the *Chinese Journal of Social Development, Social Construction, Sociological Review of China, Journal of Sociology, Zhejiang Social Sciences* and *Zhejiang Academic Journal*.

Contents

Introduction

Unit Society and Unit Village

In my opinion, it is very appropriate to use the term, "quiet revolution" to describe the social changes[1] in China's coastal rural areas since the reform. Farmers living in these areas have long been regarded as a major drag on China's modernization, but once they have a very limited free choice, they are able to conjure up magical creativity in the process of improving their living conditions, they have creatively changed the economic landscape of many regions and have even become the most positive impetus for the local modernization process. Economists, sociologists and political scientists in cities were astonished to see the changes in the countryside. It was like seeing a pile of historical ashes that seemed to run out of energy and then suddenly burst into flames or a wooden and dull, old clay figure that has become a vivid face.[2]

It is difficult for a researcher to resist the enthusiasm of observation and research when he encounters such a powerful empirical fact in his very limited life process and more limited research career. However, as usual, it is much more difficult to describe empirical fact than experience it. Once researchers want to understand, describe and analyze the changes in rural society in a less difficult way, in a less complex paradigm, it is often found that this is a very difficult thing to do. The reason is not that the researchers do not have a concise, readymade concept and paradigm that can be relied on for the social type; on the contrary, the existing theories and concepts like those

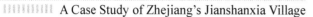
from pre-industrial society to industrialized society, from "mechanical solidarity" society to "organic solidarity" society, from "rural society" to "legal society", or from the small folk society to the large-scale urban society will certainly help us to understand and describe the rural social changes that we are facing.[3] The difficulty is that the existing concepts and paradigms, generally speaking, have more of a background in Western society, and are more static in description. Therefore, compared with the significant social changes that have taken place and are still taking place in the rural society of China, it is somewhat "separated". On the contrary, some of the forerunner achievements and research paths of Chinese rural society produced several decades ago still have active vitality up to now, but these may not be enough for the recent non-westernization and non-traditional vivid changes in rural society.

Therefore, in the process of going deeper into the rural society to feel and studying the new empirical facts, it's pretty important for us to look for the empirical facts closer to the changes of the rural society at many levels and from many angles, which can better express the various descriptive paradigms of its dynamic process. It is clear that any of the more appropriate descriptive paradigms, in the sense of meeting the general needs, should at least be able to do the following: (1) be helpful to describe the personality characteristics of the actual changes of the rural society in China; (2) help describe the dynamic process of rural social change, including its various transitional stages and patterns; (3) describe not only the characteristics of rural society but also the characteristics of rural society as a part of Chinese society, that is, it can be used to express the integration and differentiation of rural society with the whole society and with the urban society.

This book hopes to try something out although at best, it is at the micro level and can only attempt to describe the change of a village.

On closer examination, the researchers may have reason to marvel at the pace of vitality of farmers and rural change, but it does not seem right to be particularly alien to the direction of these changes. In the dramatic coastal rural areas, in addition to the changes that occurred in agricultural production after the introduction of the household contract system, I am afraid that the most exciting change is the urbanization called for by industrialization and small-scale urbanization; in the direction of change, the countryside is obviously approaching the city.

The so-called approach has a complex meaning. First of all, there is no way to know whether it is because of the call for narrowing the urban–rural gap that has been popular since the 1960s, or because urban life has always been the envy of the countryside from the 1950s to the 1980s, but the approach of the countryside to the city is often conscious; at least the result of the approach is often a willingness to see and accept change by the farmers. Therefore, the approach can be seen to a large extent as a rural-to-city imitation. At the same time, whether it is the more objective approach or the imitation with the more prominent subjective intention, it is quite extensive in scope, including various arrangements that mimic urban society in terms of social system and organization, and even consciously or unconsciously imitating a number of systems that are gradually being broken down or eliminated in the urban society.

In my opinion, this phenomenon not only makes it easy for people to describe the changes of urban and rural society from the macro perspective but also suggests a variety of new perspectives for people to describe the changes of rural society on the medium and micro levels. I have paid special attention to the process of unit-building in some villages, especially the movement of imitating urban units in some villages since the reform. As a result, the book chooses the unit system as the descriptive framework to describe the organizational changes characterized by the unit in a village, as well as other aspects of social change that are indicated by this change, accompanied by it, and triggered by it.

This choice is based on both logic and experience.

Logically speaking, the unit system and the unit institution are only a descriptive paradigm that has gradually been given importance in the study of urban organizations, industrial organizations, and governmental processes in China. But, empirical evidence suggests that it is not entirely inappropriate to use it to analyze changes in rural areas. The theory of this research can be traced directly to Kornai's theory of shortage economy[4] published in 1986 by Walder, *Communist Neo Traditionalism: Work and Authority in Chinese Industry,* which was seen as the actual beginning of the research on the unit system of Chinese enterprises and the whole urban society.

The latter found that China's socialist society has a unique institutional structure, a kind of enterprise organization that contains the means of political control in an organized way. This enterprise organization is the basic social unit of the asylum relationship between a highly institutionalized asylum provider and the asylum seeker. Since then, a number of young and middle-aged scholars in China have further studied various aspects of individual cases, macroscopic historical processes and organizational theories, and described quite accurately the following empirical facts about how Chinese urban society is organized: In the decades before the reform, the Chinese society was mainly a formal organization called unit that long existed in urban society. It was a form of organization used by the state to manage personnel in the public sector, originating from 1949 to 1956. In order to pursue production efficiency and social control, the new regime relied on a series of written systems promulgated by state machinery and administrative organization. Supported by this series of written systems, China's urban society has established an unprecedented and unique unit system through the establishment of numerous units. This system takes people's places of employment as the basic organizational unit, and assembles and classifies production management systems (or other professional management systems), personnel systems, financial systems, household registration systems, social security systems, political and ideological implementation systems, etc. As a result, the unit is not only a generalized production (private goods, services, and public goods) organization or the employment place for people in the public ownership system but also a part of the authoritative system of social control and integration. It is also a major part of the social welfare and social security system and has the triple functions of economic production organizations, political and administrative organizations, and social management organizations.[5] Since units are different from the general technical organizations in other industrial societies, they are not primarily governed by the principle of efficiency. Its legitimacy depends on its cooperation with the whole institutional environment and its ideology, and it is difficult to avoid inefficiency in the sense of economics. The whole urban society is organized by units and their complements (neighborhood committees) as knots, and the ruling party system has developed a complete set of social functions, social structures, and social production, distribution and redistribution systems on this axis, therefore, the whole urban society and even the whole Chinese society is a unit society; the law of relationship between state and unit, the law of relationship between the units, the relationship between people and units and the law of action constitute the actual operation rules and characteristics of Chinese urban society. Before the reform, China was a type of socialist planned economy and society. Its uniqueness lies not in the allocation of resources without depending on the market but in relying on a plan and a redistribution system, and is embodied in the established system of units taking the unit as a tissue cell. It can be said that the unit system is not only the microsocial organization system of urban society but also the main characteristics of the macroscopic social structure and its operation process of the whole Chinese society. In addition, the unit phenomenon and unit system have been the characteristics of China's planned economy and traditional Chinese public ownership since 1956. The reform and social change of China are also reflected in the reform and change of the unit system.[6]

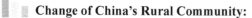

In my opinion, this is an interesting and effective understanding and description of the social fact that we have known for years. In terms of description, it actually contains the following set of concepts that can help us to approximate empirical facts. Among them, the unit is specified as a specific organization form; the system is defined as the formal and substantive normative system of social action, and the legality, nature, rules and so on of the units are stipulated in the formal system and the quasi-system,[7] which is the unit system. All kinds of unit entities, written systems, actual operation rules, and operation processes are compiled into the unit system; once society is organized in units and the unit rule is the dominant rule of the society, then this society becomes a unit society. In terms of effectiveness, it is clear that the system of units is a descriptive paradigm of the Chinese urban society. It helps to present not only the difference between society under the socialist planned economy and that under the social and market economy but also the significant difference between China as a society under the other socialist planned economy before the reform and the societies under the socialist planned economy. Moreover, the system is formed on the basis of various organizational resources, such as the institutional tradition of the red base, industrial organization of industrial society, and social organization. As a descriptive paradigm, it is quite effective in presenting what kind of non-traditional organization type and social structure the Chinese urban society grew out of a traditional society basis and what kind of way before the reform; On the contrary, it also shows as a new structure, why it can't be fully classified into the modern industrial society; correspondingly, this descriptive paradigm will also show how the target of market economy will be realized in the urban society gradually in terms of unit digestion and transformation.

The discovery and description of unit, unit system and unit institution have multiple meanings. For example, in addition to the empirical level, it effectively shows that the Chinese urban society has experienced a transitional change to the modern industrial society in the past half century; it may also have multiple linkage effects at the macrosocial theory level.[8] Of course, my particular concern here is the following: Before the reform, there existed obvious "urban and rural differences" between urban society and rural society in China, and there was obviously a consistency of social system. In this sense, is the unit system or unit society only the characteristic of organization and type of urban society, or is it the characteristic of the whole social system? Accordingly, can the unit system and its change as the descriptive paradigm of social type and social system, while being used to observe urban society and its changes, be further used to observe the countryside—at least some type or part of the countryside?

So far, unit researchers have generally not agreed to observe the countryside with the unit institutional paradigm.[9]

This, of course, is not without reason because when it comes to language habits, people generally refer to institutions, schools, social organizations, public enterprises, etc., as units.[10] The countryside has always been regarded as irrelevant to the unit. Especially in the past, when the barriers between urban and rural areas were obvious and social mobility was low, working in the unit or not was the most important mark of a person's social identity and social status. So, generally no one is going to be wrong about what is a unit, although not many people say the exact meaning of the unit; in general, farmers do not say they work in units, and people who work in units do not condescend to confuse units with rural organizations such as production teams. In this way, it seems to be inconvenient to observe the countryside with the paradigm of the unit system. In theory, as the researchers have discovered, the basic institutional content of the unit system is that the state organizes people into an administrative network. In this process, the employment places of urban economic sectors are transformed into units in the socialist economic framework. The whole rural organization, especially its grassroots organization, is at the edge of the redistribution system, and the degree of institutionalization and organization is relatively lower. In general, there is only a certain urban "unit" feature; it is not a standardized unit. Therefore, the researchers can't help but feel that the countryside cannot be effectively analyzed by unit research.

However, if further consideration is given to the following three aspects, it is logically acceptable to observe rural changes in the unit institutional paradigm, especially the relevant rural changes.

The first thing to consider is that the system of units is consistent and coherent as a social system. It may be very important to observe and analyze the system of unit system in every level (including in urban and rural societies) in the form of a unit system paradigm. That is to say, in the descriptive paradigm of the unit system, the unit itself refers to the formal organization deliberately established after 1949 to achieve a specific goal. Moreover, the researcher has made a conceptual definition of the unit from the perspective of phenomenon description, histological classification and functional analysis. For example, from the perspective of economics and sociology, the urban welfare group since 1949 has been called the unit; from the perspective of political science, the unit can be called the grassroots organization form of Chinese social economy and political life. It is not only the specialized business organization but also the "nerve ending" of the state (government), the non-governmental extension of local government, the quasi-dispatch agency, etc. In either view, the unit entity that is fully possessed does exist only in the pre-reform urban society. However, the establishment of a unit of urban society by taking the numerous units as the social knot organization and organizing the whole (urban) society with unit network is not a spontaneous process, nor a separate process, but a social project since 1949. It is a result of the state organizing the people in a planned way through administrative form, trying to integrate people's employment places, political organizations and welfare institutions into one and giving the corresponding institutional arrangement system solidification. The urban society composed of unit and unit network is the partial result or the standard result that the state intends to carry out in the process. At the same time, the countryside is undoubtedly within the scope of the state's intentions. Although the final result is different, can it be said that it is another part of the result or non-standard result that appears in the process of national intention?[11] Because of this, even if the unit does not exist in the countryside, the unit system can be used as a paradigm to observe the rural society and its changes. As for the difference between the countryside and the city under this paradigm, how these differences arise and change are not only the questions that need to be studied, but it is also important for understanding the relationship between urban and rural areas in China and understanding the units themselves. In other words, if the unit system was regarded as the main mode of implementation of the traditional Chinese public ownership society before reform, it was the main organization mode of China's planned economy and society. Then, it is necessary to observe the countryside carefully from the perspective of the system of units and analyze the connection and difference between the countryside and the city under this general system.

In the second case, there are some important unit variants in the rural society, which can be understood and described by the paradigm of the unit system. In fact, the establishment of the unit system has been one of the core projects in social engineering designed and implemented by the new regime since 1949. The intention of the state to establish a system of units is not an exception to the macroscopic and microscopic results in the process of arrangement and implementation. Microcosmic accidents occur within the unit. For example, the design intention of unit system may be to organize production efficiently, distribute welfare fairly and control social members comprehensively through the unit. However, in the absence of market mechanism and bureaucracy management, the unit is economically inefficient; also, the relationships between asylum provider and asylum seeker and between the party and the masses are implemented to the relationship between the units and the masses in the units, especially the leadership of units and the masses in units; there must be all kinds of inequalities in fact and various kinds of control and counter-control among leaders in units and between leaders and the masses. But, unexpected macroscopic result refers to the unit variant of the village. In the past, the People's Commune could be seen as the historical form of the variant of the rural unit— it was the unsuccessful or unexpected result of rural unit according to the mode of urban unit, which the new regime tried to implement after the completion of urban unit. The realistic form of the rural unit variant refers to the phenomenon of enterprise or village unit in the rural changes since the reform. This mainly refers to the measures taken since the reform, such as the implementation of the household contract responsibility system, the abolition of the People's Commune and the establishment of a system of villagers' autonomy, which meant that the country was giving up the organization of the rural grassroots by means of the unit method day by day and giving farmers more power to organize their own production and life. However, for economic, cultural, and other backgrounds to be studied, the rural grassroots in a given framework of autonomy in the country have produced many interesting unexpected results. In the process of organizing social life, some rural areas look for resources and paradigms from the relatively ancient rural clan tradition, which leads to the rise of family power and the trend of clan organization in rural grassroots organizations.[12] In other rural areas, usually areas with more developed collective economy and the rural industrial economy, it has first experienced the social mobilization that aims at narrowing the differences between urban and rural areas before the reform and has been developing the township enterprises since the reform and promoting urbanization through small-scale urbanization. Therefore, in the process of organizing production and life, they tend to get demonstration from urban enterprises and urban society. It may have something to do with this background, and this kind of rural area has been mimicking urban life and urban units. There is a case in this book which will be devoted to enterprise units and even village units. While there is no doubt that such a new and spontaneous unit or unit variant is different from the state-designed social engineering, what will be its operation mechanism and function? In the case that the urban unit is gradually fading away from the market economy, why does the countryside have the phenomenon of unitization? These problems clearly require attention. Of course, there must be a lot of difference between the rural unit variant and the standard urban unit. However, this difference is not the reason for us to dismiss the unit variants in the countryside, but it is one of the keys for further study.

Finally, there is a situation that cannot be ignored: the unit-oriented enterprise in the village or unit-oriented village is probably not a result of one or two pure accidents. In some parts of China's coastal areas, rural industrialization and urbanization are often supported by township enterprises, and the generalized and familiar "South Jiangsu Province Pattern" is one of the most significant types. From the mechanism and trend, although such enterprises have more market factors and flexibility than state-owned enterprises in the same period from the beginning in operation, distribution, labor and other aspects, the state has no interest in or has made no attempt to control these enterprises, but the original social team basis, institutional innovation environment and so on of the township enterprises in this type of development can easily promote the tendency of these enterprises to follow the example of the unit. Of course, the background and process of marketization may not allow these imitation actions to be fully realized, especially with the transformation of the former township collective enterprises in the recent years, the unit system which has been imitated seems to be facing a transformation. This whole process of change seems to enter the field of vision of unit researchers. It at least provides a vivid rural annotation for the formation and transformation of the unit system in China.

Therefore, if the unit system is approved to embody the social characteristics of socialist China in a long period of time, "unit" is the semantic habit used by people to express this unique system; therefore, it is possible and necessary to observe some corresponding phenomena and changes in rural areas with a limited use of the paradigm of units and unit systems. It can at least be a tentative paradigm for discussion and description of a transitional type in the countryside.

I have repeatedly emphasized that China's social reform and change in a sense reflect the reform and change of the society of unit system, emphasized the existence of unit variants in rural areas and also the possibility of limited use of the unit system as a descriptive paradigm to present a certain type of rural society and its changes in coastal areas. But, for the sake of personal energy, ability and the pursuit of certainty, this book can only attempt to describe a very limited object from the perspective of unit and unit system—the changes of Jianshanxia Village in Xiaoshan District, Hangzhou, Zhejiang Province. It intends to use the concept of "unit village" to represent the change process and characteristics of the village.

That is to say, although I would like to suggest that there is some consistency, uniformity and homogeneity in the social system and social structure of cities and villages, I must emphasize that I have never thought the unit village proposed and described in this book is a general concept or paradigm for describing rural change. Rather, I would like to limit it to a rural phenomenon that I found during the rural investigation in Xiaoshan, Zhejiang Province, which I think should be described and analyzed. The purpose of this is to show that there is a basis of observation and experience for the change of a kind of rural area from the point of view of the unit. However, I am aware of the limitations of individual observation and case study and prefer to consider this description as a case or local proof for the study of rural units in a more general sense.

In fact, the choice goes through a process of experience. The survey, mentioned above, began in June 1995. At that time, I applied and received funding from the "Huo Yingdong—Modern and Tradition" Foundation and carried out a study on rural modernization, especially the non-economic factors in rural economic development in Xiaoshan,

Zhejiang Province.[13] During the first two months of field visits, interviews, and textual research, I was constantly excited by the various "quiet revolutions" here, which produced a bit of an economist's impulse to summarize economic types. But, this poor ambition was soon diluted by serious depression. Because of the recent 20 years of development in the rural areas of Xiaoshan, although the initial stage can be roughly classified as the so-called "South Jiangsu Province Pattern" from the commune and brigade-run enterprises, since the 1990s, it has entered a more complex and diversified development. Economically, for example, the private enterprise, family, township or village enterprises, joint-stock enterprises, cross-village group enterprise, etc., not only exist at the same time but also in each country form a pattern of different combinations; the combination of agriculture, industry, and services in the process of industrialization varies from place to place; other social changes in towns and villages are different in terms of ways, manifestation, and changes. Therefore, trying to filter out a lot of concrete details in the sense of economic sociology, abstract out a "model" of Xiaoshan's modernization, it seems to me that it is not only very difficult but also not very strict. I feel increasingly that for such a profoundly changing countryside, in-depth observation and description is more urgent than a hurried mode induction or classification; it is not only more realistic but also more important in both academic and social aspects to delve more deeply into villages and conduct case, microscopic observation and analysis. What's more, the initial investigation work is naturally concentrated in the most developed urban and rural areas in Xiaoshan. To view from the statistics, geographic data, and field observations, the northern part of Xiaoshan is adjacent to or close to the surrounding reclamation area or sandy plain of Hangzhou, and the southern part to the lower hilly area. However, most of the economic development areas in Xiaoshan are distributed in the north and the middle sections, while the poor villages are mostly in the south area, that is, the extent of the economic leap and the extent of social change are positively correlated with geographical conditions and ecological resources. It seems that the rich are rich, the poor are poor, the developer is self-developing, and the laggard is lagging behind. This certainly confirms the ecological resources theory of the comparative economic sociology, but it is close to a bashing blow to my attempt to induce the model. I cannot but give up this attempt of my own accord.

However, this does not mean to give up the investigation. I still have a series of stubborn doubts in my mind—Is the relationship between regional ecological resources and regional economy and social development really one to one? If it is, then why is the imbalance of the natural distribution of regional ecological resources transformed into the inequality of ecological resources? What are the social consequences of this inequality? What happened to the south of Xiaoshan area? If this situation continues, will the south be placed in the future economic and social context and will it further amplify existing social inequalities? In what other ways could this inequality be changed? Are there any signs of a real change? If so, how did it change? Driven by these doubts, the field trip was not only continued but also gradually shifted to the southern part of Xiaoshan. Different from the previous study, with the shift of emphasis on the region, an intellectual concern unknowingly replaces the original interest in eager search for and induction of model. To my relief, the southern part of Xiaoshan is actually filled with villages that are developing faster and with little difference between their economic level and that of the developed regions. What is more interesting is that the economic leaps and social changes of these villages are not based on any unique regional ecological resource advantages. The economic development pattern and the barren degree of regional ecological resources of Jianshanxia Village, Yunshi Township, form a striking contrast. In fact, this contrast not only naturally arouses an interest in understanding the objects of these cases but also strongly drives the observer to sum up some new model and revise the usual ecological theory of resources; only, after the first stage of repetition, I resolved to no longer hold any extravagant hopes for the latter.

At this point, I firmly believed that any choice of a village for careful observation and description would be very valuable. Since September 1995, I have selected villages in the south area, and I have chosen Jianshanxia Village as the observation target.

There are a few simple considerations for this particular choice. First of all, the natural ecological resources of this small mountain village are very general, even close to poor. Therefore, compared with choosing other villages as a case study object, choosing this village can explain my personal questions above. Second, this little mountain village has been involved in almost every movement of the country in the countryside since 1949. If we need to investigate the relationship between rural grassroots and government level and the whole country, it belongs to a complete research model. The last reason is almost laughable: Community observation here is particularly operable. Although the small mountain village is not convenient in traffic, there are no restaurants for outsiders to room and board, most of the villagers are friendly to outsiders who observe their villages. Generally speaking, it is not too difficult to observe and understand the situation in their relationships with friends.

The remaining question is what method and what perspective to observe. Frankly, I never thought it was too big a problem, nor did I intend to turn it into a complex problem that was too pedantic. Because of my personal preference and observation and convenient narration, I mainly adopt common literature analysis, community investigation, and some historical narrative style. The general impression that I get from this is that the village is particularly like a unit in a city in a period of time; the change of the whole village since 1949 is like the unit process of a village. It happens to coincide with the general judgment I have described in the previous sections. Therefore, I would be happy to try to describe the observed facts from the perspective of the unit village, and when I finally confirmed that I wanted to use the unit village to describe the changes of the village in Jianshan, I felt that it was reasonable and true in the background.

I do call for unit observation to describe the evolution of a particular type of society or organization in coastal rural areas. But, this book is merely an illustrative study of a village. If this interpretation proves the study of rural unit variant and even rural unit system in a more general sense, I hope that this will not be arbitrarily accused of being small, with little coverage and partial generalization; at the very least, once I have entered into the process of specific description, there has been no such attempt.

The book is divided into four chapters.

The first chapter focuses on observing and analyzing the organizational resources of the village. Throughout the village history, it can be found that although the village has been located in a remote place for a long time, it has long been a place to avoid the war of soldiers and bandits, it still experiences the long historical process of the state power permeating the countryside. After 1949, the whole process of transformation from clan village to administrative village was completed. In the process, a number of elements conducive to the formation of unit villages have emerged, including the following: the existence of the village community and the rising status of the village as a rural organization, the weakening of clan organization and the exit of clan culture, the structure of the village organization, the precedent or practice of collective action (in particular, large-scale operations depend on the leadership of the village party and the "political" organization) in the village, demonstration of the organization mode and welfare arrangement of urban units, especially urban enterprises, maintenance of village resource boundaries by the state and so on. These factors constitute the organizational resources of the Jianshanxia Village after the end of the People's Commune.

The second chapter focuses on observing the ecological environment resources and policy resources and the formation process of the unit villages. It tries to show that due to the combined action of the ecological resources of the Jianshanxia Village (the land resources are not suitable for the development of agriculture, the transportation cost is not conducive to the development of industry or other non-agricultural industries in the family unit), traditional factors (emphasis on the production of handicraft and sideline industry), the state power-driven factors (restrain the clan, enforce the boundaries of villages, take administrative villages as rural grassroots, agree with village collective economy and so on), factors in the process of political organization (the village team structure with administrative function and the practice of village team organization and the collective action of the organization village), the capital requirements and technical requirements for the industry in the village, in the later stage of the People's Commune, the collective industrial development of the village team became an act of consensus within the community. After the commune system was over, the administrative village was once again recognized as the rural grassroots by the state. Due to historical inertia and enterprise technology type and other factors, until 1992, even before 1995, it continued to expand the scale of the industrial economy of the villages by expanding the size of the village collective, with evident results. As a result, the collective enterprises in the village gradually became stronger, and eventually became the majority of the village economy, and the enterprises were basically overlapped with the villages. In the process, the village also strived to learn the welfare and other operating systems of urban units to realize the management of villages and enterprises. Finally, there was comparability between the village and the industrial organization unit and the basic social organization unit.

The third chapter focuses on observing the operation condition of the unit village and analyzing the interaction between the organization mode and the village change. It is intended to emphasize that village organization is an unprecedented approach to urban grassroots organization pattern and urban life. Therefore, it cannot help but have a lot of revolutionary influence on village community. The reason seems to be obvious: Because the village enterprises in the village of Jianshanxia had absorbed most of the labor force in the village, the collective industrial economy of the village had occupied over 95% of the village economy. For the above share, the unit management by the village-level organizations and the unit management of enterprises continued to extend to the whole village, which means that the entire village community is incorporated into a new organizational process and organizational system. As a natural result, the modern resources contained in the unit often improve the villages in various ways, even quietly causing some revolutionary change to the social organization and social life in the village. Of course, these changes may be triggered more by the factory system (organization mode and labor process) contained in the unit. But, because for decades, the system of units was made up of industrial organizations, administrative organizations, social organizations, or the Chinese factory form before the market economy became dominant, these changes in the villages can still be seen as triggered by modern resources in the system of units. From an observer's point of view, such changes are often interesting. The observation of this kind of change often brings about some kind of introspection on the rural social analysis and the peasant theory (especially some traditional theories about the alienation of farmers and modern society).

On the contrary, various situations indicate that the unit village is still underdeveloped. Logically, this of course means that the unit village still retains some of the traditional elements of the village. This may be referred to as the local resource in a unit village in the usual way. The combination of these resources with the modern resources in the system often makes the dynamics and processes of village unit change very complicated. In observing such phenomena, the observer often feels a certain kind of doubt and does not know that such phenomena mean that the village is in the process of moving from the rural society to the legal society and has entered some transitional form, or does it show that the system has a natural affinity for certain traditional resources in rural society?

The fourth chapter analyzes the new problems and main problems encountered in the operation of the village and states the efforts made by the unit villages to solve these problems and the transformation trend of the unit villages produced by these efforts. I observe that no matter how the village is institutionalized, to what extent it is achieved, the urban units are different from the village units. What is particularly thought-provoking is that the risk and transformation of urban units clearly have some kind of formal and informal mechanism, which is not available in the unit villages. This means that there is almost no way out for the unit village! It is worth noting that village enterprises form the economic pillar of the village. However, because of the high risk of enterprise operation in the market economy, the village enterprises also become the fragile place of the village unit. More importantly, the village enterprises are also modeled after the unit system; the property rights system, the corresponding authority relationship, and the distribution relationship as the incentive return system adopted are all in favor of the low-efficiency production process under the system of units, rather than providing a strong support framework for companies facing fierce market competition. Finally, under the obvious pressure of survival, the unit villages were forced to loosen the ties between the villages and the village enterprises. Inside the enterprise, it was forced to start from the property rights system to carry on the system and the mechanism change. As a result, the village was finally turning to the direction of dismantling the village unit. I believe that this process provides a special meaning for the fading out or withdrawal of the unit system in the Chinese society.

Through the above observations and analysis, this book tries to focus on the following observations:

(1) A village of homogeneous individuals, nuclear families, clans and one or more families is a typical Chinese version of the so-called rural society. Among them, villages may be the joint point of "country" and society.

(2) The rural development of the industry can lead to the transformation of the so-called "rural society" to "legal society"; this change can be characterized by the industrialization of the countryside, rural urbanization or urbanization, and the non-traditional tendency in daily life.

(3) Because of natural environment factors (such as transport, geography, etc.), political factors (for example, the relationship between the state and society in the post-development countries, the geopolitics of interests, etc.), and historical factors (division between the cities and the countryside, etc.), the countryside is difficult to be fully urbanized in reality, and it is difficult to be fully integrated into legal society in the way of social interaction. Therefore, in reality, there are "village units" as some typical transitional or intermediate form.

Finally, I express my sincere gratitude to the "Huo Yingdong— Modern and Tradition" Foundation and Zhejiang Philosophy and Social Science Foundation for funding this research.

It is hoped that this book will be commensurate with the two research grants and the publication grant of the Jinshi Humanities Foundation of Zhejiang University.

Endnotes

1. Many researchers seem to be happy to use the "quiet revolution" to present the delightful changes in China's rural transition: (1) David SG, Goodman and Hooper B. *China's Quiet Revolution: New Interactions between State and Society.* Melbourne: Longman Cheshire, 1994. (2) Shen GB. *A Quiet Revolution: Industry and Society in Sunan Countryside.* Kunming: Yunnan People's Press, 1993. (3) Liu XJ. A Quiet Revolution: Research on the Adaptation of Rural Land System in China. In: Institute of Rural Development, Chinese Academy of Social Sciences.

Rural China in the Great Revolution—Research on Rural Organization and Institutional Change. Beijing: Social Sciences Academic Press, 1999.

2. This change has even caused people to actively discuss the relationship between peasants' political characteristics, farmers and modern politics. See Zheng YN. Rural Democracy and Chinese Political Process. *Twenty-First Century*. 1996(35):24–35.

3. These inspiring and admirable theories and concepts include the following: (1) In 1887, Tönnies (1855–1936) proposed the rural society and legal society (Gemeinschaft and Gesellschaft in German), *Community and society*, or community and mass organization. The former is a small, simple community, and the social life revolves around the family. Most people know each other, have intimate relationships and a sense of community solidarity, people focus on group interests, group activities and consistency, and are bound by tradition and control any unusual behavior by informal means such as gossip, individual exhortation, etc. The latter is a large individual society, where members of society often do not know each other and share no common beliefs. The relationship between people is not primarily personal, and it is often based on mutual complementary needs rather than emotional obligations. People pay attention to individualism, and tradition and custom no longer have a strong influence on individuals. Informal means can no longer effectively achieve social control. Therefore, the social order cannot be guaranteed without legal and formal sanctions. (Tönnies F. Originally published in 1887. *Community and Society*. East Lansing, Mich.: Michigan State University Press, 1957. Trans. Lin RY. *Community and Society*, The Commercial Press, 1999.) (2) In 1893, Durkheim (1858–1917) proposed a society of mechanical solidarity and a society of organic solidarity. Durkheim argues that the former is a traditional society and a homogenous society. It's a small society, where everybody's work is roughly the same, and all members of society are socialized in the same way. Social members share the same experience and share common values and norms, thus forming a "collective consciousness" of the society. It can be said that society is gathered by the basic similarity of members. The latter society is a huge division of labor, and the social basis is not the similarity of social members, but the division of labor and the difference of social members; social members belong to different organizations, play different economic roles, have

different experiences, hold different value standards, and socialize their children according to different patterns. Collective consciousness is much less restrictive to society. It can be said that society is made up of individuals who are connected and dependent on each other based on a series of highly specialized divisions of labor, which are gathered by people's dissimilarity. (Durkheim E. Originally published 1893. *The Division Labor in Society*. Trans. Simpson GG. Ill: Free Press, 1964.) (3) In 1941, the anthropologist Redfield proposed a small folk society and a large urban society. The former is combined with traditional and close personal connections, and the latter is marked by non-personal relationships and values. (Redfield R. *The Folk Culture of Yucatan*. Chicago: University of Chicago Press, 1941.) In addition, Lenski systematically stated in 1966 the social types and their respective social stratification from hunting and gathering society, farming society to agricultural society and industrial society. (Redfield R. *Power and Privilege: A Theory of Social stratification*. New York: McGraw-Hill, 1966. The Chinese version is translated by Guan Xinping *et al.*, published by Zhejiang People's Publishing House in 1988. It is a pity that the Chinese translation has deleted the original indexes and most of the notes.)

4. In 1980, Kornai's *Shortage Economics* detailed the analysis of the resource-constrained system in the socialist planned economy, the hierarchical relationship of various production organizations and the way of behavior. His account of the unique conduct of enterprises and more general social organizations in the socialist system is striking.

5. Lu F. Origin and Formation of the Unit System in China, *Chinese Social Sciences Quarterly*. 1993(5):77.

6. In addition to the Lu Feng's analysis, some of the best studies are as follows: (1) Tan S. Formation and Characteristics of Urban Unit Security. *Sociological Research*. 1991(5):82–87. (2) Li HL, Wang FY and Li LL. The Integration Mechanism and Unit Phenomenon of Urban Communities in China. *World of Management*. 1994(2):192–200. (3) Li NX. Corporatism and the Reform of China's Economic Reform. *Twenty-First Century*. 1991(7):150–160. (4) Yu XY. A Sociological Analysis of Unit Consciousness. *Sociological Research*, 1991(7):76–81. (5) Li M *et al*. Unit: Internal Mechanism of Institutionalized Organizations. *China Social Science Quarterly*.

1991(16):135–167. (6) Thomson J and Warmark B. *Chinese Politics*. Trans. Gu S and Dong F. Nanjing: Jiangsu People's Publishing House, 1994. (7) Yang XM and Zhou YH. *Unit System in China*, Beijing: China Economic Publishing House, 1999.

7. Liu Xiaojing in *A Quiet Revolution: Research on the Adaptation of Rural Land System in China*, points out that: "According to the formal degree of the system itself, it is divided into formal system and quasi-system. Formal system consists of two categories: advanced form and primary form. The advanced form of the system is the legal text and the primary form is the policy text. The quasi-system refers specifically to the chief's speech and the important policy guiding articles published in the central press. (Including editorials, commentator's articles, editors' posts, leading cadres' famous articles, etc.)" (Institute of Rural Development, Chinese Academy of Social Sciences. *Rural China in the Great Revolution—Research on Rural Organization and Institutional Change*. Beijing: Social Sciences Academic Press, 1999, pp. 3–4.) The book thinks so deeply and draws on it.

8. For example, the mixing of traditional and modern elements in the unit system is a good case study of the stability and change of Chinese social structure and general social structure over the years. It reminds us of the theoretical insights that Giddens put forward when discussing social structure and the stability and transformation of social structures: The social structure is not the invariable frame, the rigid restriction, but is the rules and resources repeatedly involved in the social reproduction process. Therefore, it is not only the premise and the intermediary of human action but also has the transformation. It can be translated into many different patterns and appearances as the actor's activities need to be transformed, and may change with the use of actors in specific situations. (Giddens A. *The Composition of Society*. Trans. Li K and Li M. Beijing: SDX Joint Publishing Company, 1998.)

9. (1) Lu F. Origin and Formation of the Unit System in China. *Chinese Social Sciences Quarterly*. 1993(5):81. (2) Li Meng *et al*. Unit: Internal Mechanism of Institutionalized Organizations. *China Social Science Quarterly*. 1996(16):94, 105.

10. Zhu GL. *The Process of Contemporary Chinese Government*. Tianjin: Tianjin People's Press, 1997, p. 348.

11. Lu Feng is very resourceful at this point. He thinks that rural organizations (such as People's Communes) and neighborhood committees in cities are not units, but embody the principle of organizing people by administrative means, so are an integral part of the unit system.

12. Qian H and Xie WY. *Tradition and Transformation: Jiangxi Thai and Rural Clan Form: A Study of Social Anthropology*. (Shanghai Academy of Social Sciences Press, 1995 provides a typical example and description. Wang HN. *Family Culture of Contemporary Chinese Village: A Probe into the Modernization of Chinese Society*. Shanghai People's Publishing House, 1991 and Wang MM. *Culture and Power in the Vision of Villages*. SDX Joint Publishing Company, 1997 also involve the revival of family forces in the countryside.

13. Since the reform and opening-up, Xiaoshan's achievements in economic development and social change have attracted some attention from researchers at home and abroad. For example: White G. Prospects for Civil Society in China: A Case Study of Xiaoshan City. *The Australian Journal of China Affairs*, 1993(1):63–87.

Village: From Natural Settlement to Administrative Organization—Organizational Resources of a Unit Village

1.1 Theoretical Viewpoint: Is There a Village Community?

Jianshanxia Village, which we will observe, is now an administrative village in Xiaoshan district, Zhejiang Province, in the southwest mountain area of Xiaoshan.[1]

The village is not large. It is composed of four natural villages, namely, Jianshanxia, Shangmen, Hongtanqiao and Changpantian. The whole village stretches from the northeast to the southwest, "hidden" in a strip valley of about 1,800 meters in length, with a maximum width of about 200 meters, and it has an area of only 360,000 square meters. In addition to the 132 mu of reclaimed land dozens of miles away, the village now has only 39.3 mu of arable land. At the end of 1997, there were 368 households and 1,353 villagers (20 of whom were non-agricultural). Among nearly 800 administrative villages in Xiaoshan, in terms of the village area (excluding the forest area) and the population size, it is a small administrative village.

But, the village's history is not too short. According to Bao's genealogical records in the village and the old man's oral information in the village, the first family settled down in Jianshanxia in the third year of Jianyan of the Southern Song Dynasty (1129). It's been nearly 890 years since then.

It seems that the Jianshanxia Village is a typical village type starting from household, family, village and finally the administrative village. Its 890-year history is a typical history from natural settlement to administrative village macroscopically. In general, this type implies more about the status and role of the village as the basic settlement of the rural area. I believe there are many such types everywhere, but this type and its implications are not usually given enough attention in social science research. In my impression, Western researchers tend to be more surprised and pay more attention to the families (clans) and clan villages (clans) in rural China (especially in southern China).[2] In the Chinese ideological circle of this century, the village, as the organizational level of the rural society, has been deliberately or unintentionally ignored for a long time in the critical discourse of household, family structure and concept.[3]

Fortunately, this vision and its inner judgment were criticized by researchers of modern history such as Huang Zongzhi.[4] Relatively speaking, the study of social anthropology in China has always focused on the status and role of the village from its forerunner.[5] In recent years, there have been a number of works on the study of village society and culture, which remedied the lack of village research after decades of interruption. All of these studies may imply a certain feeling or judgment of the researcher: The function of village in rural society in China cannot be ignored, especially after the transformation and social change of rural society since 1949, and the status of village as village community in the rural social organization system is at least not under the family.

I personally agree with the latter and believe that the village community is probably the organizational resource of the unit village to be discussed in this book. So, when I had to go back first to the history of the village in order to preserve the completeness of the narrative, I reminded myself of the following: If the family is recognized as the basic unit of society, then the village should be recognized as the basic settlement unit of the members of the rural society at the same time; it can also be said that villages include probably not only the basic range of activities of peasants' economic and social life but also a layer of organization or an organizational level of the rural grassroots, which has the significance of village community. At the very least, the village has more of the nature and function of social organization than that of the family. Of course, villages are more of a natural ecological and community organization than larger settlements.

Based on this awareness, this chapter, in its general retrospect of the history of the Jianshanxia Village, cannot but be very concerned about the following issues: If the status of the village is indeed as stated above, then the history of the village undoubtedly concerns the process of how a village is organized or the main aspect of how farmers are organized. This historical process of "organizing" is certainly different from the process of rebuilding rural organizations after 1949. However, according to Gadamer and Shields's understanding and interpretation of traditional continuity, it is natural for us to associate or speculate that the history of the specific process of change will have a continuity with the recent changes in the village. What is this relationship? Is the existing village history the historical resources of the unit villages that we will analyze later? Or, in turn, is the unit village the revolutionary base of the village historical tradition and is still an abrupt interruption? For these questions, the preconceived hypothetical opinion is mainly as follows: (1) There are village entities and village communities in history. The action structure and action habit of the village constitute the historical resources of village organization. (2) After 1949, the social engineering, especially the People's Commune movement, basically disintegrated the clan structure of the old village and consolidated the village collective of administrative unit and economic distribution unit. After the collapse of the People's Commune, it still formed the tradition and core of the village and farmer's action.

If these assumptions are finally verified, we will have a reason to think further about whether the unit village is a revolutionary extension of the traditional village or not.

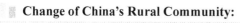
1.2   From Natural Settlement to Village Community

Let's look at the history of the village to see if these assumptions hold true.

It would be interesting to trace back the village history of the Jianshanxia, especially if it gives a complete description of its origin and evolution from the text. Unfortunately, this work has become very difficult because of the scarcity of texts on which to analyze the history of Jianshanxia. At present, there are some genealogical records that can be collected and analyzed. Among them, there are five well-preserved genealogical records of Jiang, Bao, Shao, Yang and Zhu in the village. These five genealogies were successively repaired in the later period of the Republic of China and the victory of the Chinese People's War of Resistance against Japanese Aggression. Due to the style of the old genealogy and the limitation of the later continuation, the records of the origin and changes of the villages in the genealogy are not detailed. From 1986 to 1993, the village organization, villagers and official workers compiled the *Chronicles of Jianshanxia Village*, which used to collect all the important records of the early history of the village from these genealogies under the title of "the Great Chronicles". Because it was not long, it recorded the period from the Song Dynasty to the Qing Dynasty:

Song Dynasty

Bao Wenxian and Bao Rende brothers moved to Jianshanxia from Yuhang to avoid military chaos in the third year of Jianyan of the Southern Song Dynasty (1129).

Ming Dynasty

During the Hongwu period of Ming Dynasty (1368–1398), An Sangong surnamed Jiang moved from Fangjiadun, Fuyang to Jianshanxia.

During the period of YongLe (1403–1424), Zhongzhigong surnamed Yang from Nanping Village, Zhuji saw the beautiful scenery of Jianshanxia, was happy and forgot to return, settling down in Jianshanxia.

During the period of Xuande (1426–1435), Angliugong surnamed Zhu in Zhucunqiao of Xiaoshan married into and lived with Wu family in Shangmen, his bride's family, which later became a big family.

During the period of Hongzhi (1488–1506), Liangbagong, surnamed Shao from Langlingxia, Zhucunqiao of Xiaoshan, married into and lived with Wen family in Shangmen, his bride's family, which later became a big family.

Qing Dynasty

In the early Qing Dynasty, people surnamed Cao migrated from Caojiaqiao of Xiaoshan to the Changpantian of Jianshanxia.

At the same time, Jiang Hemin and Yang Baihua built Guangsheng Nunnery and Yongfu Nunnery in Jianshanxia, respectively, which were demolished during land reform by 1950.

In the fifth year of Shunzhi (1648), Shi Zhongfang led hundreds of people on the crest of Yuqingling Mountain to fight against the Qing army. That year, Shi Zhongfang was held by the Qing army. In the eighth year of Shunzhi (1651), the remaining followers of Shi Zhongfang were dispelled. There is still the observation post, training ground, stone matrix and other sites of Shi Zhongfang's military department of the year.

During the reign of Emperor Qianlong (1736–1795), there was man surnamed Ge who moved to Shangmen from Gejia Village, Yushan of Fuyang and lived in groups. During the same period, in order to protect against strong wind attacks, villagers built high wind and flood control ridges in Yangjia and Shangmen, which were leveled for construction after 1949.

In the 34th year of Guangxu (1908), after the Qing government promulgated the Regulations on the Local Autonomy of Urban and Rural Areas, the name of the Jianshanxia Village was recorded and it belonged to Shencun Township.[6]

In addition, there are two sections of records related to the history of Jianshanxia in *Chronicles of Jianshanxia Village*. One paragraph is about the formation of the four natural villages in the Jianshanxia Village, which is a brief explanation of the above contents; another paragraph is about the historical "building zoning" of the Jianshanxia Village. It is also excerpted below:

Formation of villages

...

Shangmen

The original name was "Shangwen", because later generations had been misinformed, it is called "Shagnmen". The natural village of Shangmen was formed in the third year of Jianyan of the Southern Song Dynasty (1129). At the time, Wu's and Wen's families settled in Shangmen and Xiamen during the Southbound Retreat of the Song Regime. But, Wu's, Wen's people were not prosperous and more women were born. During the period of Xuande (1426–1435), Angliugong surnamed Zhu in Zhucunqiao of Xiaoshan married into and lived with Wu family; during the period of Hongzhi (1488–1506), Liangbagong, surnamed Shao from Langlingxia, Zhucunqiao of Xiaoshan, married into and lived with Wen family; during the reign of Emperor Qianlong (1736–1795), there was a man surnamed Ge who moved to Shangmen from Gejia Village, Yushan of Fuyang. So Zhu, Shao and Ge became large families in the natural village. As the children had the surname of the father, the son-in-law by adoption and the married would not be surnamed Wu or Wen. So, the people surnamed Wu and Wen declined each year, and later, Wu's and Wen's surnames were lost and there were no villagers surnamed Wu or Wen.

Jianshanxia

In the third year of Jianyan of the Southern Song Dynasty, Jin
Dynasty invaded Jiangnan. To avoid military chaos, Bao Wenxian and Bao
Rende brothers (the second and third sons of Bao grandfather) native to Xi
Zhou, Anhui moved to Jianshanxia from Yuhang and gradually developed
into a large family. During Hongwu period of Ming Dynasty (1368–
1398), Ansangong surnamed Jiang moved from Fangjiadun, Fuyang to
Jianshanxia with children due to falling in love with the beautiful scenery
in Jianshanxia of Xiaoshan. During the period of Yongle (1403–1424),
Zhongzhigong surnamed Yang from Nanping Village, Zhuji saw the
picturesque scenery of Jianshanxia while travelling, was happy and forgot
to return, settling down in Jianshanxia. In this regard, Bao, Jiang and
Yang families gather and live in the area of Jianshanxia, forming a natural
village.

Hongtanqiao

During the Tongzhi period of Qing Dynasty (1862–1874),
people surnamed Sheng with former residence in Xizhuang Village,
Yiqiao Township, bought a hill with woods in Pulianwu and settled
in Hongtanqiao near Pulianwu so as to manage the mountain. During
this period, some of the people, surnamed Bao, who lived at the foot of
Jianshanxia, moved to Hongtanqiao (thus, it is said that there are two Bao
families). People surnamed Sheng and Bao gather and live in groups here,
forming a village.

Changpantian

Changpantian village is the southernmost village. In the early Qing
Dynasty, people surnamed Cao, migrated from Caojiaqiao of Xiaoshan
to here. During the reign of Emperor Qianlong (1736–1795), villagers
surnamed Yang in Jianshanxia settled here to manage the mountain villa
in Changpantian. It has been handed down for 12 generations; later, due
to population increase, part of villagers surnamed Jiang in Jianshanxia

lived in Changpantian. After several years of development, villages formed.

Building zoning

In the third year of Peace and Rejuvenation of the Country of Song Dynasty (978), Jianshanxia was the annexed territory of Mageli of Xuxian Township.

In the 16th year of Zhiyuan in the Yuan Dynasty (1279), the township was changed to Du, Li to Tu. It was the annexed territory of Seventh Du and Fifth Tu.

In the Ming Dynasty, it followed the system of the Yuan Dynasty and still belonged to the annexed territory of Seventh Du and Fifth Tu.

In the seventh year of Yongzheng in the Qing Dynasty (1729), Tu was changed to Zhuang. It was the annexed territory of Seventh Du Banli Zhuang. Later, Zhuang was changed to Tu again and still belonged to the Seventh Du and Fifth Tu.

In the 34th year of Guangxu of the Qing Dynasty (1928), the Qing government promulgated the Regulations on the Local Autonomy of Urban and Rural Areas, which stipulated to set up township under county. The name of the Jianshanxia Village was recorded and it belonged to Shencun Township. The early Republic of China followed the Qing system.

In the 17th year of the Republic of China (1928), the government announced the county organization law to promote the village system and set up District, Village and Li under County. Jianshanxia Village started to have a village system. It was named Jianshan United Village and belonged to the fourth district of Xiaoshan.

In the 19th year of the Republic of China (1930), Village and Li were changed into Township and Town, under which there were Lü and Lin. At that time, Jianshanxia belonged to Yuntan Township, in the second district of Xiaoshan County and had four Lü and 20 Lin.

In the 23rd year of the Republic of China (1934), the Baojia system was implemented. Those under the township and town were Bao us and Jia. At that time, Jianshanxia belonged to Shencun Township, Daicun District. The whole village had three Bao, namely, the 18th, 19th and 20th Bao in Shencun Township, and had a total of 26 Jia. Shangmen was the 18th Bao, which had six Jia; Yangjia to Xiaoqiao was the 19th Bao with 10 Jia; Xiaoqiao to Changpantian was the 20th Bao and had 10 Jia.

In the 30th year of the Republic of China (1941), the township system was adjusted and Shencun Township was divided into Shencun and Changtan Townships. At that time, Jianshan Village belonged to Changtan Township, Daicun District. The whole village had two Bao, namely, the 5th and 6th Bao in Changtan Township. Shangmen to Xiaoqiao was the 5th Bao and Xiaoqiao to Changpantian was the 6th Bao. Each Bao had 10 Jia.

In the 36th year of the Republic of China (1947), townships and towns were reorganized. Shencun and Changtan were merged into Changtan Township. At that time, Jianshanxia Village was the 20th Bao of Changtan Township and had 20 Jia (When the War of Resistance against Japanese Aggression began, on the eve of the liberation of Xiaoshan, because of the war turmoil and famine, the peasant households moved out by more than half year by year, so the original three Bao became one Bao).

In the 37th year of the Republic of China (1948), Jianshanxia Village belonged to Changtan Township, Heshang District and was still the 20th Bao.

In July 1950, Baojia system was abolished and administrative village system was promoted. It was called Jianshanxia Village, Changtan Township of Daicun District, administrating eight administrative teams.[7]

Apart from being sentimental, time devours the details of history; these brief but almost boring records obviously cannot provide us with a complete picture of the history of the Jianshanxia Village. However, if we try hard, we may still be able to learn and analyze the following:

(1) In Xiaoshan, the Jianshanxia Village is a non-single-surnamed, secluded village with a multi-family name embedded over the time.

Although the village can be called a basic type of human settlement, it is a kind of group settlement method[8] with a long history. The process of its occurrence is still quite different. The ancient village researchers believe that the village can be classified into five types from the angle of village origin: primitive settlement type, regional development type (for example, in the Qing Dynasty, immigrants developed many villages in the Northeast), ethnic migration type (especially in the late Western Jin Dynasty, the late Tang Dynasty and the late Northern Song Dynasty, there were three large-scale southward migrations of the Han population due to the minority nationality entering the Central Plains), retreat type and diachronic type (first, it means a place in which immigrants are embedded in an already populated population and second, it means to move in or embed at different times).[9] Xiaoshan, where the village is located, may have been a human settlement 6 or 7,000 years ago.[10] Because of its long history, there are not only a large number of ethnic migration villages[11] formed in the process of the southward migration of the Song Dynasty but also a large number of ancient villages that originated from the Wu and Yue Dynasties in the Xiaoshan region. There are also many regional development villages along with the successive reclamation in the south bank of Qiantang River. In contrast, the village obviously belongs to a diachronic embedding type where a single family or small family moved in to shelter from the world with a number of families embedded in over a period of time.

We may be able to make some limited inferences: This village is mainly a community as Fei Xiaotong calls it, while Skinner's so-called market significance, the rural market network, has very little significance. That is to say, in the general sense, villages may assume two basic functions: market and community. As a market, villages are used as the distributing centers of market transactions. As a community, villages may have taken a kind of protection in ancient times to protect the functions of village members, including the following: Village members cooperating to supplement the function of the family as a group; the boundary of existing water and soil resources being preserved outside the village, so that outsiders are excluded from entering the village for a long period of time, or competing with other villages for water and soil resources. Usually, villages as markets have community functions, while remote villages located far from the center of the network in the so-called market network by Skinner do not always have the functions of markets. However, as long as such villages have the latter protection, safeguard function, they can always exist as a community of community members.

As for the Jianshanxia Village, it has been in a secluded place since its escape from the world, and the meaning of the market is basically absent, but it does not prevent it from becoming a "community" as Fei Xiaotong defines.

However, from the current record, we cannot know in detail how the village community in history has been used for the protection and safeguarding of its members. Frankly, we don't know or even speculate about most of the things that happened after the Bao brothers first came to the village. What was the geography of the village at that time? How many people did the Bao brothers bring when they moved in? How did they build homes? Where did they get their wives? When the new settlers arrived, how did the settlers protect their "territory" under the mountain? What about the people who came after? How did the newcomer occupy the land? Was there any conflict with the settler? Who coordinated and how? Where was the market? What items were exchanged and how? What did the families do for a living? What about land distribution? How about property status and property relation?

What was the relationship between the adjacent natural villages? The four natural villages in Jianshanxia clearly showed that this type of village was a fixed space unit for multiple households, multiple families and multiple surnames for a long period of life, settlement and reproduction with clear boundaries rather than simple expansion of households and families of the same surnames in space. Not only that, in terms of social function, although there is no evidence of the common economic interests of the villages, and there is no record of the fact that these villages and their "union" can be used for the purpose of external defense, due to multiple clans and surnames inhabiting a space unit, it is difficult to envisage that the large-scale projects, such as the renovation of nunneries, bridges and high wind and flood control ridges in the village, could be implemented and shared by the residents without collective cooperation. When there was a need for cooperative action in the village, and the state power had not been as deep as it has ever been in this remote place, there was not only some common interest in the village but the village itself had acted as an independent social organization, namely, being complementary with household and family in the space unit in the village as civil society. This may be a very weak community of villages. It is also difficult to imagine that there is no conflict in the village because of multiple clans and surnames living in a space unit and experiencing a long process of embedding (although it is impossible to envisage any conflict between the families or clans in the four natural villages, how to gain the upper hand in the village and control the leadership of the village). However, the macroending of these four natural village histories at least shows us that such conflicts can be controlled within the limits of the collapse of the village community.[12]

(2) Although the village is far from the town in history, it is not always a small community of civil society. Even in ancient times, official forces had been trying to intervene. This intervention, while strengthening the community of villages, has contributed to the dual structure of village power with the family or clan.

The study of ancient history has already found that whether from the perspective of guaranteed income taxation, supplementary troops or local security, state power had been trying to use some kind of administrative approach to integrate China's vast countryside into a formal social system. But, the country's administrative ability is limited, for the vast countryside under a county and large population, state power often was not as good as in the human and financial resources to afford the management control of costs. It controls the connection of rural grassroots, in addition to the use of the household registration system, directly for the legal subjects, having more and more reliance on employing certain "proxy" rural grassroots organizations to carry out tasks. For example, the Qin and Han Dynasties had administrative systems at district and township levels, Wei, Jin, Southern and Northern Dynasties had a three-head system, the Sui Dynasty had the secondary township and district system,[13] Tang Dynasty had Lin, Bao, Li and Township system, Song Dynasty had Baojia system and Ming Dynasty had Lijia system; for most period of the Qing Dynasty, Baojia system and Li and Zheng systems might have been parallel to the rural base, but gradually turned to the former.[14] The "official" position of the township also changed with the above changes. In general, the township officials after the Western Zhou Dynasty were low-grade petty officials. The township officials of the Qin and Han Dynasties can still be described as inferior but respected. The two old ranks of the township, Sefu and Youjiao, "all have rank and salary".[15] After the Qin and Han Dynasties, township was abandoned, to the Sui and Tang dynasties, and the status of township officials was not as good as the past. In particular, when Emperor Wen of Sui abolished the township system, he did all he could to dismiss the township officials. From then on, the township officials gradually changed into the township posts, functioning in an acting capacity to service. After the Song Dynasty, counties became administrative organizations at the grassroots level. There were no township or village officials. "Head" "chief" in the grassroots organization under county were filled by the villagers in the form of servitude.

Although the Jianshanxia Village is remote, it is no exception. The brief account of the village is consistent with the above changes (after Song Dynasty). Therefore, we should have reason to infer that it also has the village-level organization formed by the state system in the hundreds of years from the Song to Qing Dynasty. The following general features were also inherited in terms of composition and functions of such an organization: (1) The scale standard was generally based on households and 100 households formed a li. Therefore, before the late Qing Dynasty, due to the small number of village households, Jianshanxia Village had not been independently formed into "li" or "tu" for a long time but was formed into the same "li" or "tu" with a nearby village as an annexed territory. This confirms that the designation of Lijia or Baojia was only based on territory, but not directly on the boundary of existing natural villages. Generally speaking, the institutional arrangement of this kind of household for legal subjects was different from the natural village framework based on family name and blood, which helped to weaken the various forces in natural villages that may have resisted the intentions of the state. At the same time, when the national forces intervened in the rural grassroots, they could avoid completely mixing with the various forces in the natural villages as far as possible. (2) When the national forces arranged the rural organization of the system, the original intention was to facilitate the collection of taxes and the distribution of Corvée. Gradually it was entrusted with the functions of advising farmers and assisting public security. Therefore, the rural organization had increasing support, and intermediary, agency administrative functions. On the one hand, it should cooperate with (or cope with) the government to persuade the villagers, to civilize the people and to maintain order; on the other hand, it was mainly to meet the public needs of the villagers, including statistical accounting, land measuring, levying taxes and apportion of Corvée and public facilities, production collaboration, dispute mediation, providing security and religious worship. (3) The state could not but rely mainly on the local gentry to run these rural organizations and tried to give corresponding benefits.[16] At the same time, in order to give full play to the functions of the rural organization's intermediary and agency, rulers generally avoided or minimized direct contact with the general family, which meant respecting the authority of rural organizations and their leaders and also saving some manpower and material resources.

(3) The legitimacy and power of the village organizations set up by the state, such as Lijia and Baojia, are derived from the state power and its regulations. However, the clan, clan village or the non-single-surnamed village, which is dominated by one clan, like the natural villages in Jianshanxia, is usually organized spontaneously with the acquiescence, tolerance and sometimes encouragement of the national forces.[17] However, in history, this dual power structure is usually complementary or mutually supportive, thus providing a minimum guarantee for the existence of this weak community of villages in the absence of a strong village common economy in ancient villages.

Of course, from a macro point of view, the relationship between this dual power structure is not static. The situation of the Northern Song Dynasty was acutely observed by the authors of the *Family History* from a cross-cultural perspective. "To some extent, the insertion of two foreign dynasties of Jin (1115–1234) and Yuan (1206–1368)", might have accelerated the rise of the folk clan power in the Han nationality residential area: "Clan cohesion is strengthened, Confucian morality is deeply rooted in the hearts of the people, characterized by the filial piety of men and the virginity of women".[18] This change was generally supported by the court and the local government. After the 15th year of Jiajing of Ming Dynasty, the government also provided the people with the legitimacy and impetus for "combined branches of clan and temple building".[19] Folk ancestral temples were built, and clan culture almost became the system culture supported by the government. The degree of support given to folk clan organizations and clan cultures after the Qianlong period in the Qing Dynasty was even stronger than before. The original ancestral halls in the Jianshanxia Village, namely, Shao Family Ancestral Hall, Yang Family Ancestral Hall, Jiang Family

Ancestral Hall and Bao Family Ancestral Hall (also known as the Hall of Peaceful Pleasure, the Hall of Four Wisdoms, the Hall of Land Granting and the Hall of Recognizing Talented People), were all built during the Qianlong period, and related to this background. Since the late Qing Dynasty, the relationship of the above dual structure in the village has changed. By and large, after the Qing Empire was gradually involved in the modernization process, the administrative machinery of the country became increasingly lax and could no longer effectively control the population of 400 million. Starting with the Taiping Heavenly Kingdom and the Westernization Movement, the state had increasingly handed over civil and rural management to some intermediary organizations. It was characterized by "compromise with local dignitaries and recognition of the role of family connectivity". On the one hand, the existence and strengthening of rural clan organizations and cultures were recognized. On the other hand, Baojia system without considering the connection between villages or wealth or status was promoted. The latter kind of system setting constituted some kind of restraint to the former; the possible conflict between the two was often solved by selecting appropriate Head of Bao and Head of Jia, who were usually smart, flexible, organized and capable and able to buffer the contradiction between residents and government, Baojia and clan.[20]

Of course, it was not necessarily consistent between the clan organizations and their standards of conduct and the official power and their agencies; such intermediaries in villages were not necessarily strong enough to handle all public affairs in the village. At the same time, the local government, which represented the national power, did not necessarily intervene in the villages, or only handed over the affairs of the villages to the clan organization. In this respect, a dispute over the high wind and flood control ridge that the village built during the Daoguang period is interesting. It was said that this ridge was built by Zhu Dajin, an old man in the village. It was more than 2 meters high, 5 meters wide and about 95 meters long. The ancestral hall of Shao family was linked to the foot of Wugong Mountain, and trees and bamboo were planted on the ridge. At that time, the construction of this ridge mainly considered the location of Shangmen at the breach in the northern village, which had no obstruction for the high wind, endangering the house and the ridge could prevent wind. When he was constructing the ridge, he moved the creek path to the foot of the mountain to prevent the water from drowning passerby. In the village, a diversion channel was opened to introduce Ling Creek water to the village residential area so that the women with bound feet could wash rice and laundry nearby. After the ridge was finished, Zhu Dajin's reputation was greatly increased. As a result, the squire, Jiang Keshu, was outraged. Jiang complained to the county magistrate, prosecuting "ten crimes" against Zhu Dajin, including privately opening an inland river, building a "city wall" without permission (high wind and water-proof ridge), building Official Avenue secretly (creek path) and destroying "feng shui" of Jiang family. As a result, after the county government came to the village to visit and investigate, it was decided that what Zhu Dajin had done was beneficial to the people, and that the "ten crimes" were false accusations, and Zhu Dajin was judged to win the lawsuit.[21]

Today, it is just a common case that the rich in the village are bullying the good and finally being held back by the officials. Perhaps because the project was huge at that time, especially because the people of the Jianshanxia Village were always simple and uncomplicated without any big dispute, the event was finally seen as a major event, and it was eventually recorded as an important historical story. Of course, although the event was common, we can still vaguely see the way the clans, squire and ordinary residents of the village acted at that time and their relations with the official forces outside the village: (1) Among the characters involved in the incident were villagers, the squire, Zhu Dajin, who had public prestige in the village, and the county government. Organizations such as Bao and Jia did not seem to play an organizational and mediation role. (2) The related factors include the reputation of the squire's personal authority, the self-interest of Jiang clan and the public interest of the other natural villages in Shangmen and Jianshanxia. (3) When the selfish interests of the clan were too aggressive or incompatible with the public interest of the village, the official would eventually act as the arbiter of arbitration, and was highly likely to support the public interest of the village. (4) Most of the villagers were bound to participate in the project and support the maintenance of the village public interest in this event.

Although we are unable to obtain further reliable details, it is impossible to confirm whether such organizations, such as Baojia, had played a mediating role in this event. Thus, it is difficult to discern the relationship between the national strength and the rural organization required to be set up and the relationship between the rise of the patriarchal clan and the village community. However, the existence of the so-called village community at the psychological level, and the utilitarian level, sometimes supported and protected by the state, can be more or less confirmed from the incident. The incident may also be used to explain the following: The clan organization and strength which are completely independent of the influence of national power may not be conducive to the formation, maintenance and strengthening of the village community in the non-single family name villages. However, clan organizations and forces that are completely independent of the power of the state do not seem to exist; in addition to the patriarchal clan organizations accepting the influence of the state, they established the Bao and Jia organizations required by the state and accepted supervision of the state power; it was hard for villagers to know only a family or a clan without knowing villages.

(4) During the period of the Republic of China, the weight of the administrative community in the dual structure of the village continued to rise to the level of institutional legitimacy.

The Kuomintang government has been trying to use the state power in the countryside, and from the 1930s, it has been trying to review the clan power and its power channels in the ruling area. One of the most important means is to strengthen the zoning work reflected in the previous record. In 1928, the Kuomintang government promulgated the constitution of the county and set up the District, Village and Li. In the countryside, the Township, Town, Lü and Lin system were successively implemented, and finally the township and the Baojia system were implemented. The work was the same as in the past, regardless of the clan standard, but still depended on the number of households by referring to village distance. These changes affected the Jianshanxia Village, resulting in the village construction system of Jianshanxia (in 1928, it was called Jianshan United Village). The substantive impact of this change may be in two areas: First, the original village community began to move from the natural village to the administrative village in connotation and boundaries. Both inside and outside the village, the official government and the folk were more accustomed to the existence of this administrative village rather than the original four natural villages. At the very least, officials preferred the newly established village as a unit of administrative management, and the villagers' acceptance of such arrangements seemed to cause little inconvenience. This was the case from the establishment of the Jianshan United Village in 1928 to the 20th Bao in the village of Changtan in 1947. Second, such zoning became a habit and was respected. That is why, after the establishment of the new regime in 1949, although in 1950 the Baojia system was abolished and the administrative village system was established, and the village name was officially designated as Jianshanxia Village, it still respected the old habits and actually followed the original division.

In addition, the Kuomintang government promulgated the civil law in 1934, trying to establish a new type of western-style marriage and family relations and deliberately advocated the "new life" campaign in the countryside to provide a new model of behavior. In some rural areas, it also tried to conduct land reform or to determine the ownership of land in order to clear the relationship between the landlord and tenant farmers, and on this basis, it began to establish a fair tax system and so on. These works constituted a major reform of the original dual structure of the village, which helped to further strengthen the function of the village as a community rather than as a clan. It was not clear what effect the latter two actions had on the Jianshanxia Village. On the macro level, however, these jobs, especially the latter two, were clearly enormous. After 1937, during the Chinese People's War of Resistance against Japanese Aggression, the army was also objectively canceling the possibility of these jobs or canceling its performance. So, although the Kuomintang regime explicitly set up new zoning in the ruling area, and these settings were largely continued after 1949, it was difficult to assess exactly how the Kuomintang regime had performed in its efforts to scour the countryside. On the contrary, the village was in the core of the Kuomintang regime in Zhejiang, but it could still be a red guerrilla area because it was located in the hills and dozens of miles from the county. In 1927, the CPC Xiaoshan local party organization and later the Jinxiao Detachment of the eastern Zhejiang guerrilla column had many activities in the village.[22] The records of these activities indicate that the Kuomintang regime had inadequate control capacity and low system performance in such rural areas. Therefore, even if it had planned to brush up the original dual power structure in the countryside, it would not be possible to realize the direct control of the rural grassroots by the state power. As a matter of fact, the existing family trees in the Jianshanxia Village were renewed in the later period of the Republic of China; the four ancestral halls of the village were not interrupted during the Republic of China. This point almost prompts us that the village community in this village actually moved from the natural village to the administrative village, and the elements of clan organization were basically excluded from the village community, after the establishment of the new national regime in 1949.[23]

In this way, before we continue to analyze the history of Jianshanxia after 1949, we have reason to stress that as early as before 1949, a remote mountain village such as Jianshanxia Village, like most villages in the whole country, experienced the evolution from the natural village to the administrative united village; in the rural life, the village had already been one of the most important social communities; this change and the villagers' recognition of it provided organizational and psychological resources for the establishment of administrative villages after 1949 and even for the formation of unit villages.

Some Western researchers have apparently paid attention to such phenomena and appear to very much agree with Fei Xiaotong's concentric circle, namely, a summary of the differential order pattern.[24] However, it seems necessary for these researchers to pay attention to the following: (1) Before 1949, villages were important and basic levels of these concentric circles. (2) In villages such as the Jianshanxia Village, there are families of different surnames, clans, and administrative unit villages outside. Therefore, the village is no longer the synonym of the family (clan). (3) Villages are entities that exist at the same time as families. As a way of settlement, it clearly includes the population of the organization in the family, the land with clear boundaries, and the specific natural resources, residential buildings, intangible cultural composition (such as the concept of clan, Fengshui consciousness), and social and market contacts. This not only makes community public activities and public interests exist in the village but also makes it possible for the so-called "co-village" value to be a standard in village life and for a member of the village to carry out social action. (4) The foundation of supporting the village community seems to come mainly from two aspects. The first is that the village, as a community, has the function of protecting and safeguarding the members of the community, while excluding the members outside the community. The second is that the national forces usually take the village as the basic level in the management of rural areas and generally do not directly face the countless families. Therefore, as long as the two foundations, especially the former, do not disintegrate, the village as a community of rural society will always exist. The power to weaken or counterbalance the village as a community, of course, comes first and foremost from the families in the village. The latter, as the basic production unit, settlement unit and living unit of the farming society (or as the primary group), obviously bears more protection and safeguard functions than the former, and is a more "grassroots" community in the farming society.

1.3 Significance of Administrative Village: Village Community Becomes a Formal Social Organization

The historical changes of the village after 1949 are relatively clear.

One of the most striking changes is the unprecedented integration of the village into the official network of the state. It can be said that compared with the state power's efforts to expand rural areas through various channels (such as business groups, brokers, temple fairs, folk religions, mythological and symbolic resources)[25] after new policies of the latter stage of Qing Dynasty, the expansion of state power to the countryside after 1949 was clearly more conscious and straightforward. For Jianshanxia Village, although the Kuomintang regime was unable to control it completely because of its remoteness, the new regime has carried out a systematic and comprehensive construction of grassroots organizations in the process of transforming highly organized rural production relations, cooperated to transform the traditional "function in an acting capacity to service", successfully realized substantial extension of the party and administrative organs at the village level and directly incorporated villagers into the official organization network set up by the state. For the village's original blood, geographical and industrial organizations, the country no longer depended on the intermediary, but made a devastating transformation. The whole process of organization construction mainly includes the establishment of four connected channels, namely, administrative organ, party affairs organization, production organizations and farmers' mass organization. After this transformation, the dual power structure of the rural grassroots before 1949 was finally attributed to a single structure under the leadership of the state.

As a result, Jianshanxia Village, along with hundreds of thousands of villages across the country, quickly became a village community directly connected with state power. This community, of course, has a new meaning and new functions. In this regard, it is particularly noteworthy that the village reconstruction movement was an integral part of the huge social project launched by the new regime after 1949: (1) The new regime intended to lead it to become a formal social organization as soon as possible, as a city unit, in order to form a unified social system within a larger social scope. (2) From the beginning of the administrative village, the new village community had been rapidly pushed to the unit system in practice, although because of the difference of the urban and rural conditions, the new village community could only form a variant different from the urban unit. This action had reached its peak during the formation of the People's Commune. (3) After the final disintegration of the People's Commune, the village community, as a unit variant, was still the organizational resource for the collective cooperative action of the village, including the organizational resource for the Jianshanxia Village to turn to the unit village.

Of course, the above process was implemented in two stages. Among them, the time limit for the first stage was roughly from the land reform movement to the completion of agricultural cooperation. The second stage was the People's Commune period. In the first stage, the state focused on promoting the establishment of administrative villages and their organizational structure, the land reform movement and the cooperative transformation movement. The village became a new village community—a formal social organization incorporated into the national network.

Let's look at the first project. Because the area where the village is located was a new area after the army had crossed the river south, the new regime naturally regarded "organizing" as the prerequisite for all other work according to the experience of the old liberated areas. Therefore, the establishment of the administrative village organizational structure became the first important thing to do in Jianshanxia Village after the establishment of a local government. The basic process was as follows: In May 1949, the Kuomintang government retreated from Xiaoshan. From May to June, after the successive establishment of the CPC Xiaoshan County Committee and the People's Government, in terms of administrative substitution, the provincial government established the township People's Government in the native rural areas and protected areas in accordance with the Provisional Organizational Directive of the Rural Regime. Then, under the responsibility of the township people's government, the Baojia system was abolished at the village level. The Village Administrative Committee not out of production elected by the villagers' assembly was to be composed of the Head and Deputy Head of the village, and the 15–25 households were to set up administrative groups. In May 1951, the Regulations on the Trial Organization of the Township People's Government of Zhejiang Province and the Regulations on the Trial Organization of the People's Congress of Zhejiang Province were implemented to organize the meetings of the people's congresses of townships and towns and to elect the people's committees of townships and towns. The Village Head System was to be abolished under the township, and one person or one deputy director and one director were to be promoted to be responsible for the administration of the village, and the administrative team leader was to be held by the other village representatives as an additional post. In the aspect of mass organization, after Xiaoshan County Committee was established, it soon led to the establishment of the Xiaoshan County Farmers Association to prepare construction of the farmers' associations of townships and villages from top to bottom. According to the General Principles of Farmers Association, which was passed by the Government Administration Council in July 1950, the farmers' association was stipulated to be a mass organization of a voluntary union of peasants. At the same time, it was clearly stipulated that it was the legal enforcement mechanism of land reform in rural areas. Before the land reform was completed, it was a fighting organization of peasants against feudalism. (The organization was replaced by a cooperative.)

The organizational construction of the village was completely synchronous with the whole organization construction process in the county area. In June 1949, with the help of the head of Changtan Township, the Village Farmers Association was established, with one elected director and four members. In October, the Village Security Committee and the villagers' militia company were established, with three platoons and nine squads, with a total of 108 militiamen. The Village Farmers Association was responsible for all the work of the villagers before the township government appointed the village leader the following year, including land reform, counter-revolution, War to Resist U.S. Aggression and Aid Korea, and the formation of a mutual aid group. In December 1949, the People's Government of Daicun District, Changtan Township was established. In July 1950, the administrative village-level organization of Jianshanxia was established, which belonged to Daicun District, Changtan Township and was called Jianshanxia Village with eight administrative groups; Baojia system was abolished at the same time. The People's Government of the township appointed the village head and deputy head, who were responsible for the work of the whole village. In addition, party organizations, women's organizations and so on were established. Among them, in October 1949, the Youth League branch of Changtan Township was established, and three members of the Youth League from Jianshanxia were included. By 1951, the independent village Youth League branch was established, with 25 members. (After July 1957, it was called the lower branch of China's Communist Youth League of Jianshanxia.) The Women's Meeting in the Jianshanxia Village was established in the beginning of 1950, and the following year it was changed to the representative system and called the Women's Representative (Women's Congress) of the Jianshanxia Village. In addition to organizing women to participate in the mobilization of the army, supporting the army and giving preferential treatment to the families of the army men and martyrs of the War to Resist U.S. Aggression and Aid Korea and other activities, another major event of the Women's Congress in the early 1950s was to organize and publicize the Marriage Law of the People's Republic of China published in 1950 and publicize marriage autonomy, wedding simplification, family harmony and so on, which had a great influence on the customs of the village at that time. Gu chengxiang, the representative of Women's Congress, was awarded "the County Agricultural Labor Model" in 1953 because of her outstanding achievements in all aspects. In contrast, the construction of the village party organizations was a little slower than those of the above-mentioned organizations, because local party organizations were more concerned with the recruitment of party members at the village level. At the beginning, in general, the higher party organizations were in search of poor peasants and farm laborers with "high consciousness, ideological purity and good working attitude" as the development object in the fight against the bandits and the land reform movement.[26] By the end of 1952, there were four CPC members in the village, and a party group was established under the party branch of Yunshi Township; in July 1956, the party branch of the Communist Party of China (CPC) of Jianshanxia was formed after another four CPC members were recruited in the cooperative movement.

Then, in a short time, Jianshanxia Village established a village administrative organization, militia, public security organization, party organizations, Youth League organizations, women's organization and farmers' organization on the basis of the original village domain according to the requirements of the new regime. Moreover, in this construction process, the following characteristics were almost obvious: (1) The new regime basically respected the local traditions of the original townships and villages, and at the same time made it clear that the village level was the rural grassroots level. This was further strengthened in the subsequent land reform movement. Several years later, primary cooperative, advanced cooperative, production brigade and so on came into being

in the process of collectivization, and people's communalization and
other movements were also organized by the village boundaries, or were
the direct alternative names of the administrative village. In fact, by
the time the socialist transformation of the rural relations of production
was completed, the major organizations took the administrative village
as the actual unit to complete the construction. Land, manpower and
other resources were also delimited by administrative villages (or
cooperatives, brigade, etc.) to demarcate and occupy the boundary.
Finally, even production and distribution were realized by using village
territory as the boundary and unit (or one of the units). In a word, the
interests of the countryside were localized, which had been implemented
for the village area. In this sense, if the establishment of administrative
villages in the countryside, the organization of land reform, and the
promotion of cooperatives and People's Communes by the new regime
after 1949 were almost a process of continuous strengthening of the
village community, then the starting point of this process was to build a
village-based organization. (2) In terms of system, these organizations
were composed of mass organizations and state formal organizations (or
quasi-formal organizations), with the former as the core. The legitimacy
of both organizations, however, came from the explicit provisions of
the new regime, and both were subject to the support and control of
the government. Among them, the functional role of mass organization
was also increased and decreased by the state government as necessary.
Therefore, the relationship between the village organization and the
state power should be quite close. (3) The comprehensive management
and control of rural society were implemented through the organization
of sub-categories. With the exception of organizations with productive
management functions like the later cooperatives, the seven organizations
mentioned above covered almost all aspects of the villagers' lives.
According to the relevant population information of the village, in
1949, the population of the whole village in Jianshanxia was only 164
households with 707 people. On the basis of this population scale, the
degree of organization in the village should be quite high. This, of course,
means that the traditional villages have been completely reorganized,

thus changing the content of the village community, and especially in the psychological sense of the original village community, the connotation of organizational security has greatly increased. (4) The distribution pattern and relationship pattern of village organization were basically established. Figure 1.1 and Table 1.3 in this chapter show the organizational structure and organizational function of Jianshanxia Village in the 1990s. It was the same as or similar to the structure and function of the village organization just established in the early 1950s. (5) In the construction of village-level organizations under the new regime, clan organizations did not receive any support from the new regime. As a result, the legitimacy of clan organizations in villages began to wane, although patriarchal concepts and other clan cultures still existed. (6) Of course, the establishment of the above-mentioned organizations was not directly organized to produce and improve the life of the villagers, so the overall organizational advance had no direct benefits on the improvement of villagers' lives. At that time, because of the shortage of land resources in the village, many villagers were living in a state of incapacity. Most of the labor force in the village mainly relied on going to Xiaoshan town and Yiwu County to serve as temporary workers to build railways to support the family.

In fact, the reconstruction of rural organization was only an integral part of a large social project on the national level. For the new regime, the reconstruction of the village community was unlikely to be complete without a land tenure system and a change in the whole production relationship. More importantly, the community itself was not the purpose. It was the real need of the new regime to rapidly stabilize social security, restore production and raise the economic income of members of the society so as to expand the legitimacy of the regime. Therefore, with the establishment of the above-mentioned organizations, the second rural social transformation project, the land reform movement, came quickly. As with almost all the villages in Xiaoshan, the Jianshanxia Village was quickly following the timetable set by the local government, and entered into the eliminating bandits and land reform movement. At that time, there were also bandits in the Jianshanxia Village, but the task was accomplished quickly and smoothly,[27] and the land reform movement had also been pushed forward by a timetable set by the government. The whole of Xiaoshan took the village as a unit for land reform from October 1950 to May 1951. To this end, the government sent 51 civil reform teams and 535 cadres. In the village, the land reform began in late December and ended in May. Due to the poor natural resources, the total area of arable land in the whole village was very small. In addition to 1,451 mu of bamboo, the village had only 7 mu of paddy field and 117 mu of hillside miscellaneous land. Per capita grain cultivated land was only one fen and seven li. The remaining 1,336 mu of sparse forest mountains and 2,559 mu of barren hills were of no benefit to speak of. As a result, there was a polarization between the rich and the poor in the village, as shown in Table 1.1. On the one hand about 35% of the bamboo forest and the field were held in the hands of three landlords and five industrial and commercial households, and about 75.4% of the farmers had only 70 acres of arable land and 372 mu of bamboo forest; on the other hand, the landlords and industrialists did not have much absolute property in their hands, and the polarization between the rich and the poor, social stratification and so on were more meaningful to the village. Therefore, the focus of Jianshanxia Village land reform also was shifted to redistribution of the bamboo forest, as the significance of average distribution of arable land was not usually so great. The main situation was as documented in the *Chronicles of Jianshanxia Villages*.

In late December 1950, the People's Government of Changtan Township sent Chen Quan'an to the Jianshanxia Village to carry out the land reform movement to abolish feudal land ownership. The villagers elected to form a land reform group. The group leader was Yang Binghai and land reform representatives were Yang Maotang, Shao Guanshui, yuan Shuixian, Yang Zhengming, Yang Guanqi, Shao Shuizeng, Bao Wuqian, Gu Renxian, Chen Fenqin, Jiang Guanxian, Shao Xingan and Jiang Ankun. The main content of land reform was to redistribute the bamboo mountain according to the situation that mountain forest was the main means of production in the Jianshanxia Village.

After studying policy, publicizing education, land registration and investigation, the whole village had three landlords, five households, 34 middle peasants and 129 poor farmworkers. According to the policy of land reform, the reform of bamboo forest was as follows: no change to the middle peasants, confiscating all the bamboo hills of the landlords and then distributing one to each according to their family population; expropriate redundant bamboo forests of individual and commercial households in the same way; the confiscated and expropriated bamboo forests were distributed among the poor and farmers without or under them. The housing reform was as follows: The landlords set aside three main housing blocks and one Long, four side housing blocks, three hall buildings and some household necessities for the poor, farm laborers; there was no change to the middle peasants and individual and commercial households. The possession of bamboo hills after land reform was as follows: Poor peasants and farm laborers occupied 52.6% of the village bamboo forests from the previous 25.7%; landlords occupied 3.6% of the village bamboo forests from the previous 25.7%; individual and commercial households occupied 4.2% of the village bamboo forests from the previous 9%. In May 1951, the land reform movement ended in the Jianshanxia Village.

In the cooperative period, the tools of production, such as the shovels, chisels and Tangtan of the landlords and industrial and commercial households, were owned by collectives.[28]

There were two phenomena of land reform in the Jianshanxia Village that need to be given attention. In one case, researchers discovered that the state called for the implementation of the township as the unit for reducing the excess and increasing the deficiency in the policy of land reform. But, in fact, land reform in many parts of the south was carried out in the same way as the Jianshanxia Village by taking the village as the unit. Article 11 of Chapter III of the Law on Civil Law Reform stipulated the following: "The allocation of land shall be carried out in an administrative unit of a township or a township. On the basis of the original cultivated land, the adjustment method is used to distribute land according to the population based on the quantity, quality, and location of the land". According to this regulation, the land adjustment method should take the township as the scope and the unit, the rural land and rural population as the base, calculate the average amount of land per person and then compare it with the original amount of land in each household to draw out over the average, or make up the average. The purpose of implementing this method was, of course, to take into account the uneven quantity and quality of land occupied by the administrative villages, try to reduce the excess and reverse the deficiency with the aid of the government in the land reform, achieving the average and equality of land distribution and other property in a larger rural area than the village area.[29] However, the policy and its ideals encountered obstacles in many places that had existed for many years in the village community. The adjustment between villages was far more difficult than that between households. Although the area of arable land per capita in Jianshanxia Village could not be compared with other villages in the countryside, it was impossible to divert cultivated land from other villages at all; it was difficult to realize land exchange of the old bamboo forest with land of other villages. Finally, they could only adopt the methods used in the above records to carry out a very limited land reform in the village (see Table 1.2). Such flexible methods not only meant that the former village community was the most basic social community in the countryside but also showed that the new regime recognized the great difficulty in the allocation of land and other resources. Thus, some unequal distribution of land and other property between villages had to be accepted. This recognition in fact established the boundary of the village (such as the boundary of land occupation, the boundary of population employment, the boundary of benefit distribution and so on). At this starting point, the subsequent collectivization movement took the village as a collective unit, which was the logical thing. Then, within the Jianshanxia Village, due to the limited resources available for allocation of land and other property resources, comparatively speaking, the land reform had a more obvious effect within the village community on equalizing the property of the village members and strengthening the average and equality of community members. In this way, the original village community was reconfirmed and strengthened by the new regime along the geographical boundary (and regional interests). In the village, an unprecedented interest equalization adjustment was made through the unity of administrative organization. The meaning of the village community was highlighted here. The status of the villages and other organizations in the village community had been further established.

Table 1.1. Prior-land reform possession of production means of all social classes.

Class	Hou.	Pop.	Paddy field (mu)			Dry land (mu)	Bam. land (mu)	Open forest land (mu)	Tro. Sho.	Eng.	Pond beach	Mat. War.	Mil.
			Sum	For. Vil.	Nat. Vil.								
Poor peasant and farmhand	129	470	8	4.8	3.2	67.3	372	431	3	2	1	4	
Mid. peasant	34	189	21	17.2	3.8	40.3	575	51	19	5	4	28	5
Ind. and com. household	5	38	1	1	/	3.7	130	113	5	2	2	11	
Landlord	3	32	41	41	/	5.4	374	282	5	4	5	12	1
Sum	171	729	71	64	7	117	1,451	1,336	32	13	12	55	6

Notes: Hou. = Household; Pop. = Population; For. Vil. = Foreign village; Nat.Vil. = Native village; Bam. = Bamboo; Tro.Sho. = Trough shove; Eng. = Engraver; Mat.War. = Material warehouse; Mil. = Millstone; Mid. = Middle; Ind. = Industrial; com. = commercial.

Paddy field in foreign villages was still plowed by non-local villagers after 1949. Ownership of the land was also sent to non-local villagers during collectivization. Therefore, there was simply 7 mu of paddy field in this village in the early 1950s.

Table 1.2.   Prior-land reform changes of bamboo land and houses of all social classes.

Class	Hou.		Pop.		Bam. land				House			
	Num. of hou.	Per. (%)	Num. of village	Per. (%)	Prior-land reform		Post-land reform		Prior-land reform		Post-land reform	
					mu	%	mu	%	Bui.	Bun.	Bui.	Bun.
Poor peasant and farmhand	129	75.4	470	64.5	372	25.7	762	52.6	168.5	60	178.5	60
Mid. peasant	34	19.8	189	25.9	575	39.6	575	39.6	72.5	39	72.5	39
Ind. and com. household	5	3	38	5.2	130	9	62	4.2	16.5	13	16.5	13
Landlord	3	1.8	32	4.4	374	25.7	52	3.6	16.5	16	6.5	16
Sum	171	100	729	100	1,451	100	1,451	100	274	128	274	128

Notes: Hou. = Household; Pop. = Population; Bam. = Bamboo; Num. = Number; Per. = Percentage; Bui. = Building; Bun. = Bungalow.

The end of land reform did not mean the completion of village reconstruction, at least for the new regime. The third rural social transformation project, the cooperative movement, came quickly. From the macro point of view, the new regime had accumulated the experience of establishing rural mutual cooperation organizations and carrying out labor mutual assistance in the period of the red base and had always regarded cooperation and collectivization as the necessary preparations for socialism.[30] In addition to the collectivization of agricultural production materials such as land, they also cared about the cooperation and collectivization (centralization) of labor organization and management mode. Therefore, although the land reform had just ended, the state did not abandon the rural economic production and life of the organization. In contrast, the experience of the base areas had been rapidly applied and promoted throughout the country. The difference was that the cooperative movement had a higher level of self-conscious organization from top to bottom. At the same time, the purpose of the organization of the cooperative movement was to improve production,[31] and focus on production cooperatives, implementing the rural collectivization to realize socialist transformation of rural areas.[32]

Under such a design, the cooperative movement, which started from the establishment of the mutual aid group, was moving very rapidly. As a local party organization, Xiaoshan County Committee like the party organizations in neighboring areas established the goal to increase production and prevent polarization, organize farmers to run mutual aid groups and try to push the decentralized operation into collective operation according to the central view, shortly after the completion of the land reform. From the subsequent historical process, this move could actually be understood as a complementary production management organization based on the established village organization and was the first step to further reform the land system. The next year, the participating farmers accounted for 54.71% of the total number of farmers. Xiaoshan County Committee then began to run the first semi-socialist agricultural production cooperative. By 1954, there were 22 primary cooperatives in the county, of which only two were spontaneous. In autumn of the following year, under the guidance of Mao Zedong's "on agricultural cooperation" work was carried out. By the end of the year, the number of primary cooperatives increased sharply to 2,247, covering 52.6% of the total peasant households. In the spring of 1956, with the approval of the Provincial Party Committee, four advanced agricultural cooperatives (collectively owned and distributed by labor) were started. At the end of the year, there were 313 advanced cooperatives and 1,163 primary cooperatives in the county, and 92.5% of the total farmers had joined the cooperative households (53.2% of the advanced cooperatives). In the spring of 1957, there were more than 5,000 farmers from 114 advanced cooperatives asking to withdraw. In autumn, according to the Instructions on Rectifying Agricultural Production Cooperatives of the CPC Central Committee, the County Committee sent the working group to the grassroots level to consolidate and develop. By the end of the year, the number of cooperative households accounted for 98.1% of the total farmer households, basically completing the "Socialist Transformation of Agriculture".[33] Jianshanxia Village was not far behind the process at all. Perhaps because the first two rural social reconstruction projects had already established some kind of mechanism of the national model and guidance, whether or not the villagers in Jianshanxia were really accustomed to the new changes, they were almost fully guided by the state, accelerating their slide into a cooperative movement that they were not familiar with. In October 1952, the village set up eight mutual aid production groups. Slightly different from other places, because of the small per capita occupation of mountain forests and land, they were owned by individuals and were cultivated by individuals; villagers only joined the mutual aid group of bamboo hills with grooving tools to produce handmade paper in partnership. The distribution was said to be according to work. A total of 139 households participated, accounting for 81% of the total number of households in the village. In the spring of 1955, the whole village established five primary agricultural production cooperatives, namely, Jianguo, Jianan, Xinmin, Jianzhong and Zhongshan, and one mutual aid group, similar to the other mutual aid group. In other words, members joined the cooperative of bamboo hills with grooving tools, and the land was still cultivated by the individuals. In July 1956, the two representative directors of the village (The constituency system was introduced by universal suffrage in 1954. The Jianshanxia Village was designated as the 5th and 6th constituency in Changtan Township, two district representative directors were elected and the village head system was abolished). And the party members of the village were required by the county government to implement the process envisaged in Mao Zedong's *On the Cooperative Transformation of Agriculture* by studying concretely and plan the cooperative transformation problem of this village. By the end of the year, five primary cooperatives in the village, one production group, and 32 individual households formed the Changtan (soon to be renamed Jianshanxia) advanced agricultural production cooperative. The cooperative was divided into eight production teams, which organized the papermaking group and the agricultural group to carry out the handmade paper and grain production. The forests and land were in public ownership, and were clearly not allowed to be traded, pawned or rented. The principle of distribution was fixed pay and distribution according to work. Obviously, from cooperatives to advanced cooperatives, it involved not only the change of property relations from the occupation of the land and the main means of production to the possession of the collective (village) but also the change of the mode of operation from the scattered labor of the peasant households to the collective work.[34] This was undoubtedly the basic transformation of the traditional village relationship and constituted a huge psychological span for the villagers of Jianshanxia. However, because the process of every major link was organized by the Xiaoshan county party committee and government according to the instructions of the central and provincial party committee and the provincial government, and mass movement was always organized by the corresponding organization set up, when it was necessary to speed up progress or solve problems such as the failure of the lower-level organizations, the task force would usually be sent to lead the work directly on behalf of the superior organization. Therefore, in the whole movement in the top-down implementation process, the national forces appeared to be very strong, the villagers did not have any resistance to this and finally, as in most villages, the process of cooperative transformation was completed in a uniform manner.

Of course, unlike previous village reconstruction efforts, the country's policy texts on the cooperative movement defined the purpose of the cooperative movement as changing the form of productive organization and even the entire production relationship, and thus developing the rural production and preventing polarization. However, each link of the cooperative movement clearly meant the overall reconstruction of the economic organization, political organization and social organization of the village. Therefore, the completion of the cooperation indicated that the village reconstruction work had finally completed a stage.

In this way, it was almost possible to say that from the establishment of administrative villages to cooperation the social reconstruction work was initiated and led by the state at the village level. It was of great significance to realize the effective extension of state power in this remote mountain village. After this process, as a community of villages, the Jianshanxia Village community had clearly acquired some noteworthy new features:

First, through the intervention of the state power, the new village-level organization structure had been established. This organization took village party organization and village administration as the core, and guaranteed the top-down connection with the ruling party's superior organization and local government and organized the village members into seven or eight collective organizations (among which the farmers associations gradually disappeared in the cooperative process) in accordance with social roles and activities for centralized management. When the system was put into practice, it only made the village power structure unified, established the new organizational authority and eliminated the legitimacy of the original clan organization and large-scale activities in the village at the institutional level; at the same time, it also caused important changes in the functions of the family in the village, for example, after the completion of the cooperation and until the 1980s, the family was no longer the unit of economic production organization for decades, but the unit and social control unit that was mainly responsible for reproduction. Thus, in institutional arrangement, the collective members of the village play a primary role of the social members in the village. The widespread impact of the reconstruction of village organizations meant that its significance was actually far beyond the organizational level itself. It was combined with the following changes, which meant the reconstruction of the village's social structure and social order. At least, it had an important influence on social relations, the way of activities, the consciousness of village and so on. In other words, the reconstruction of the village organization and the great changes in the village social structure were the same process here, although the latter change was not as easy to measure as the previous one.[35] On the basis of this change, a variety of systems, symbols and activities that regarded the village as a community and the members of the village as members of the village collective were often encouraged or readily accepted while a variety of systems, symbols and activities that could break down the village community and focused on clan or family were suppressed, even loss of legitimacy. For example, the ancestral temple gathering and sacrificing ceremony in the village was quickly abandoned during this period. Shao, Yang, Jiang and Bao's four ancestral halls were either removed or used for other purposes.

Second, in general, the land reform movement, which is centered on the average land rights within the village area, and the continued cooperative movement to any village meant to reorganize the land relationship and property relationship of the village, and establish the average degree of village community membership in the village; in the form of administrative division, the village members were locked in the village, and the village became the integration of community and workplace with a personal social identity card for external recognition of village boundaries. From then on, the country, which was represented by local party organizations and local government representatives in rural land rights adjustment, interest adjustment and various income redistribution, usually took villages as units or reference units. For example, on November 23, 1953, the Council of State issued an Order on the Planned Purchase and Supply of Grain for implementation of the unified purchase and marketing of grain, according to the state policy and the severe shortage of farmland in Jianshanxia, using which the local government decreed that the whole grain ration of the whole mountain village should be settled from the state. Until 1979, when the state increased grain sales by more than 100,000 catties in order to expand forestry production in the village, the village was supplied by the state with more than 500,000 catties of original grain every year. The policy did not stop until 1993 when food prices were lifted. Where the village area was increasingly clear and closely linked to the distribution of benefits, the relationship between the village and the party and government organizations at the higher level, and with other neighboring villages (such as land, mountain and forest ownership), had a great impact on the members of the village; as a community of interests and interest unit, the status of the village greatly increased. From then on, it was not only a question of region and community for being a villager in Jianshanxia or not, but it meant the number of cultivated land per capita, whether it was supplied by the state and other practical interests, while the surname or clan of the villagers in Jianshanxia is not a factor affecting these interests.

Third, the village and social organizations had more and more legitimacy to organize the economy and business activities; as compensation, the state also supported villages and social groups by providing low social security for village members. Subsequently, the village as a community had a new economic foundation. In this regard, the impact of cooperatives was the most significant. In view of the overall situation of the country at that time, the purpose of promoting the cooperative movement, in addition to the development of production and the prevention of polarization as indicated in the policy text, a relatively secret and more urgent task, which Hu Sheng pointed out more than 30 years later, was to solve the urban food supply crisis caused by the development of industrialization. In order to solve the crisis, the state began to adopt the harshest policy of grain purchase and marketing since 1953,[36] namely, closing the original grain market and the government was responsible for carrying out the exclusive sale. Farmers must sell their crops to the state in accordance with the quantity, variety and price set by the government, which could not be exempted even in the year of famine. If farmers were underfed because of years of famine or excessive government procurement, the government shall, after the approval, sell the grain to the peasants, as appropriate, rather than return of grain. (City residents used vouchers to purchase grain from the national grain department according to the

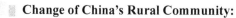
quantity, type and price of the ration determined by the national factors, such as sex, age, occupation, residential area, etc.) Since this system was obviously mandatory for farmers, also due to the dispersion of housing and management of 110 million farmers at that time, technically any administrative organizations didn't know the changes in harvest and could not ensure correct door-to-door collection. The state could not help but think that the relations of production under individual ownership could not guarantee a large supply of grain. In order to solve the contradiction between individual operation, the mutual aid group and the policy of purchasing and marketing, in December 1953, the CPC Central Committee adopted a resolution on the development of agricultural cooperatives and decided to promote cooperation. It said that, first of all, the peasant households should be absorbed into a number of large-scale agricultural primary cooperatives. Although the primary cooperatives had not abolished the private ownership of the means of production, they had realized a unified operation and the products were first owned by collectives. After deducting the state agricultural tax, public welfare fund, accumulation fund, and other taxes, they were distributed to the members in the form of land compensation and labor remuneration. Then, on the basis of the primary cooperative, it constructed advanced cooperatives on a larger scale, and fully realized collective ownership of the means of production, the unified management of labor and means of production, and the uniform distribution of labor products.

The actual process did show that, through the construction of the primary and advanced cooperatives, the state had finally eliminated the contradiction in the struggle for the control of the products with the rural families in a way, realizing the complete control of the state. One of the most significant results of this change was not only the individual farmers and families, who no longer had the right to control the means of production, but also the fact that the economic base of the family's control of agricultural products in the village had been removed. However, it is worth noting here that the state's control over agricultural products was still achieved through villages, cooperative organizations and their village and community cadres. Thus, for village-level organizations and village communities, the state implemented the system of unified purchase and marketing and cooperatives, as well as supplied farmers with food for sale as a compensatory state and implemented low social security in the countryside, which meant that the country provided stronger institutional support and economic support from outside the village. In this context, the completion of the cooperative movement meant that the village and community organizations, established under the guidance and organization of the State after 1949, with formal social organizational significance and administrative functions finally had the most critical economic foundation as the village community organization. In this respect, compared with other nearby villages, the only special point was probably because there was very little arable land, and there was little contribution to help the country solve the supply of commodity grain, but it had benefited from the state far more than other rural communities in addressing minimum food needs; but in the aspects of release of production management and product control in the families and unified organization of production and management and product distribution within the village and cooperative, the situation in the village was no different from that of other villages. Because of this, although the village and cooperative of Jianshanxia could not play a big role in increasing the food production of the village, there was no inferiority in the aspects of the collective management organization, control of agricultural products for the state and the implementation of the low social security. For example, after the establishment of the cooperative, the village began to implement the "five guarantees" system for the elderly who had no dependents in life, namely, collective guaranteed food, clothing, housing, medical care and funeral. In August 1956, the village was hit by typhoons and rainstorms. After the disaster, the state subsidies were based on households (30–40 yuan per household and 100 yuan per household for relief loans), but the work was also organized by the village community. In terms of the type of production, before the "Great Leap Forward" in 1958, the main production activity in the Jianshanxia Village was using bamboo as raw material to process local paper. In 1956, the village of 470 whole and semi-labor force produced about 24,000 pieces of paper a year. These products were mainly purchased and operated by the supply and marketing agency, and each year, the supply and marketing agency would issue loans and pre-order deposit for the paper; however, the whole paper raw material supply and production of the village was organized by the collective organization of the village community after the establishment of the cooperative. It was not subject to decentralization management of farmers, but directly traded with the supply and marketing cooperative and belonged to the collective economic action of the village. Therefore, if the cooperative movement provided the basis and demonstration for the collective action of villages in the later rural economy, then, the tradition of the Jianshanxia Village might be more than that of the general village.

Fourth, according to the requirements of the state and the ruling party's ideology, the village community also attempts to organize unified action in the aspects of thought, emotion and customs. Since the establishment of the local party organizations and local governments in Xiaoshan, the general social mobilization by the CPC Central Committee and the central government or the local decree of the local party and government could be implemented in the village at least in form as long as necessary. Since the 1950s, this top-down implementation had begun to involve many aspects of ideology and ethics. In the village, in addition to the movement to resist U.S. aggression and aid Korea propaganda, increasing production, and joining the army to support frontline activities, the most prominent example of the village might be organizing women for propaganda and activities mentioned earlier. Women who gained social status by supporting national policies and ideological propaganda even appeared in the Jianshan troupe. During the Spring Festival, there were performances in and out of the village every year for seven years.[37]

In addition, although it was not an exhaustive discussion, it was clear that a new organizational model of the relationship between villages and countries was formed in the process, including how to accept the country's guidance for major actions in the village, the nature of village cadres, the selection mechanism, the strategy of action, etc. Thus, it provided the organization mechanism, psychological habit and cadre team for the further action of the country in the villages. Putting these things together, it's not hard to say the following: From the establishment of village-level administrative organizations to cooperative village reconstruction, the foundation of village community and collective action had been laid.

1.4　People's Commune: The Unit Variation under a Strong State

Although rural reconstruction had reached a remote mountain village like Jianshanxia in just a few short years, in the eyes of the new regime, rural reconstruction was a small step toward urban renewal. Because the new regime had put the organizational experience and principles of the base areas into full play in the city, it eventually created the unit system and realized the unit management of the city.

The subsequent historical process showed that the system, which had accumulated in 6 or 7 years, had indeed wrapped up the members of the urban society, so that after nearly 40 years, the researchers had a chance to take a slightly more nuanced view of the unit system and the urban unit society when the unit system was transformed. These researchers had found some very important facts: (1) The unit was the form of organizational unit set by the state to manage the personnel in the public ownership system since 1949. It was the system of the state, which originated from the written system established by the state in the way of promulgating rules, regulations and party policies. (2) In the type of system, the unit system was the basic organizational unit of people's employment place and brought together the production classification management system (or other professional management systems), the personnel system, financial system, the household registration management system, the social security systems, and political and ideological systems.[38] In terms of institutional content, the unit system was a set of systems for production organization and management, social organization and social control, power and welfare redistribution. (3) Units established by the formal system of the state had compound functions. As some researchers have found, from a histological point of view, the organization was the organization of people in the public system. Its organizational elements took public officials as subjects and formed the basic cell of the state power balance mechanism according to certain macrostructures. From an economic point of view, the unit has always been an important entity to control the lifeblood of the state, guarantee and accommodate the cultural and material productivity. From a sociological perspective, the unit is a social group that marks the difference between urban and rural areas, and is the core of city life. It determines a person's occupation, identity, consumption ability, values, way of life and social status. (4) The purpose of the state in formulating and implementing these systems is to effectively control society, organize production and distribute welfare, and lay down and expand the legitimacy foundation of the new regime. But, while these institutional expectations had been achieved, a number of unintended consequences, or incomplete institutional expectations, had been produced. Among them was a large urban welfare group and power group, comprising about 10%–20% of China's population, which was made up of people with public ownership, public office and public service, the urban unit society of this group, various factions, action strategies in the unit, etc.[39]

In general, starting from 1949, the unit system and unit society had been established around 1956, after years of accumulation and gradual change.[40] As a result of this process, generally carried out by the state by formulating and promulgating rules and regulations, the promulgation of relevant policies of the party and the state had also become the periodic mark of the formation of the unit system and the unit society. Without assessing the performance of these institutions and the degree to which people depend on them, by observing the scope and activity of some of the written rules, we can see the broad and deep influence of these written systems on urban society.[41]

In order to avoid complications, the detailed processes of creation and implementation of the urban unit system will not be discussed here. In general, the establishment of the unit system in the city through these written systems did not pay much for the construction cost at that time. Although it was later proved that it would require significant operational costs, all problems were latent or minor in the early days of the system. The new regime and members of urban society had just shared the benefits brought about by the system of units, including the rapid recovery and development of industrial production and the continuous growth of national revenue,[42] the maintenance of social order, the improvement of people's living standards, the high level of public loyalty to the ruling party and the state, and the political views of the party and the leader being popularized overnight to every part of the city. Almost all of these changes were what the new regime sought after its founding. As long as there was an appropriate opportunity, the new regime would be very happy to bring the urban unit system to the whole society, including to the vast rural society.

History did provide this opportunity. In July 1958, with the encouragement of the central leadership and the leadership of Henan Province, there were some examples of the large merged commune and organization of communist "commune". The new commune was not only large but also a new system. It not only had the power to control production but also had the power of administration, and it was also a social institution and charity, and even responsible for the morality and thoughts of the members. Mao Zedong quickly responded to this and described it as the model of communism. It was the integration of the township and commune and managed everything. It was the basic unit

of society. In early August 1958, Mao Zedong said, "it is better to run a People's Commune". Then, during the summer meeting of the CPC Central Committee in Beidaihe, the committee proposed the Enlarged Meeting of the Political Bureau of the CPC Central and called for the Whole Party and People to struggle for the Production of 10 million 700,000 tons of steel while passing the CPC Central Committee's Resolution on the Establishment of a People's Commune in Rural Areas. Mao Zedong was excited to announce that communism was not a distant future, and that a concrete way of transition to communism should be explored in the form of People's Commune. Under such a strong mobilization, the People's Commune movement rushed to the national countryside.[43] The first People's Commune was opened in mid-September in Xiaoshan, which administered the Jianshanxia Village. It implemented the "unity of the political community" and "unity of workers, peasants, businessmen, students, and soldiers". Other villages quickly followed and caught up. In the last stage, administrative organizations and production organizations, official organizations and mass organizations, which were separately constructed, went into unity. The network of village organizations established in the previous stage clearly provided a strong administrative implementation channel for the government to rapidly promote the People's Commune. At the end of September, Xiaoshan announced the full realization of the People's Commune, according to the requirements, "large in size and collective in nature", setting up a total of 17 rural communes, with 83 teams and 1,381 production teams. Free call of production data by the commune was recorded; at one time, some communes were engaged in battalion, company and platoon systems according to the military establishment; in the production, the labor force was unified, and the food supply system, the collective canteen and the basic wage and reward system had been implemented for some time. So far, farmers had been incorporated into the national strength of a single grassroots organization far more than urban residents. In February 1959, the CPC Central Committee made the Provisions on the Management

System of the People's Communes (Draft) and then subsequently made Eighteen Questions about the People's Commune and Five Provisions on Agriculture, which limited the contents and terms of reference of ownership of communes, production brigades and production teams, required to protect the interests of members and restore the members' private plots. The above-mentioned military communism in Xiaoshan had been adjusted. However, after the Lushan Conference, the practice of free misappropriation, running canteens, the development of the community economy and so on rose again. After the establishment of the district branch in 1961 and implementation of the CPC Central Committee in 1962, Amendments to the Working Regulations of the Rural People's Commune (60 clauses) and Instructions on Changing the Basic Accounting Units of Rural People's Communes, it formed "rural means of production owned by three levels and production team is the foundation"; according to the work regulations, the scope of the sideline business of farmers had been expanded, and the sideline products were owned by the peasants, including the sale at the market. Because the work regulations no longer carried public canteens, the public dining halls in Xiaoshan district had been dissolved, and the peasant household economy and family life had been restored. At this point, the system adjustment of the People's Commune was finalized, and before the household contract responsibility system was implemented more than 20 years later, there was no significant system modification.

After the establishment of the administrative organization, land reform and cooperative movement, Jianshanxia Village became accustomed to all changes required by the central government to the county and township governments. Therefore, Jianshanxia Village has also joined the process of people's communalization in Xiaoshan without delay. At the end of September 1958, the advanced agricultural production cooperative of the village was rebuilt into the Changtan production team of Daicun Town People's Commune, and the production team was established with one head and three members. Soon, it was renamed the Jianshanxia production team with 8 production teams. This pattern continued until 1984 when the county withdrew and restored the village.

From 1958 to 1984, it might have been a mere swing, just over 20 years at the macro level. However, from the establishment of the People's Commune to the abandonment of the People's Commune, it was not a simple matter for the state, for the local government, and for the villagers in the village. For the country, this at least meant that the process of keeping farmers closely organized (especially the integration of peasants into unity and organization) after the founding of the country had finally been abandoned and no longer considered that the unified management and the collective ownership of the village community would support the industrialization of the city, which was regarded as socialism. It took more than 20 years for the country to prove that the People's Commune was an untimely construction, and it was economically and politically costly. As for the villagers in Jianshanxia, these two decades had consumed the energy of a whole group of cadres in the village, and the prosperous life of a generation; when the new generation of villagers did not know what it was like before the commune, the older generation of villagers almost felt that being a member of the community was a matter of course. However, the state encouraged the villagers to disintegrate the People's Communes and engage in the household contract system for agriculture and mountain forests. This made people feel that history had gone round in circles for more than 20 years and had returned overnight to a time before the commune and even before the cooperatives.

Of course, aside from the feelings of the villagers at that time, history was in fact just like a circle, but far from a true return to the original place. Instead, the commune's history left much of the legacy that influenced the village's subsequent progress.

Here are three items of commune legacies that I personally consider important.

First legacy: After the establishment of a strong state pattern, the countryside unconditionally accepted the national norm as a villager's practice.

When the People's Commune was established, the members of the village in Jianshanxia heard about its benefits during the mobilization of People's Commune[44] and felt the passion of Kangsheng spread nationwide—"communism is heaven, and People's Communes are bridges". Members seemed to quickly enjoy some of the benefits of being a city dweller. For example, no money was needed for dinner, the children were brought to the nursery and the labor force was concentrated in iron-making like the city dwellers. In theory, before long there should be upstairs and downstairs, lights and telephones, medical treatment, books and going out in the car without having to pay personal money. In fact, however, entering the People's Commune was not only unnecessary for the country's economic development and political stability[45] but also less necessary and beneficial for the villagers in Jianshanxia. To be sure, the new systems and practices had made the villagers feel uncomfortable. For example, other villages might have been happy for a while at the beginning of the communal dining hall, but the rations of the villagers in Jianshanxia were supplied by the state since 1953. The People's Commune asked the villagers to move the table food from each household into the canteen, but it did not change the source of grain in the village, nor did it increase the grain supply in the village. The rigid change was only the habit of eating at home, which was taken for granted by individual households.

There were two other things that made the villagers feel the injustice. One thing was that at the beginning of the commune, there was an equal distribution of the means of production and personal property of a collective organization (that is, to allocate the means of production and personal property of a collective organization for free and to transfer the labor force of the production team at no cost). In principle, it had destroyed the unit of accounting of the original village community and the resources occupancy boundary to realize the average redistribution, which should be in favor of the poor village community such as the Jianshanxia Village. However, in the actual implementation process, only those not rich in property and manpower of village community were easily transferred under various reasons and pretexts, and a considerable part was also used to some project that made people feel heart-wrenched. The elderly villagers still remembered very clearly that in the process of constructing the Changtan Power Station, Changtan Highway, and smelting iron and steel, a lot of funds, labor and property were transferred and many mountain forests were cut down indiscriminately in the village. Among them, the Zhongshan Reservoir, which started construction in June 1958, had drawn a lot of manpower and material resources after the establishment of the People's Commune. When more than 900 meters of drainage channels along the mountain were completed, the entire project began to contract because of the construction of the Tianling Reservoir in Taicun District. It was completely shut down in 1960 and the reservoir power plant house was sold off in 1963. According to the economic capacity of the village at that time, it was not surprising that manpower, money and things were injected in vain. The rules of the commune were scary.

Second, in 1958, the State promulgated the Regulations of the People's Republic of China on Household Registration, which divided Hukou into agricultural Hukou and non-agricultural Hukou. The country took two kinds of Hukou as the benchmark and implemented the supporting employment, the food supply, the social security, the housing and so on.

Because of the changes in household registration and the extremely strict system of migration, this household registration system had clearly caused a gap between urban and rural areas, stopping the rural population from entering the city freely for employment. At the beginning of the founding of the People's Republic of China, the free movement of the rural population to the cities ended completely. When it came to influence, though the villagers in Jianshan still lacked arable land as in the past, since then they had been working in the cities, but have been restricted from going out for a living, unlike before when they had been able to do so.

Together, the two things that happened during the commune seemed to give the villagers a strange feeling that was not clear. The previous one clearly told villagers to forget that they were family members, village people, and only remember that they are members of the community. The latter, however, made the villagers almost remember that they were always country folk. Of course, this was at best the private feelings of the villagers. In the process of entering the People's Commune and various subsequent adjustments, villagers were objectively forced by the state power and the policy system, but this kind of compulsion was not as strong and obvious as it was when the cooperatives were founded. The reason was that it has gone through the major links of rebuilding villages after the founding of the People's Republic of China, the pattern of a strong country had been established in the countryside, and it had been accepted by the villagers to follow the policies of the ruling party and accept the government's guidance. Rural affairs needed to be determined by the state, at least with government support.

Naturally, after the collapse of the People's Commune, this relationship was still accepted as a practice in both the country and the villages. Therefore, the country's macrocontrol strategy for the rural areas after the People's Commune continued to be supported by the farmers. The system and activities of various villages' self-governance should be given and encouraged by the state. Major activities including village-run enterprises and unit village also needed to seek national support, and could only be smoothly implemented with the support. These could almost be seen as the lag effects of the social relations model of the People's Commune period.

Second legacy: State-driven villages and villagers have experienced more than 20 years of unit variation.

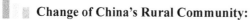
Although some historians pointed out decades later that it was not necessary to set up a People's Commune, using the political, economic, military, cultural and various ways to organize the people were some of the social ideals that Mao Zedong and the ruling party had established on the eve of the founding of the People's Republic of China. Therefore, the more a way was realized for the organization in the whole country at that time, the more it was attractive to the ruling party. In the choice of the specific organization mode, because the city had already achieved the unit society quickly through the unit system and attempts were made to construct units in rural areas, at least to provide preparation for the organization, it was a natural choice that the ruling party was happy to face. The original idea and method of organizing were to turn the rural organization into a unit of urbanization. However, the social productive forces had put forward the restriction on the effective expansion of the system. The reason why the country could not bring the whole society into the management of the urban public officials was that the social productivity at that time could not provide the country with such economic strength. In other words, at the time of the establishment of the People's Commune, the State was in fact faced with a dilemma as to how to organize society: The organization of public officials into urban units was considered to be a satisfying and powerful organizational system and organizational way, and the whole society realized the ideal blueprint of unitization. However, allowing peasants to go to cities to become public officials would break the urban unit society. To this end, the central government had to start to implement the household registration system, so as to divide the urban and rural areas and prevent the rural population from entering the city for employment. On the other hand, it was still an attractive goal for the country to promote the farmers to the organization that was consistent with the urban units while protecting the city. Perhaps because of this, the state had reason to be excited about the emergence of the People's Commune, because the People's Commune seemed to produce the benefits that the country was very willing to see: First, the countryside and farmers were highly organized; second, it might lead to the complete elimination of all kinds of private ownership remnants;

third, the disappearance of the family as a rural consumption place should reduce the production cost significantly. Fourth, it organized the farmers while realizing the social protection of urban units.

Under this background, a strange paradox occurred at the beginning of the establishment of the People's Commune. In the case of Xiaoshan, where Jianshanxia Village is located, on the one hand, under enthusiastic publicity and strong administrative promotion of the ruling party and the government, the People's Commune was at one time much more violent than the city in achieving the strength of the unit organization. In accordance with the spirit of the Central Committee, the People's Commune was an organization that integrated government and society, including workers, peasants, businessmen, students and soldiers. Therefore, it was not only the economic organization for organizing and managing rural economic life but also the grassroots political organization for organizing and managing rural political life, as well as the social organization for organizing and managing social life in rural areas. In this organization, the degree of public ownership was very high, the property was basically under commune public ownership, and production brigades and production teams had only partial ownership. Members had no private property other than housing. At the same time, the commune achieved a high degree of centralization and unity of production and life, and some People's Communes adopted the strongest militarization or quasi-militarization mode at the beginning of the establishment of the commune, and organized and directed the labor force according to the army's squads, platoons, companies, battalions and regiments; in addition to the unified arrangement of entertainment for farmers, unified office public canteens, nurseries and nursing homes, in order to abolish the life of a single family, even the male and female labor were organized into male and female dormitories and family reunions could be arranged only once a week and so on. On the other hand, because of the low production capacity, the People's Commune could not provide welfare security as the urban units. Although at the beginning of the People's Commune's establishment, the commune

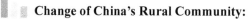
once implemented the system of wage and supply, some communes also carried out the reimbursement system for the basic living expenses of the members, such as medical treatment, study, marriage and funeral. The state has decentralized banks, shops and some enterprises owned by the whole people in rural areas to communes for management in order to improve the economic capacity of the communes, but this would not solve the problem of inadequate welfare protection in the communes. In this regard, the particularity of the Jianshanxia Village, probably lay in its remote location and traffic inconvenience, with the commune eventually unable to execute completely like other brigades demanding military establishment and management.

This kind of abnormally developed system ability and serious insufficient safeguard ability of the People's Commune appeared too uncoordinated. Of course, a series of serious problems quickly occurred. These included, as historians are familiar, "equalitarianism and indiscriminate transfer of resources" depriving farmers, low productivity among members, waste in public canteens and political involvement of cadres. Therefore, it was imperative to adjust the People's Commune system. The adjustment of the system and policy, as mentioned earlier, began from the Zhengzhou conference in February 1959 to the implementation of the Amendments to the Working Regulations of the Rural People's Commune in 1962. These adjustments are directed in the opposite direction to the unitization at the beginning of the establishment of the commune: changing the commune level for all the production team as the basic accounting unit was to reduce the degree of public ownership; allowing farmers to retain their own land and to operate sideline activities aimed at restoring to some extent the family economy and family life of farmers; the abolition of public canteens was in fact a recognition by the state that the commune did not have the capacity to provide members with basic social welfare and so on. As a result, there were obvious differences between the People's Commune and the urban unit, the members of the commune and the members of the unit. Prior to this, the country had implemented a strict household registration system, defining the separation between cities and the countryside. Therefore, if it was said that the basic tendency of the People's Commune at the beginning of the establishment of the cooperative was to turn the peasants into local units, then the completion of the adjustment of the People's Commune marked the consolidation of the urban–rural dualism established from the household registration system.[47]

It should be noted, however, that even in this case, the People's Communes should, in general, be seen as a variation of the unit in the countryside. After the adjustment of the People's Commune, it formed the so-called urban–rural dualism, but the adjustment of the People's Commune was only partial, so there were many things that had not changed, including the unity of the political and social institutions, organizing social members by administrative means and administrative organization, the pattern of oneness of employment place and social intercourse place, and the channels and means of achieving political control in the workplace. Therefore, such dualization could also be understood as the two outcomes of the efforts of the state to organize the social member organizations in the urban and rural areas. The urban unit was the standard unit and the People's Commune was the unit variant of the village. Moreover, the biggest difference between the two systems might not be that the specific system types of urban units were detailed, comprehensive and specific. Rather, it might be that urban units, through these specific systems, strictly integrated the work, political participation and social exchanges of public officials in employment places and realized the management of units and provided a guaranteed return on basic benefits through the unit, including priorities in full employment, health care, education, housing, etc. It was important to note that the presence of these differences clearly showed that the city unit welfare was far beyond the rural People's Communes and clearly showed that the unit members' country's proximity to political power and participation possibility were far greater than that of the People's Commune members. Therefore, these differences naturally made the members of People's Commune yearn for a secure life like the members of urban units. Thus, it provided a kind of psychological drive for the conscious imitation of urban units in rural areas.

Third legacy: The People's Commune left a precedent for team organization and mass collective action.

Generally speaking, the public ownership of the People's Commune, its organizational scale and management mechanism, the service habits of its members to its superiors and the state, and the atmosphere of "Great Leap Forward" when the People's Commune was established together led to the People's Commune's keenness to organize large-scale collective action by taking brigade and commune as a unit from the beginning. In these operations, brigades, or later villages, generally acted as primary or important level-one units and formed a routine. In the more than 20 years of entering the People's Commune, there were four main types of collective action in the Jianshanxia Village.

The first type of action was a large-scale campaign organized by the formation of brigades or by individual execution called upon by a superior, including steel smelting, large-scale water conservancy and power construction, the Qiantang River reclamation and learning from Dazhai in agriculture. These projects were huge projects for the Jianshanxia Village. Among them, in September 1969, it joined the Yunshi Xiangtianling Reservoir project, which was jointly funded and labored by six villages, namely, Zengxiang, Pingshan, Qingong, Fengshan and Jianshanxia. The reservoir project was not completed until 1976. In November of the same year, except the old and the young, all the village personnel participated in the Qiantang River reclamation project, 80 kilometers away from the village of Jianshanxia. After two months, after completing sections six and seven of the pond embankment with other villages, they got a share of 310 mu of saltwater land. Since then, due to the heavy salt and alkali composition of the plot, the entire brigade transformed the soil for producing grain. Eight production teams built houses here, dug rivers, built ports, diverted fresh water for irrigation, fed pigs for compost and created ploughing beds. By

1971, there were 132 mu of cultivated land and a pig farm, which supplied the village with some food, vegetables and pork since then. In addition, from 1968, the village began "learning from Dazhai in agriculture", until after 1977. In the meantime, in order to change the dry land of the village into paddy fields, five dams and two sand wells built. Moreover, they also built a goose dock reservoir with the Zengfeng team, with a total of 57 mu of new paddy fields. (Later, most of them were used in the construction of villages.) In 1975, members of the Yunshi Commune Committee organized the construction of the Jiaxi road project from Yunshi Bridge to Xiamen Bridge. The team organized the labor of the village to participate according to allocated labor input based on the population of that year as stipulated.

The second type of action included the village (brigade) unit, which involved various public facilities in the village, including water conservancy, transportation, education and other public works. Among them were the following: the great hall of Jianshanxia, which was built in 1957; Xiangtianling reservoir built in 1958; the brigade health station built in 1958 (closed due to personnel transfer in 1959). In 1962, 10,000 yuan was invested to relocate and reconstruct the original Jiang family bridge and rebuild it as Zhongshan bridge, and the local opera troupe were invited to perform for three days after the completion of the new bridge. In 1964, there was a broadcasting branch in the village, with 90 radio speakers installed; the village primary school was converted into a complete primary school in 1962. In 1969, according to the government's "junior high school within the brigade", one junior high school was required to be established (closed after two sessions). In 1974, the night school for adults was established, and there were three classes in lower primary school, higher primary school and junior middle school, with over 100 students. In 1969, the whole village implemented the cooperative medical care system and connected the electric wire, each household using the electric light. In 1974, Xiashiling was flattened and a 4-meter-wide yellow mud road was built. In October 1977, the Xiamen Bridge was built to connect the road to the entrance of the village hall, about 620 meters in length, the following year, the road section of the hall extending southward was widened again and so on.

The third type of action was the economic activity of setting up the sideline and industrial enterprises. Since the 1950s, the scarcity of cultivated land in the village had not really changed, so the village labor force had always been more into sideline activities (mainly traditional local paper production and bamboo product processing) in order to address the labor surplus and shortage of purchasing power for essential necessities such as food. Because of the low level of economic income of the villagers, they seldom relied entirely on the funds or manpower of one farmer and one household to produce local paper and bamboo products. After cooperatives, especially after entering the People's Commune, these two sideline productions were organized and set up by the village (team). Among them, Dongcun village bamboo products factory was established in 1969 with 250 bamboo workers, until it closed in 1976. In 1974, the village had founded a dyeing shop. In September 1975, the first industrial enterprise, Xiaoshan Filter Paper Factory, was completed and put into production. In fact, this enterprise started the process of setting up industrial units in the village of Jianshanxia, although the larger enterprises were mainly established in the late 1980s and early 1990s. Before the withdrawal of the People's Commune in 1984, the village set up a paper mill and a carton workshop.

The fourth type of action was a village (brigade) political movement directed by a superior. The establishment of the People's Commune and subsequent policy adjustments provided an atmosphere, practice and mechanism for the political movement of the ruling party and the government in the village (brigade). By 1964, during the "socialist education campaign to overhaul political, economic, organizational and ideological matters", the country's political penetration of villages had been unimpeded.[48] Since then, for every larger national political activity, there would be a reverberation in the village. Once the country considered it necessary, it would formally transmit the political information to the village or organize the corresponding activities in the village through the network of commune teams. In this way, formal political activities became one of the important ceremonies for members, not only increasing the types of large-scale collective action in villages but also strengthening the power and authority of the organizations leading these activities. The most important of these activities since the socialist education campaign to overhaul political, economic, organizational and ideological matters included the following: In March 1965, some problems were raised in the socialist education movement in rural areas and the Central Committee implemented a system in the whole village (that is, "23 clauses", the document points out that the focus of the movement is to rectify the establishment of the capitalist party within the Party). In October, it set up the Jianshanxia brigade branch of the Poor and Lower-middle Farmers Association of Yunshi People's Commune. In 1966, according to the style of the city, it swept "four olds" (old ideas, old culture, old customs, old habits), even confiscated or burnt some carved stones and ancient poems and calligraphy in the village. In 1967, the United Rebel Headquarters and the Rebel Command Headquarters of the Poor and Lower-middle Farmers Association of Jianshanxia Brigade were subsequently established; in June 1968, it followed the wave of power grab and set up a group of leading revolutionary leaders, replacing the party branch and the team management committee (the party branch was resumed in May 1970, and the brigade management committee was resumed in May 1978). From February to May 1970, the commune sent the working group to carry out "one combat and three against" campaigns (to combat the current counter-revolution against corruption, theft, speculation and extravagance) in the village and members of the party branch were adjusted at the end. In October 1971, cadres above the production team leader went to the commune to listen to the central document on the question of Lin Biao. In 1972, the general assembly of the whole village communicated the relevant documents of the Central Committee on the struggle against the anti-revolutionary coups of Lin Biao and Chen Boda. In April 1973, party members and village cadres participated in the party's basic line education and held the whole village membership conference twice. In 1974, a team for criticizing and struggling against Lin and Sun was set up in Jianshanxia. In January 1976, cadres of production team leader or above went to Xiaoshan to attend the conference on learning from Dazhai in agriculture in the whole county; in October of the same year, the villagers gathered for the "Gang of Four". In 1977, the village cadres and party members participated in the conference on learning from Dazhai in agriculture. In November of the same year, the village carried out a survey of people and matters involved in the "Gang of Four". In January 1979, according to the decision on the label removal of the landlords, the rich peasants and the problems of the children of the landlords, the rich peasants of the central government, approved by the county revolutionary committee and evaluated by the masses, the four villager label of landlords and rich peasants were removed.[49]

During the People's Commune period, it seemed natural that the above four types of action became collective actions organized by commune teams. This was not only because commune teams had gained further control over fields that had traditionally been the responsibility of families or clan organizations on the basis of cooperatives and had become the only legal organizations in the countryside that were recognized by the state, but also because after the socialist transformation of the means of production, the above-mentioned large-scale actions could only depend on the commune, the brigade and the production team in terms of the financial burden. Especially in Jianshanxia Village, as the original economic strength was relatively weak, none of the above actions could be undertaken by one or more families in terms of working hours, financial resources and coordination ability. From 1977 to 1987 alone, more than 500,000 yuan was spent on the construction of village roads. From 1962 to 1992, 141,000 yuan was spent in demolishing old bamboo and wooden bridges and rebuilding 17 new bridges.

As for the effect of these actions, to view from the process of the dissolution of the People's Commune, on the one hand, it mainly added and improved the public infrastructure and the financial resources of the village; on the other hand, it formed a habit of action, in particular, the improvement of public facilities, and greater economic action on a large scale was always more dependent on the village community, and they had to rely on the collective, rather than relying on an authoritative individual, family, or clan that had lost their organization in terms of financial burden, resource ownership and organizational capacity. In other words, in the period of the People's Communes, village (team) collective organizations increasingly enjoyed unmatched authority and organization in the aspects of organizing of village public activities for farmers and large-scale economic and political, cultural activities.

On the whole, if the above three commune legacies are established, then we can at least consider the inclusion of the Jianshanxia Village as a part of the history of the People's Commune, which confirms a problem: One of the major influences of the People's Commune is that it is not only the organizational basis for consolidating collective life and collective action in general but also more importantly it may have laid the organizational foundation of the village unit after the People's Commune. As Zhe Xiaoye discovered when discussing the changes in Wanfeng Village, since the reform, in the process of industrialization, the countryside has been scattered and disintegrated while there is also the type of village convergence and farmers "to realize the integral transformation to non-agriculture locally". Again in the latter type, "the farmer's cooperation is not a pure process of self-organization, commune system legacy-village administrative organizations and village collective after the marketization reform, is still the pillar and the kernel of the new cooperation system operation".[50]

1.5   The Spontaneous Unit Orientation of Villages after the People's Commune

After 1978, the countryside all over the country began the economic system reform one after another. The production organization was separated from the administrative organization. As the basic production organization unit in rural areas, the family has become the core content

of this reform. Of course, this kind of reform could fail to cause the reconstruction of villages.

Zhejiang Province was relatively slow in the early stage of promoting the household contract system. So, in September 1980, the CPC issued the Circular on Issuing and Printing Several Issues on Further Strengthening and Perfecting the Responsibility System for Agricultural Production, and Xiaoshan County Committee was able to legally promote this change. A total of seven working groups had been piloted and promoted in various districts by the County Committee. In 1983, it basically realized the contract system of multiple forms, which was mainly based on family contract. The following year, the County Committee reorganized 60 working groups to implement the Notice of the CPC Central Committee on Rural Work in 1984, to stabilize the household contract responsibility system and grant farmers the long-term use of land certificates. On the administrative organs, the adaptation changes were made according to the policies and regulations that had been promulgated since 1981, for changing the rural management mode and accelerating the development of rural economy. Finally, in May 1984, the political organization was separated from the commune, and the township and village were restored, and the People's Commune was abolished. It was re-established as township. The People's Congresses of townships and towns elected the township chief and town chief, and two to four persons for the deputy posts and no government committees were established; the production brigade was renamed as the administrative village, the villagers or residents' committee was formed, set up with the head/deputy head (director) and members of the village, the nature of which was clearly the grassroots mass autonomous organization. From January to March 1987, in accordance with the Constitution and the Local Organization Act, the People's Congresses were elected at the regular county and township levels. After the establishment of the city in 1987, and "withdrawal, merge and affiliation in 1992", it formed 34 townships and 795 administrative villages.

The change of the Jianshanxia Village was still being driven by the party and government of the county (city) and the commune (township). In October 1983, with the help of the task force of the People's Government of Xiaoshan County and the Party Committee of Yunshi People's Commune, the household contract responsibility system of farmland and mountain forest was implemented. Among them, 51.5 mu of hillside miscellaneous land was identified as the villagers' household plot, and 46 mu of cultivated land in the village and 132 mu of reclaimed land were contracted by each household on free will. In 1984, the land contract period was extended. However, unlike other villages, after 1988, in order to implement the unified planning of village construction, the 46 mu dryland was reclaimed by the village committee for unified deployment, of which 35.5 mu of miscellaneous land was used for the construction of schools and workshops. In view of the long way to reclamation and the difficulty of farming, the village collectives reclaimed the land and set up agricultural workshops to carry out production. In total, 5,382 mu of forest hills, bamboo hills and wild mountains were subject to a double-layer management system, of which 41% of forest hills and bamboo hills, totaling 2,205 mu of land, was contracted to households, with an average of 1.68 mu per person. A total of 1,173 mu of forest and barren hills covering a total area of 21.8% were allocated by the population to their own mountain, and a total 2,004 mu of the remaining forests covering a total area of 37.2% were managed by the professional mountain forest team of the village. As for the decomposition of the People's Commune system, the arrangement was unified throughout the county. In 1984, the management committee of the Jianshanxia brigade was abolished, and a Villagers' Committee was established, administering four villages and eight villager groups.

At this point, the village began to enter a new period of political autonomy and economic autonomy with relatively independent development choice. However, the new pattern of village organization actually maintained an important continuity with the previous stage. Especially in the process of decomposing the People's Commune System and rebuilding the village organization from top to bottom, although during the commune period the brigade was turned into a village, the party organization in the commune period was retained. At the same time, a number of new organizations had been put into place in the system of villager autonomy with rural family village organization characteristics, and the following structures (see Figure 1.1) were finally formed:

Obviously, no matter how much it is implied or emphasized that after the reform state forces still maintain control over villages through

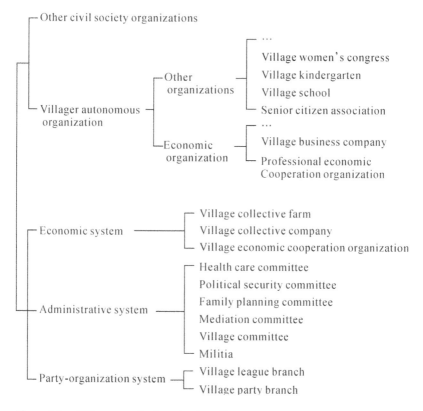

Figure 1.1.   Village organization structure diagram.
Notes: Village party branch and village committee are collectively referred to as "two village committees", often known as Village Party and Government Organization.

local parties and political institutions, with the establishment of the village autonomy organization in law and the establishment of the family as the basic production unit in policy, the village has obtained unprecedented freedom of choice after all. However, it is important to stress again that it is possible that the above changes have provided an extended framework for the commune organization for villages like Jianshanxia. It could also mean giving the country an opportunity to spontaneously mimic the city, including the establishment of welfare conditions. At least, because of the unit variation of the People's Communes in the previous decades, the members of the rural society did not enjoy the preferential treatment of the members of the city in accepting the institutional constraints. In the immediate new period, as long as conditions permit, there is a tendency to imitate urban units more fully in the extended framework (see Table 1.3). In a sense, it can be said that under the pressure of the state, after the attempt to organize the unit village directly by the state had failed, the state created the conditions for farmers to imitate themselves and construct themselves into units through the reconstruction of rural grassroots organizations.

Table 1.3.　Characteristics of village organization.

Level of organization	Village and town	Village-level organization	Organization below village level
Name	Party committee and government in village and town.	Village party branch and village committee.	Family and other organizations.
Property	Party and government grassroots leading organ; secondary group formal organization; members are state cadres.	Including party grassroots organization and formal villager autonomous organization; incomplete traditional primary group organization or incomplete bureaucratic formal organization; members are not state cadres but serve as deputy.	Primary group organization.

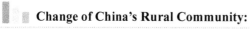

Table 1.3.　(*Continued*)

Level of organization	Village and town	Village-level organization	Organization below village level
Formation	Elected by Congress of Party Representatives, people's deputies, and superior appointment.	Respectively elected by party members and villagers under the instruction of party committee and the government in village and town; submitting the election results to the superior organization for approval; the superior organization takes charge of the general election.	Family is formed in a habitual manner; other organizations are formed under the leadership, instruction or tolerance of the party branch or village committee.
Main responsibilities	Responsible for the superior; issuing all sorts of directive plans (plantation, family planning, conscription) to all administrative villages; encouraging the growth of local economy; supervising village-level organization general election; responsible for public security within the jurisdiction; establishing village companies; implementing taxation policies; joining in or approving major policies in village organization and so forth.	Receiving and implementing the directives of party committee and the government in village and town; leading other village organizations; establishing collective companies; formulating major village policies under the supervision of the superior organization; organizing other mass village activities; village public security, civil mediation and so forth.	Family or joint household operation; joining in village-level organization election as a party member or voter; weak control ability on village-level organizations.

So, the two assumptions we put forward at the beginning of this chapter are valid in Jianshanxia Village. Although the village has been located in a remote area for a long time, it has long been a place to avoid war and bandits, we can be sure that it has still gone through the long history of the country's power to permeate the countryside. After 1949, the transformation process from clan village to administrative village was completely experienced. In this process, a number of factors that are beneficial to the formation of villages were produced. Among them, we will continue to cover the following: the existence of village community and the continued ascent of status of villages as rural organizations, the weakening of clan organization and the exit of clan culture, a precedent or practice that relies on village collective action, especially on a large scale, demonstration of the organization and welfare arrangement of urban units, especially urban enterprises, state maintenance of village resource boundaries, etc.

These factors formed the organizational resources of the unit villages.

Endnotes

1. Xiaoshan is located in the north of Zhejiang Province and on the south bank of the Qiantang River. It is adjacent to Shaoxing in the east, Zhuji in the south and Fuyang District in the west. It is adjacent to Hangzhou city and is directly under the city of Hangzhou, the capital city of Zhejiang Province. Xiaoshan belongs to the economically developed area of Zhejiang Province. Since the reform, Xiaoshan has run a large number of township enterprises. Since the mid and late 1980s, the government has re-advocated the "second round of entrepreneurship" and achieved considerable economic benefits by focusing on the scaled rural industry and scaled agricultural operation. As a result, Xiaoshan has been in the top 10 richest counties in the country for eight consecutive years, and has been in the top 100 counties in

China for three consecutive years (the second largest county in the country). In the economic structure, agriculture is its foundation, the rural industry is the main body. The national well-known Wanxiang Group, the Aviation Village, Hongshan Farm and so on are all in Xiaoshan area. In 1996, industrial output accounted for 94.9% of Xiaoshan's gross national product (of which only 2.7% were state-owned) (see (1) *Xiaoshan Today*, Hangzhou: Hangzhou University Press, 1994. (2) Evaluation Index of the Third National Top 100 Counties (Zhejiang). *Qianjiang Evening News*, February 13, 1996. (3) Xiaoshan Bureau Statistics Bulletin 1994–1996).

2. See (1) Baker HDR. A Chinese Lineage Village: Sheung Shui. *International Affairs*. 1969, 45(4):766–767. (2) Freedman M. *Chinese Lineage and Society: Fukien and Kwangtung*. London: Athlone Press, University of London, Humanities, 1966. The western scholars who have studied Chinese society in modern times may have an especially profound impression of the family status in Chinese society based on the background of individual social units in western society and paid relatively little attention to the status of villages in Chinese society, and even not regarded the village as an independent basic living unit. For example, when Fei Zhengqing discusses the nature of Chinese society, he thinks that the Chinese family is a miniature state. The unit of Chinese society is the family, not the individual: the family is responsible for the local political life. The Chinese people in the village were mainly organized in the family system until recently, and the village is usually composed of a group of families and family units. Every farmer is a social unit, an economic unit and so on (Fei ZQ. *The United States and China*. Trans. Zhang LJ. Beijing: The Commercial Press, 1987 pp. 17–20).

3. Since the beginning of this century, Liang Qichao has criticized the Chinese people for being family centered, lacking national consciousness and civic morality. In the New Cultural Movement, Wu Yu, Chen Duxiu and others directly criticized family centrism. More and more people were willing to comment on family, family (clan) structure and family concept in traditional Chinese society with a critical attitude. It was generally regarded as a manifestation of the congenital inadequacy of Chinese society, which was regarded as an obstacle to the formation of national awareness, citizen consciousness and national consciousness. First, however, critics seemed less concerned that self-sufficient family structures were a long-term

presence not only in China but also around the world. Even functional families and clans were not Chinese specialties at all (see Bilkier A *et al*. *History of the Family*: Vol. 1 Trans. Yuan SR *et al*. Beijing: SDX Joint Publishing Company, 1998 pp. 74–85). Second, critics are often happy to quote Professor Fei Xiaotong's interpretation of the "differential order pattern", that is, the grassroots structure of China's rural society is a "network of individual connections", and social relations are "the increase of private connections" (see Fei XT. *Rural China, Fertility System*. Beijing: Peking University Press, 1998, pp. 30). It seems that Fei Xiaotong did not negate the existence of villages and their functions as community units in rural China when quoting this generalization to emphasize the family centeredness of Chinese rural society. On the contrary, in the social sphere of Fei Xiaotong's so-called "from self to outside", the village is the most important concentric circle of the family. In his own words, it is only in a rural society where the population is not mobile and completely self-sufficient that it can be said that the family community has a regional meaning and "the concept of village can be said to be superfluous". At the same time, "business cannot exist in a close consanguineous society," and their transactions are carried out as human beings and as gifts to each other. But population mobility exists after all. Therefore, villages exist and are meaningful. People also establish a commercial base in addition to blood relations, establish a variety of professional trade activities in the local community and so on (*Rural China, Fertility Systems*, pp. 70 and 74).

4. In his study of the geographical space of the Chinese countryside, Skinner emphasized that the traditional Chinese social structure was based on the close connection between the folk market network (such as village and town bazaars) and the formal administrative geographical space (such as the government, county, du and li system) with the former as the basis. His research criticized the village studies of anthropology and sociology on another level and from another angle (Skinner. *Market and Social Structure in Rural China*. Trans. Shi JY and Xu XL. Beijing: China Social Sciences Press, 1998). In his view, the market structure is both a system of space and economy, as well as a system of society and culture. "The economic function of a settlement is consistent with its position in the market system, which arranges itself at a fixed level" (p. 5). In this particular way of thinking, the term village is used "specifically to refer to residential settlements

where there is no market" (p. 7). It is not so important that various village entities have been placed in larger trading systems by him. "If you can say that farmers are living in a self-sufficient society, the society is not a village but a grassroots market community," he said (p. 40). Obviously, Skinner's research on the existence and importance of private market networks and informal social networks is indeed a very creative discovery. However, he assessed the village by settlements, somewhat biased toward one side. As a very interesting contrast, Huang Zongzhi emphasized the significance of the village community. In his view, even if the village was incorporated into a larger trading market or an upper administrative system, it was possible for farmers to "act only with the identity and consciousness of the whole village" (Huang ZZ. *Small-scale Peasant Economy and Social Change in North China*. Beijing: Chinese Book Bureau, 1986, pp. 21–26). Du Zanqi, another researcher, thinks that the interests of the village are different, but at the same time, he still attaches importance to the existence of the village as an independent basic living unit and its role in the social and cultural network at the grassroots level (Du ZQ. *Culture, Power and the Countryside of North China 1900–1942*. Trans. Wang FM. Nanjing: Jiangsu People's Publishing House, 1994).

5. Fei Xiaotong has pointed out in his early studies, "The village is a community, characterized by the concentration of farmers in a compact residential area, separated by a considerable distance from other similar units. (In some parts of China, farmers are scattered, but this is not the case.) It is a group of various forms of social activity, with its specific name, and is a recognized *de facto* social unit" (Fei XT. *Jiangcun Economy: The Life of Chinese Farmers*. Trans. Dai K J. Nanjing: Jiangsu People's Publishing House, 1986, p. 5).

6. Hong YY. *Chronicles of Jianshanxia Village*. Beijing: Unity Press, 1993, pp. 7–8. Hereinafter referred to as *Chronicles*.

7. *Chronicles*, pp. 25–28.

8. Settlement refers to a place where humans settle in groups. There is the so-called "Settlement is formed by people living together in groups in one year, Yi is formed in two years and Du is formed in three years" in *Historical Records of the*

Five Emperors; there is so-called "Without disaster for a long time, people will build home, then form a settlement" in the *Book of Former Han. Irrigation Ditch Record.* The ancient village researchers deduce that the meaning of "settlement" is the place where people live, which is equivalent to settlement in English. Later it expanded into a place where people live in compact communities. As the settlement population increases and the settlement pattern changes, and the settlement is divided into villages and cities due to the emergence of the city, and the market town in between. The village becomes the abbreviation of rural settlements and becomes a space unit of long-term living, settlement and reproduction in a clear and fixed geographical area for agricultural population (Liu PL. *Ancient Village: Harmonious People Gathering Space.* Shanghai: SDX Joint Publishing Company, 1997, p. 1). The Chinese urban history researchers also believe that the form of human settlements has undergone the transformation from the primitive group, primitive village, primitive market and primitive bazaar. Then, on the basis of division of labor, the rural areas dominated with agriculture and the city dominated with the handicraft industry and commerce (Gu CL. *The System of Cities and Towns in China-History, Status-quo, Prospect.* Beijing: The Commercial Press, 1996, pp. 7–18).

9. Liu PL. *Ancient Village: Harmonious People Gathering Space.* Shanghai: SDX Joint Publishing Company, 1997, pp. 56–63.

10. In the surrounding area of Xiaoshan, Yuyao Hemudu cultural site and Hangzhou Liangzhu cultural site have been found. The stone sword and stone arrows unearthed in the northern part of Xiaoshan and Xianghu Lake indicate that there have been human activities in the age of the Neolithic Age in the present Xiaoshan area. During the Spring and Autumn period and the Warring States period, it belonged to Yue. According to the ancient books such as the *Geography of the Former Han*, Xiaoshan was named Yu Ji. County was established not later than the second year of Yuanshi Western Han Dynasty (Compilation Committee of Xiaoshan County Records. *Xiaoshan County Annals: A Study on the Time of Xiaoshan County Construction.* Hangzhou: Zhejiang People's Publishing House, 1987, p. 1068).

11. Wang ZB. *Pu Liancun Chronicles.* Beijing: China Book Publishing House, 1996, pp. 1–9. The village is now designated as Binjiang District, Hangzhou City.

12. In fact, Goode had provided some appropriate, logical macro explanation. When he discussed the "extended *family*" in ancient Chinese society, the clan system as an organized lineage group (sole heirs) or the family system (partly based on the whole lineage heirs), and villages above the clan, he believed that the function of such family based organizations was to provide social services that were lacking in non-urban and unindustrialized areas and to mobilize a considerable number of people (see Goode W. *Family*. Trans. Wei ZL. Beijing: Social Sciences Academic Press, 1986, pp. 148–153, 165–168 and 177–178). Of course, the theory is also a kind of macro hypothesis, which only logically explains the function of the family and the family village, and does not explain the clan, why the village originated and how it came into being.

13. Ma Duanlin, in *Literature Research: Official Service of Rural Party*, says, "100 households form a Li, five Li is a township, four households form Lin (neighbors), and five households form Bao".

14. Sun HQ. On the Evolution from Lijia to Baojia in Qing Dynasty. *The Study of Chinese History*. 1994(2):50–62.

15. Du Y. *Tongdian: Township Official*. Shanghai: Shanghai Classics Publishing House, 1983, p. 117.

16. For example, the local grassroots administrative officials in Wei and Jin, "all chosen by the county guards and county governor from the local rich. Many of them are also competing for the posts, because they can be exempted from garrison, and later on, they may even be exempted from all servitude..." (Zhang ZL. Township Legacy Rules—The Structure of the Village Community. In: Du ZS (ed.), *Our Land, Our People*. Taipei: Lianjing Publishing Company, 1982, p. 196). In fact, this is not the only case of a generation.

17. In the pre-Qin period, there was the hereditary system, so the patriarchal clan had overlapping relations with the regime, and the social status of the clan was determined by the status of the regime. From the Qin and Han dynasties to the Sui and Tang Dynasties, especially the Wei and Jin Dynasties, after the implementation of the nine-rank system, the patriarchal system was flourishing, and the overlapping

relationship between clan and regime was lax. The clan status was decided by the family status. Since Five Dynasties and Ten Kingdoms, the tenancy contract system and the imperial examination system were gradually routine. The folk also began to emphasize the clan, pay attention to the blood relationship and advocate the establishment of the ancestral temple to worship the ancestors. It was increasingly common for rural communities to live together. The village became the most important carrier of clan system and clan culture.

18. Bilkiere A *et al. Family History*, vol. 1. Beijing: SDX Joint Publishing Company, 1998, p. 715.

19. It is said that in the 15th year of Jiajing in the Ming Dynasty, Xia Yan, Minister of Rituals presented *Order the subjects to worship their ancestors and set up a temple*, "Order the subject of the world to pay tribute to the ancestor on winter solstice...order officials to set up home temple". Emperor Shizong of Ming Dynasty agreed. From then on, the people began to combine branches of clan and set up temples, respect ancestors and unite people. In the past, the folk ancestral hall was transformed from a family temple to an ancestral temple (Liu PL. *Ancient Village: Harmonious People Gathering Space*. Shanghai: SDX Joint Publishing Company, 1997, p. 21).

20. Bilkiere A *et al. Family History*, vol. 2. Beijing: SDX Joint Publishing Company, 1998, pp. 305–308.

21. See *Chronicles*, pp. 109–110.

22. After 1949, the village and its subordinate Yunshi Township were identified by the government as "revolutionary old areas". The *Chronicles* recorded a number of "history of revolutionary activities". In the spring of 1928, Zhong Ama, a member of the communist party committee of the CPC, organized the "Iron Group" in the village of Yunshi and he started bamboo chopping riots in October of the following year. Affected by the movement, the villagers were also organized to strike the paper factory owner and joined the peasant movement. In November 1944, seven youths from the village came to join the New Fourth Army. In 1948, the main force of the Jinxiao Detachment of the Communist Party of Zhejiang Province in the east

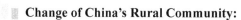

of China was often active in the area of the village. In October, in the battle against the Kuomintang Xiaoshan militia in Yuqingling, Shao Shenlin and Jiang Wangzhai, villagers in Jianshanxia transferred a wounded soldier in Jinxiao detachment. In the same month, the villager Bao Yagen joined the CPC and became the first communist party member of the village. In October and November of the same year, the Xiaoshan and Fuyang district committee and the district government of the CPC were established and Jianshanxia was under the jurisdiction. In November, Xiaoshan and Fuyang district's armed forces were established, and after that, they often cooperated with the Jinxiao detachment to fight and organized peasants to struggle against hegemonism (for details, see *Chronicles*, pp. 8–9, 45 and 51–52).

23. On the macro level, it was in the red base of the communist party, which, as Mao Zedong said, put the power, clan, theocracy, and manus as four feudal ropes (Mao ZD. Hunan Peasant Movement Investigation Report. In: *Selected Works of Mao Zedong*, Vol. 1. Beijing: People's Press, 1991, p. 31). Since the 1930s, there has been experimentation with the reconstruction of village organizations on the basis of land reform. These efforts have not only been relatively effective but also accumulated experience and the rudiments of the basic principles in reorganizing society in a unit manner after 1949, as will be described in section 3 and 4 of this chapter.

24. People even note that "in all relations with the outside world, the Chinese always give priority to the inner circle at the corresponding level. In other words, it fights adjacent villages the family, counters towns through neighboring villages, and combats ethnic groups through the provincial union or union of dialect areas", which is true in economic life or in political life (*Family History*, Vol. 2, p. 308).

25. Du ZQ. *Culture, Power and the Countryside of North China 1900–1942*. Nanjing: Jiangsu People's Publishing House, 1994. The book provides a regional case study.

26. *Chronicles*, p. 52.

27. At that time, banditry took place in Daicun Town and the Yunshi area. In August 1949, Zheng Zhenting, the township head of Daicun Town, and Cai Lin,

home secretary, were killed by bandits. In April 1950, three persons including Jiang
Bing, the former head of Bao in Jianshanxia Village, plotted with Wu Xiaoshui,
Lu Ziquan and other bandits to kill Jiao Fude, the township head of Changtan,
and were arrested. In November, three people were executed by law enforcement
agencies as counter-revolutionaries, according to the Regulations on the Punishment
of the Counter-Revolution of the central people's government.

28. *Chronicles*, p. 69.

29. See (1) Cao JQ *et al. Social and Cultural Changes in Rural Areas of
Northern Zhejiang*. Shanghai: Shanghai Far East Press, 1995, pp. 38–39. (2)
Zhe XY. *Rebuilding Villages-Social Change in a Super Village*. Beijing: China
Social Sciences Press, 1997, pp. 53–54.

30. Starting from the second domestic revolutionary war, among the base
area, in order to solve the shortage of manpower caused by peasants joining the
army and supporting the front lines, and the shortage of livestock power of many
peasant households, the CPC once, on the basis of the farmers' spontaneous mutual
cooperation, organized labor mutual assistance. For example, during the second
domestic revolutionary war, the labor mutual aid group, the plough cooperative,
mainly helped the families of the red army to carry on the work and help each
other within the support group, and charged a small amount of wages. During
the Chinese People's War of Resistance against Japanese Aggression, 24% of the
labor force of Shaanxi, Gansu and Ningxia, 37.4% of the labor force of Shanxi
and Suiyuan, and 20% of the labor force of Shanxi, Shandong and Henan were
organized in various forms of mutual assistance and cooperation organizations.
During the War of Liberation, the number of peasants joining the army and the
task of supporting the war attendance expanded rapidly. In the liberated areas,
half the men's workforce and the auxiliary labor force, such as the elderly and the
children, were usually organized into mutual aid and cooperative groups to carry
out mutual assistance work. Taihang District only had 18,936 mutual aid groups
in 11 counties in 1946 (see Lu XY, Wang CG and Zhang QZ. *A Study on the Road
to Rural Modernization in China*. Nanning: Guangxi People's Publishing House,
1998, pp. 64–67).

31. The Government Administration Council of the Central People's Government claimed in The Decision on Rural Production in 1951 that mutual aid cooperation was not only aimed at solving the shortage of manpower and means of production but also at further improving production. Therefore, it was necessary to carry out the instructions of Chairman Mao to "organize and be the only way to be rich". We must oppose the idea that labor surplus and mutual assistance should be disintegrated.

32. As early as 1953, the CPC Central Committee's Resolution on the Development of Agricultural Production Cooperatives had clearly expressed the design of the pace and road of changing the individual production mode of farmers: temporary mutual assistance teams through simple common work and some division of labor on the basis of common work, a perennial mutual aid group with some small amount of public property for the implementation of land equity, unified management with more public property, finally implementation of more advanced agricultural production cooperatives with complete socialist collective peasants' public ownership.

33. Sources: (1) *Xiaoshan County Records*. Hangzhou: Zhejiang People's Publishing House, 1987. (2) *1949–1992 The Record of Important Party and Government Affairs in Xiaoshan*. Hangzhou: Zhejiang University Press, 1994; Xiaoshan Statistical Bureau. *Xiaoshan Statistical Data 1949–1990*.

34. Lu XY, Wang CG and Zhang QZ. *A Study on the Road to Rural Modernization in China*. Nanning: Guangxi People's Publishing House, 1998, pp. 67–71.

35. When discussing the social changes in Japan by Nakane Chie and analyzing the changes in Wanfeng Village by Zhe Xiaoye both of them proposed to distinguish social organizations (such as industrial organization) from social structures (such as village structure) and believe that the establishment or introduction of industrialized organizations does not mean the elimination or disappearance of the endogenous structure of villages and the habitual means of village society (such as identity commitment, familiar credit, relationship strategy, community consciousness).

Both are often interwoven, parallel, symbiotic and co-flourishing (Nakane C
The Japanese Society. Trans. Xu Z *et al.* Tianjin: Tianjin People's Publishing
House, 1982, p. 8; Zhe XY. *Reformation of Villages—Social Change of a Super
Village.* Beijing: China Social Sciences Press, 1997, pp. 336–339). This view was
indeed very relevant and important, in line with the actual conditions of the rural
industrialization process since the reform. However, the timing and meaning of this
situation was not the same as that of rural reconstruction in the early 1950s.

36. Since the founding of the People's Republic of China, the country had been
already facing a food supply crisis with the recovery and prosperity of industrial
production and the rapid expansion of the organs of political power, the expanded
urban population, and the gradually increased number of people eating commodity
grain in the countryside, and the increased per capita grain consumption of the
peasants. It was said that in 1953, the urban population that ate commercial grain
had reached 78.26 million, and the rural population had reached 100 million. The
state had a total of 27.35 billion kg of grain, an expenditure of 29.3 billion kg and
a deficit of 2 billion kg (see Lu XY, Wang CG and Zhang QZ. *A Study on the Road
to Rural Modernization in China.* Nanning: Guangxi People's Publishing House,
1998, pp. 68–69). Since the state supplies had been used to offset the deficit of grain
balance, there was little left, just enough to sustain the city for two months, and the
situation was already very tense. It was said that Chen Yun, who was asked to solve
the problem, described the situation as picking up a load of explosives: Without
grain, the city dweller will explode; imposing grain levy, the peasants are going
to explode. But, in 1953, wheat was damaged and farmers were reluctant to sell
grain. Summer grain purchase was expected to continue to decline, while industrial
construction and urban development would require more commercial grain and
agricultural surplus after the start of the First Five-Year Plan. In accordance with
proposals of Chen Yun and others, the CPC Central Committee adopted the most
stringent unified purchase and marketing policies in the measures to solve the food
supply and the Administrative Council issued the Order on the Implementation of
the Grain Program Requisition and Supply Plan (see Ling ZJ. *History is No Longer
Wandering—The Rise and Failure of the People's Commune in China.* Beijing:
People's Publishing House, 1996, pp. 40–45).

37. It is said that the troupe stopped later, because the band was difficult to organize, because all the girls who were actresses were finally married. Thus, we can also imagine the role of the women in the village when the drama club was built.

38. See Zhou YH and Yang XM. *Unit System in China*. Beijing: China Economic Publishing House, 1999, pp. 37–59.

39. Zhou Yihu and Yang Xiaomin believe that the group has state public office and has obtained special rights and interests that other groups do not have by controlling and distributing all the resources of the country, such as economy, politics, culture, science and technology, education and health, including the general employment right guaranteed by the constitution, the relatively perfect welfare security system, the stable wage income and more cultural and educational opportunities. On the contrary, the establishment of a unit through a written system reflects the government's strategy to determine the social status and lifestyle of people through the development of various institutions. In particular, when the planned economy is created out of nothing by rigid rules and regulations, these systems represent not only a combination of social resources but also a decisive entity. It developed and expanded according to its own logic and gradually separated from the original intention of the original designers to become an uncontrollable huge entity. In the process of transforming the planned spirit into a planning phenomenon, China's urban community has gradually evolved into a unit society, which has made fundamental changes in the basic structure of Chinese society (*Unit System in China*, pp. 3 and 5).

40. According to Lu Feng's detailed research on the origin of unit system in China, the unit system was initially formed when the First Five-Year Plan was completed. See Lu F. Origin and Formation of the Unit System in China, *Chinese Social Sciences Quarterly*. 1993(5):77.

41. Establishing a system of party directly controlling the administrative power and the management of state cadres, the CPC Central Committee released the Decision on Organizing the CPC Party Committee of the Central People's Government and the Decision on the Establishment of the CPC within the Central People's Government in November 1949 and decision on Strengthening the Central

Government's Decision on the Leadership of the Government (Draft) of the CPC Central Committee in March 1953.

In March 1950, establishing a system of state sector and unifying financial and economic work, the central people's government decided to establish committees at all levels; decided that all public grain (except local additional grain) and all taxes (except the approved local taxes) shall be used by the ministry of finance of the central people's government under unified dispatching; decided that all companies in the country fall into three categories and instructed the financial and economic committee of the administrative department of the government to clarify the management responsibilities of various state-owned enterprises; appointed the people's bank as the general organization for the state capital dispatch; decided that the ministry of finance of the central people's government must take care of the expenditure of the army and local people's government, the investment necessary to restore the people's economy, etc.

Concerning the establishment of the system for the trade unions (unit), the masses, the public security organization under the leadership of the party, from July to August 1949, the National Conference of the All-China Federation of Trade Unions decided to set up a labor union in the employment place within one year and organize the workers nationwide. In June 1950, the central people's government promulgated the Trade Union Law. In April 1950, the CPC Central Committee issued Instructions on Strengthening the Work of the Youth League and Other Mass Organizations. In August 1952, the ministry of public security promulgated and implemented the Provisional Organization Regulations of the Security Council of Public Security. In December 1954, the standing Committee of the National People's Congress adopted and promulgated City Sub-district Office Organization Ordinance, Regulations on the Organization of Urban Residents' Committees and Regulations on Police Stations.

For employment, length of service and wage system, in June 1950, the Administrative Council issued Instructions on the Relief of Unemployed Workers; in the case of government arbitration of labor disputes and strict restrictions on the dismissal of workers, in April 1950, the Administrative Council approved

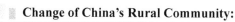

the announcement of Directive of the Ministry of Labor on the Establishment of Industrial and Labor Consultative Conferences in Private Enterprises, in June 1950, the Ministry of Labor issued Organization and Working Rules of the Municipal Labor Dispute Arbitration Commission, in November 1950, the Administrative Council approved the release of Provisions of the Ministry of Labor on Procedures for the settlement of Labor Disputes; published in August 1952, decision of the Administrative Council on the Issue of Labor and Employment stipulated the government labor department intervene in the employment of all enterprises; in terms of labor insurance and seniority that require enterprises to assume unlimited liability for employees, and to prevent the workers from moving freely between enterprises, in January 1953, the Administrative Council amended and promulgated the Labor Insurance Regulations of the People's Republic of China. In January 1953, the ministry of labor announced the trial of the Draft Amendments to the Rules for the Implementation of the Regulations on Labor Insurance of the People's Republic of China (some of them were revised after they were taken into public ownership). For example, the length of service in this system was defined as continuous service in Interim Provisions of the State Council on the Industry and Retirement of Staff Members in 1958 and Regulations of the Ministry of Labor on the length of Service of Workers and Workers (Draft) in 1963 more explicitly preventing the free movement of workers.

There was a system for controlling market relations with State planning and administrative powers and of putting economic organizations under the jurisdiction of the state's administrative power and of the administration of enterprises' organizations. After the unification of financial and economic work in 1950, the state budget became the basic financial plan. In December 1950, the Administrative Council promulgated the Interim Regulations on Foreign Trade Administration to exercise the control of foreign trade and to establish a highly centralized state-owned commercial system within the country. Subsequently, it carried out the processing and ordering, purchase and underwriting of capitalist industry and commerce and cut off the links between private enterprises and the market, as well as the grain purchase and marketing after 1953, transforming the market exchange between urban and rural areas into the planned allocation of state-administrative power control. (After September 1954, the purchase and sale of cotton cloth was further carried out.) After the socialist transformation of industry and commerce was completed, many enterprises were merged and reorganized by the state, implemented the network of administrative organizations composed of the Central Ministry of Industry and the local industrial bureaus and their subordinate industrial companies with all enterprises incorporated into the administration of the government, and eventually led to the national "strip" administrative organization structure.

For a system by which the state sets standards and distributes employee benefits and controls personal life through units, in 1956, the State Council led the second wage reform, officially issued Decision on Wage Reform, Provisions on Certain Specific Issues in Wage Reform and Notice on the Procedures for Implementing the Wage Reform Programme in July of the following year, and implemented the monetary wage system according to the nature of workers and staff, industries, departments and regions in a unified manner. The wage plan was managed by the national labor department, and the enterprise had no right to decide on its own. But, after the plan was issued, the concrete promotion of worker salary was decided by unit according to seniority of workers such as length of service. In addition, started during the First Five-Year Plan period, on the basis of the original supply system, the collective welfare system of state organs, institutions and enterprises began to be implemented (of which the funds of state organs and institutions shall, according to the provisions, be allocated by the financial authorities for administrative undertakings). The contents of welfare include basic means of living for workers, such as housing, facilities to facilitate workers' life, such as canteens, nurseries and bathrooms, welfare benefits such as paid family visit, commuting allowance, winter heating and hardship allowance and cultural and recreational facilities such as cultural palaces, clubs and libraries. Of course, salary evaluation and welfare distribution were in the scope of the unit, and all were connected with the place of employment, the individual wanting to obtain these goods and the service could only do so through unit and the employment place.

42. For the relationship between the strengthening of national financial capacity and the unit system in the early years of the People's Republic of China, see *Unit System in China*, pp. 136–141.

43. See *History is No Longer Wandering—The Rise and Failure of the People's Commune in China*, pp. 59–72.

44. See Bo YB. *A Review of a Number of Major Decisions and Events,* Vol. 2. Beijing: CPC Central School Press, 1993, p. 731.

45. Lu Xueyi and others believe that if the important intention of establishing and promoting cooperatives was to give the state absolute control over agricultural products and control of the countryside, then, after the establishment of the advanced cooperative, the State had indeed turned all the means of production information of the family of farmers into public property, at the same time, successfully realizing the intention through the establishment of a batch of advanced cooperatives responsible to the state. "In this regard, the advanced cooperative could no longer be upgraded to the People's Commune" (see Lu XY, Wang CG and Zhang QZ. *A Study on the Road to Rural Modernization in China.* Nanning: Guangxi People's Publishing House, 1998, pp. 70–71).

46. The "rural autonomous system" implemented by People's Commune was basically given by the state, especially the political system. In essence, the state not only reduced the control range in the countryside but also changed the way of controlling the village—At best, it reduced the excessive and direct involvement of rural social affairs while changing the way of economic control. But, even when it came to rural social affairs, the state could control power at its will. (Strictly speaking, it was only a reduction, not a withdrawal. Once the government deemed it necessary, it would continue to take strong administrative control over rural social affairs. For example, from 1995 to 1996, the various levels of governments of Zhejiang Province performed a massive cleanup against the construction of temples and monasteries in rural areas and a large number of tombs, which was carried out on a large scale.) Based on the customs of the relationship between the state and the countryside formed and continued in the People's Commune, the peasants did not resist it.

Due to the current rural development strategy and its contradictions, the state power will still consider and implement the autonomy and autonomous process of the rural autonomous organizations, and maintain the direct framework. Specifically, this rural development strategy focused on the development of rural economy, and there were two basic points. One was to lighten or relieve the country's burden of rural development as far as possible. As mentioned earlier, the two stages of rural political and organizational reconstruction, from cooperation to the People's Commune, economically, were related to the realization of the national grain purchase and marketing policy and its basic targets after 1953, and to the funds and raw materials needed by the state to support the industrial development mainly from the agricultural aspect. This long-term binding of chicken to get eggs made the country obtain profits while directly bearing the burden of the rural economy. A great change in the country since the reform was to mobilize the enthusiasm of farmers to unload this burden. The main way to implement it was to give peasants a certain space to earn their own living by changing the way of controlling the villages, and in the form of organization, policy and publicity, it tolerated and encouraged rural development of township industry and self-accumulation of wealth. On the other hand, there was still a need for rural stability to continue to provide food, some industrial goods and industrial raw materials, and a limited supply of cheap labor for the modernization of cities and the country as a whole. The State therefore attached great importance to the production of food crops and the control of the movement of rural populations, still guaranteed the proportion of agriculture in the rural industrial structure by issuing the plan instead of relying mainly on the market price, and ensured the basis of grain production and supply while adopting the household registration system to restrict farmers from changing their professional status to getting rid of regional subordinate relationships and household registration status. (Fan Ping, Wang Xiaoyi's *Basic situation of Peasants in 1995* put forward the objection to replacing professional identity with user status. See *Social Blue Book, 1995–1996, Analysis and Forecast of China's Social Situation.* Beijing: China Social Sciences Press, 1996, p. 297. But, I believe that this situation was related to the national rural strategy and would not change in the short term.) It is clear that this development strategy needs to maintain State policy control over rural grassroots organizations not only at the internal end. Moreover, it is necessary to maintain the state's political control over the rural grassroots organizations as the basic guarantee in the sense of maintaining the internal contradiction between the implementation way and the control. This is why the

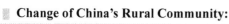
stability of the countryside and the peasants and the influence of the national power in the countryside are again and again placed in the political stability of the country and the stability of the regime.

The above problems were clearly reflected in the early slogan of "no labor, no wealth, no agriculture, no stability", and the concrete methods of guiding peasants to enter the market and maintaining their control and intervention in the market. If the concept of "separation of powers" is applied here, it is clear that the separation of powers by the State is far from a transfer of power; economic decentralization, in these circumstances, may require the strengthening of political control and the corresponding organization cooperation. For the rural organization, it is not only the township, the township government, but also the center of the village-level organization, and in fact, it cannot but be endowed with the dual functions of developing economy and grassroots power. The government agency of the township and town is, of course, the legal base of the government. But, on the one hand, township and town party committees and governments can alone or with the village establish enterprises, serve as enterprise owners or shareholders, and make full use of government effectiveness in the enterprise financing, raw material supply, product sales process and so on to gain convenience. On the other hand, direct involvement in the village-level economy is even more necessary in order to implement the planned targets of various countries, such as taxation and planting. Compared to township government and township cadres directly involved in rural families, establishing a close relationship with a subordinate organization or through a village organization is a more general and effective approach, which can be referred to as the external organizational relationship or the second organizational system. I found that this phenomenon is very common in the interview and work observation of village leaders in Daicun, Yunshi, Ningwei and other townships and towns of Xiaoshan. At the end of the village organization, the party branch of the actual power center is closely connected with the organizational structure of the party and the township and town party committees. Moreover, the village committee, as an autonomous organization, has the responsibility and obligation to accept the leadership of the township and township governments, and to carry out and complete the national policy tasks assigned by the township and township governments. It is through the double transformation of such functions that the two levels of township and village have formed the coherence of the organization. Village cadres have the role of the "function in an acting capacity to service" in the democratically elected process.

Therefore, neither in my own field investigation nor in logic can the village after the People's Commune be assumed to enjoy full autonomy in general terms. Moreover, based on the historical heritage of the relationship between the state and the countryside left by the People's Commune, farmers generally have no resistance to accepting this special background and special sense of autonomy.

47. See Lu XY, Wang CG and Zhang QZ. *A Study on the Road to Rural Modernization in China*. Nanning: Guangxi People's Publishing House, 1998, pp. 84–112.

48. According to the *Chronicles of Jianshanxia Village*, in 1964, "in October, Yunshi People's Commune dispatched work team to enter and be stationed in Jianshanxia Village to study and implement the Decision of the CPC Central Committee on a Number of Issues in Current Rural Work (Draft) (later referred to as the 'First Ten Points') and carry out 'clear accounts, clear warehouse, clear finance and clear work points' movement. Then, they implemented the Provisions of the CPC Central Committee on Specific Policies in the Education Movement of Rural Socialism (draft amendment) (later referred to as the 'Later Ten Points'). At the same time, it carried out the A Summary of the Experience of the Socialist Education Movement in One Brigade (that is, Taoyuan experience) forwarded of the CPC Central Committee. It emphasized that the 'Four Clear' in the socialist education work was to initiate the socialist education campaign to overhaul political, economic, organizational and ideological matters, put forward the slogan of opposing 'new exploitation' and 'new oppression', which made many village cadres be subjected to undue blows" (*Chronicles*, p. 12).

49. There is a little thing about the slogan, which can be an interesting proof of the country's political penetration into the village. In 1996, when I was in the village for interviews, I found slogans for bringing down Liu Shaoqi and Jiang Hua (Secretary of Zhejiang provincial party committee at that time) during the

cultural revolution and the title of learning from Dazhai in agriculture, slogans about "Wise Leader-Chairman Hua" as well as innovative slogans for advocating family planning, saving land, saving electricity, opposing gambling and others on several prominent walls in the village that were suitable for painting slogans. Some of the walls had been peeled off, and there was an earlier slogan about the "Four Clear" (socialist education campaign to overhaul political, economic, organizational and ideological matters), the "Great Leap Forward", the movement to resist U.S. aggression and aid Korea and so on. It was the opening of the Fourth UN Conference on Women in the distant suburbs of Beijing. The village actually put up many propaganda slogans along the road to greet the World Women's meeting, which shows that the slogan politics was still going on. If these slogans are classified, it is believed to be a pillar of the political process after 1949. The slogan politics and the political connection between the state and the village behind it are deeply lamentable.

50. Zhe XY. *Reformation of Villages—Social Change of a Super Village.* Beijing: China Social Sciences Press, 1997, pp. 13–16.

Chapter 2

Village-Run Industry and Village Unitization—Analysis of Ecological Resources and Policy Resources

2.1 Turning Background: Termination of the People's Commune

According to the history of Jianshanxia Village stated earlier, the formation and organization of this village also indicated that, though traditional operation techniques and modes maintained the family as a basic unit of a village for a long time, as a form of rural organizations, villages have been ubiquitous over a long period of time and their status has gave through a continuously rising process. After 1949, the country gradually attempted to build villages as units. At the same time, families have continued on doggedly. However, old-fashioned clan organizations have basically been hidden from view. Of course, this is directly because the country gradually strengthens its infiltration into and control of rural grassroots and makes great efforts to remove old-fashioned clan organizations and also because the country cannot conduct completely effective administration of organizations below villages (such as rural families). Even today, China's national power only effectively covers more than 900,000 organized villages, and the country indirectly manages rural families via these villages. It is impossible for the country to deal with each family directly.

The last section discussed the long-term existence of village entities or village communities as well as the organization structure and action structure taking a village as an organization unit in the history of Jianshanxia Village, which has generally been supported and strengthened by the country. However, this section is about a turning background: Termination of the People's Commune, which obviously showed that usage of village organization, was abandoned by the country in 1949 and the country discontinued direct organization and control of villages (including organizations below villages). In other words, it stopped the intention of organizing and regulating villages in a covert mode of city unit management. During this turn, the state force reset grassroots units of state power as townships (towns). Afterwards, though the state maintained its organization and control of rural grassroots through the extension of Party and League organizations in villages and function adjustment of villagers' autonomous organizations such as village committees, this turn signified the termination of continuous strengthening of village organizations governed or supported by the country, and villagers regained some freedom for production and to live in accordance with their conditions within villages. In other words, termination of the People's Commune means that villages go through a process of reorganization. On one hand, control of state force was relaxed obviously and the organization mode changed distinctly. On the other hand, as villages still perform their basic functions as rural communities and functions of villages have been strengthened by the country for nearly 40 years, villages naturally exist and continue to play a role. As a result, characteristics of reorganization of villages after termination of the People's Commune are as follows: direct intervention of the state weakened, and villages started their reorganization and transition in accordance with their resources and conditions on the premise of the community status of villages.

Influences of this turn on village organization were obvious and general. However, due to different conditions in different regions, specific changes in different regions were varied. In general, compared with village organizations during the People's Commune, village organizations after termination of the People's Commune showed a trend of scale and function reduction, but the status and function of other organizations within villages were promoted. For example, as most villages were based on the family contract responsibility system, a family was a basic unit for agricultural production and other economic production activities. As a result, families became more important from the perspectives of both economy and consciousness. In some villages, clan organizations that were concealed for several decades exerted important influences on social activity in villages again.[1] As for the most common changes in Xiaoshan, where Jianshanxia Village is located, they are probably part of the so-called "South Jiangsu Province Pattern" put forward by scholars. Particularly, village organizations often preserved economic strength, scale and social influence on the basis of original communes and groups. Generally, due to the original industrial foundations of communes and groups, some funds accumulated by rural families through the family contract responsibility system (which were not abundant), local customs about operation and support for development of rural industry to digest rural labor force from the country, etc., in these regions, after termination of the People's Commune, most villages set up enterprises through collective fund-raising and one worker in each household went to seek wealth and nurture agriculture by industry and remove labor surplus in rural families. By the mid-1990s, the basis and the main features of the economic structure of Xiaoshan were the agriculture and rural industry, respectively, and gross value of industrial output accounted for 94.9% of GNP of Xiaoshan (where state-operated industry only accounted for 2.7%).[2] On the whole, organization paradigms of various villages were based on proportions of their village industry and household economy to form several types of village communities. Villages in the middle and northern parts of the Xiaoshan municipal government region are close to Hangzhou geographically, and a village collective industrial economy dominated in these villages, supplemented by household economy. Some of these villages are famous. Collective economy, especially collective industry, took shape in these villages, so that trans-village joint group operations were formed, leading to nearly super-villages. Correspondingly, village organization was characterized by outstanding village communities and clear family units under village communities. Meanwhile, there is another common type of village in these regions, and the basic difference between these two types of villagers is that household economy and family units dominated in the latter type, supplemented by the large village collective economy and village communities. In the southern part of Xiaoshan, although the overall village industrial economy was weak and small, two paradigms basically covered its village organization.

Against this background, the change of Jianshanxia Village seems interesting. In general, before the termination of the People's Commune, the organizational process, types and functions of Jianshanxia Village and the change history of the whole countryside, especially the history after 1949, synchronized. However, after termination of the People's Commune against the same background of national policy, the change of Jianshanxia Village became obviously different from that of other villages nearby. The first difference is that, in view of natural resources of this village, its economic and social development was once significantly quicker than that of other villages nearby. The second difference is that economic and social changes or the organization mode of this village was different from those of other villages. Further strengthening of organizational function of this village even led to the unitization mentioned in this book.

2.2 Impression of Village Unitization

Frankly, when I first visited Jianshanxia Village in September 1996 for investigation, the first thing that I noticed was the rapid economic development of this village after termination of the People's Commune only. At that time, this village had been rid of the People's Commune for 12 years, and 8 years later, i.e. in 1988, it built the plant for electric warming mosquito incense, which was the leading industrial enterprise of this village. Similarly to other villages in Zhejiang that focused on the establishment of township enterprises, during this period, the organizational and institutional reform of the People's Commune ended and economic benefits caused by industrial development in villages quickly changed the economic structure of this village. As a result, the appearance of this village and quality of the villagers' life, as well as social influences of the village on the city, were unprecedentedly improved. In addition, in contrast to slightly slow development of other villages and originally weak economic basis and barren natural resources of this village, the so-called social progress attracted the attention of foreigners and delighted the villagers. Both villagers and foreigners regard this period as the best time. Therefore, when the Provincial Office of Local Records got in touch with the Office of Local Records of Xiaoshan to select villages and towns and send professionals for composition of records of villages and towns in early 1993, this village was naturally recommended, and most villagers accepted this. Both the office and the villagers thought that Jianshanxia Village had achieved great accomplishments, and so it should qualify for the record in line with the tradition of writing history and records in times of peace and prosperity.[3] Before I visited the village, I got the published *Chronicles of Jianshanxia Village* from the Office of Local Records of Xiaoshan. After reading the book, I was impressed by the industry history and macroscopic influences of this village. Still, after I visited the village, I was moved by some scenes of economic development there. In my opinion, compared with the historical overview of this village before the People's Commune in accordance with the book, economic strength and types of the village at that time were quite different than before. For example, in the process of economic change of the village, villagers had a high income and reached a high living standard.

Let's look at Tables 2.1 and 2.2.

Table 2.1.   Classification of villager income in 1993–1997.

(Unit: 10,000 yuan)

Year	Township company	Village company	Collective operation	Joint household operation	Family operation	Sum	Agricultural population	Per capita net income (in yuan)	Annual growth amount (in yuan)
1993	4.41	231.58	8.56	21.05	86.96	352.56	1,360	2,592	780
1994	4.00	214.26	30.50	10.94	140.96	400.66	1,349	2,970	378
1995	3.00	339.49	13.51		157.50	513.50	1,349	3,804	834
1996	1.20	348.00	8.70		243.10	601.00	1,338	4,492	688
1997	3.50	283.00	14.00		350.10	650.60	1,333	4,880	388

Table 2.2.   Villager household production and living goods in 1993–1997.

Year	Aut.	Tra.	Mot.	Tri.	TV Sum	Color TV	Ref.	Ele.	Was.	Air.	Sew.	Pho.	Cel.	Cam.	Bic.	Bee.
1993	4	6	15	14	350	97	140	715	25	9	265	4		20		3
1994	12	7	24	12	370	135	157	826	30	13	271	37	4	41		35
1995	6	7	30	12	380	143	160	830	35	20	275	107	7	40	665	25
1996	14	7	35	15	425	183	173	830	36	20	280	107	14	23	665	102
1997	21	8	54	22	593	283	264	1,082	70	34	332	134	14	99	650	102

Notes: Aut. = Automobile; Tra. = Tractor; Mot. = Motorbike; Tri. = Tricycle; Ref. = Refrigerator; Ele. = Electric Fan; Was. = Washing Machine; Air. = Air conditioner; Sew. = Sewing machine; Pho. = Phone; Cel. = Cellular Phone; Cam. = Camera; Bic. = Bicycle; Bee. = Beeper.
Source: Overview from 1993 to 1997 in *Jianshanxia Village of Yunshi Township*.

As shown in Table 2.1, villagers' per capita net income in Jianshanxia Village is obviously far higher than the average level of Zhejiang Province in the same year and the national peasants' per capita net income.[4] Admittedly, it was nothing new for peasants to have such a high per capita net income in the eastern region of China in the late 1990s. However, southern Xiaoshan City where the Jianshanxia Village is located is actually an underdeveloped area. If you drive from Hangzhou downtown to the remote Yunshi Town, you would experience the change from plain to mountain area. Meanwhile, you would also see the fast switch from rich to poor rural areas, as if the development of rural areas in Xiaoshan was rewound. Hence, the performance of Jianshanxia Village at the end of this course would surprise you.[5]

Therefore, at least from the perspective of time, it seemed that Jianshanxia Village indeed obtained some freedom of development after termination of the People's Commune and successfully transformed the freedom into acceleration of economic and social development.

However, as an observer, I not only marveled at the economic performance of this village after termination of the People's Commune but also noticed the shortage of land and other economic resources in this village, which is not very conspicuous. As a result, due to interests in general theory and methods of seeking wealth, I wondered what technical means and organization modes were adopted by villagers to accomplish the development above. The observer found out that, neither the individual scale, which was commonly used by urban citizens, nor family units, which were common in rural areas, were employed by Jianshanxia Village to understand and fulfill the freedom of development released after termination of the People's Commune. In other words, economic development of this village was not fulfilled through individual economy and family management. In addition, it seemed that living conditions and lifestyles of each household in this village were not regulated on the basis of families only, which is quite different from the general theoretical imagination of economists.

In fact, I found that there is a unitization of organization and welfare of villagers in this village. In other words, the development mentioned above was mainly realized through village unitization that takes a village as a unit.

Let's see Table 2.3 first.

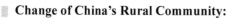

Table 2.3.　Village labor force employment distribution in 1993–1997.

(Unit: person)

Year	Tow.	Vil.	Joi.	Ind.	Han.	Bam.	Bui.	Tra.	Sto.	Hea.	Rec.	For.	Oth.	Sum
1993	9	597			21	6	35	28	7		9	6	120	838
1994	8	588	14		25	4	34	46	7	8	13	6	63	816
1995	4	556		63		4	34	43	7	8	12	6	80	817
1996	2	600		28			40	38	11	8	11	6	57	805
1997	4	420				10	37	47	11	9	10	6	351	805

Notes: Tow. = Township company; Vil. = Village company; Joi. = Joint household operation; Ind. = Individual company; Han. = Handmade paper-making; Bam. = Bamboo product industry; Bui. = Building industry; Tra. = Transportation industry; Sto. = Store; Hea. = Health welfare; Rec. = Reclamation; For. = Forestry; Oth. = Others.

The boring figures in Table 2.3 roughly tell us that about three-fourths of the more than 800 able-bodied people in this village worked for the village industry for a long time before 1997[6]; though most villagers lived in a rural area or belonged to an agricultural population in line with the household registration system, few of them were only really engaged in agriculture. As can be seen from Table 2.1, it was found that, before the system transformation of village industry in 1997, the primary economic income of villagers was their salary from village enterprises, followed by the income from family-run operations. In addition, the income from traditional agriculture was negligible.

Of course, the table surprises foreigners. During interview and observation, it is found that the situation reflected in the table is largely true. At least, it was true that the power of the village collective for important affairs in the village was centralized and considerable; the economy of the village collective dominated; the most able-bodied villagers worked in village factories; the main source of income for each household was wages and few villages undertook farm work (or no land was available to be tilled); public facilities and public welfare relied on village industry and the village collective tried to provide basic living security for villagers on the basis of village industry; and even behavioral patterns and strategies of people in village industry were similar to those in city units. So, the following characteristics are absolutely clear: (1) This village and its enterprises were almost common production units for villagers, and the most able-bodied villagers worked in village enterprises. In addition, the main income for most families was from enterprises. That is to say, farmers' net income from the family operation was secondary, and family agriculture (sideline production) was simply a supplementary source of income. The main operations of agriculture (sideline production) were conducted in village agricultural shops with common production facilities and common services before, during and after production. Meanwhile, nuclear families remained as consuetudinary interest units and income comparison units. Spare family-run operations and a small household industry made up for the village industry. Hence, the village turned into a karmic community based on nuclear families and division of labor (see Figure 2.1). (2) It is a geographical community based on public possession and usage of land, where general unit members were villagers and new members joined through marriage and parenthood. Foreign technical and operating personnel were temporary, and were not completely approved by villagers. Affinity was further integrated with geographical relationships, strengthening the concept of village public welfare. In addition, economic benefits of the village industry influenced each family and concerned village public welfare, causing problems relating to enterprise expansion, tolerance of foreign labor force and selection of technical and operating personnel. (3) It is a community maintaining the shared values of villagers. Due to the unified house-building system, increasing intermarriages within the village resulting from good economic benefits and similar employment opportunities and operating modes of factories, the significance of clans and caste was further removed. On the basis of occupational generality, the similarity of most nuclear families was enhanced. In combination with rural characteristics, including a limited village

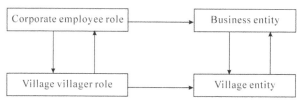

Figure 2.1.   Similarity between village and company in jianshanxia village.

scale, rural interpersonal relationships and a high interpersonal transmission rate, nuclear families in the village generated new community features. (4) Enterprise leaders and cadres of party and government in the village formed a new elite class and had an elite evaluation criteria. Villagers respected the irreplaceability of elites. They paid more attention to the operating ability of elites than their fairness and other characteristics and showed unprecedented tolerance for them. The possible evaluation of villagers also affected the decision-making and behavior of elites.[7]

I think that these not only show a strong village industry and the high economic strength of a village but also are similar to a city unit. In other words, this village is like a unit.[8]

This forced me to think: After termination of the People's Commune, village organizations of most villages were weakened. But why were village organizations of this village further strengthened? Can this case reveal a general mechanism of village organization change after termination of the People's Commune? For example, what is the relationship of village unitization with village organization tradition, national policy and technological types of a village, respectively? That is to say, though we have stressed the powerful role of a country in changing village organizations, the unitization of Jianshanxia Village after termination of the People's Commune at least prompts the following: the state power is not the only force that can affect modes of village organizations. There are some other interesting issues. For instance, we wonder whether the economic change of this village caused village unitization or if economic change was realized through village unitization. According to simple deduction based on general knowledge, the total amount and types of natural resources were fixed at least during the People's Commune. So, did the introduction of other social resources and social capital, including village unitization, cause change of economic production?

I happily find that this assumption is confirmed by related research of economic sociology. Therefore, I can put forward some possible risky explanations for the questions above: (1) According to economic sociology, ecological environments–development technology–social organizations, is a generally positive continuous mechanism. In other words, a specific ecological environment can regulate appropriate development activities or proper development technology for the ecological environment. Application of technological development for an ecological environment allows technology users to form corresponding production organizations and promote other social organizations. In addition, with limited environmental resources, organization modes and organization processes show decisive effects on technology selection and application. In economics, technology application can be included in social capital and its application. (2) For Jianshanxia Village, if running enterprises and industrialization is a reasonable choice because of severe scarcity of resources for agricultural production, it is natural to choose village unitization to realize the industrialization process. In order to realize this choice, the effects of the ecological environment and social resources are equally important.

These assumptions may be a little abrupt, so we have to provide some relevant interpretations in this Chapter. Then, we will observe whether these assumptions can help us understand the change in Jianshanxia Village.

2.3   The Interpretation Method of Economic Sociology

In fact, the preceding chapter emphasized the state factor in village location transformation and village organization mode transformation

Figure 2.2.   Mutual interaction of all factors in village transformation process.

process, but overlooked other factors in its narration. However, there also exist many other determinants which could affect the alteration of village status and village organization mode. According to general experience, the research expresses some of the most important or most distinct factors and their mutual interaction in the village transformation process, as shown in Figure 2.2. This diagram shows the mechanism of various factors and involves two basic preconditions.

The first precondition is to regard the administrative Jianshanxia Village as an independent rural community or even a small regional society. This precondition attempts to draw a conclusion that due to different actual conditions of different small regions, it is completely possible that different changes take place in different regions against the same national background, especially when the state gives necessary discretionary power to various regions. There are four main reasons for regarding Jianshanxia Village as a small regional society. First, according to both the historical tradition of village inhabitation of villagers and the pattern of administrative villages formed by the connection of natural villages, villages are the most common independent communities in rural areas all the time. Second, the state supports that villages continue to serve as small regional societies. As analyzed in the last chapter, the government retained a clear village division after termination of the People's Commune, which usually took natural regionalism into account. In this division system, so-called village autonomous organizations, such as village committees, are clearly entitled to the lawful right of village management regulated by national laws, such as Organic Law of Village Committees of the People's Republic of China, to maintain actual village organization.[9] The state makes great efforts to fix this pattern. Hence, China has taken various measures, especially stuck to registration stipulations of rural population via the household registration system and retained various methods of population management based on registered permanent residence, which greatly restricts free mobility of villagers between villages and city and countryside. Under this condition, although the natural function of villages greatly changes with the economic development, the pattern of taking a village as a regional unit is maintained. For example, the traditional rural market network and the town and village pattern in the network stated by George William Skinner have gradually changed with the development of rural economy and transport improvement. Market transactions between the town and country become increasingly smooth, and more and more functions of rural towns are replaced by those of cities. In addition, there is no need for many market towns to serve as distributing centers any longer. However, although the marketing function of towns or villages was weakened, they still exist naturally without any sign of decline. Third, as the state has clearly defined and maintained the boundary of villages and exactly regulated the modes of village management organizations and their power of controlling village resources, it has basically approved and defined the boundary of village resources. There is no power relation between villages, and one village cannot allot or use resources of another village for free, which, in fact, supports village-based profit division and specific economic settlement. Last but not least, due to the tradition of village inhabitation by villagers, village customs and the interest pattern of village-based occupation and use of resources, villagers universally accept village units and villagers' roles.

Therefore, we have reasons to regard the change of Jianshanxia Village and its unitization as a special type of rural regional economy and social organization.

The second precondition is that though we stressed the influences of the state power on organizational change in a region and hoped to explain or highlight the direct motivation of continuous strengthening of village organizations before the People's Commune, an economic sociologist may think that a regional society always has an ecological characteristic, namely ecological resources and environments are closely related to characteristics of behavior and organization of a regional society. Therefore, an economic sociologist tends to remind people to pay attention to how regional ecological resources restrain types of production organizations and other social organizations by restricting types of production technology.

Specifically, in economic sociology, natural environments, ecological environments, ecological resources, etc., can be regarded as different expressions of the same concept.[10] Of course, ecological resources may show rethinking of latent and apparent economic functions of "natural habitats" over the recent 30 years,[11] as stated by Pierce and Waldorf, or imply influences of specific resources in specific regions on types and processes of people's activity and affirm the role of nature in human economic activities and other social activities. It attempts to express one idea: the correlation between natural conditions and social structures. Each society is organized on the basis of a specific mode of production, and each mode of production is an exchange with nature. Thus, the production mode of a society depends on how to develop nature through its technology and its natural conditions: what resources nature can offer. In this chapter, the concept of ecological resources is used to clearly stress that "resources are environmental characteristics of human activity that can be used to produce valuable objects". In order to solve the various problems brought about by environmental characteristics, the production mode and economic structure of a society should be approved.

However, to stress the correlation between natural conditions and social structure or acknowledge ecological characteristics of a society is not an edition of ancient geographic determinism or climatic determinism. This is because its core is to consider resource distribution and resource technology as well as resource demands for production activity. Hence, resources refer to environmental characteristics of human activity that can be used to produce valuable objects, especially types and quantity of resources in a specific region that can determine possible and proper human activities. In addition, as Stinchcombe said, existence of objects in an environment depends on the activity that people want to conduct; resources used in an activity depend on the technical level and organization mode of activity. In general, technical progress always increases the availability of a particular environment and the value of resources. Therefore, within the measure of availability of resources, there is close interaction between resources and technology.

Meanwhile, social organizations define applicability of technology to affect solutions for natural problems.[12]

Naturally, due to stability of resources, external economy of people's behavior and ecological characteristics of the society also have a certain stability.

Furthermore, Figure 2.2 shows a process involving the application of ecological resources, operation technology, organization of operation units and adaptive changes of other social organizations, and social life, which may be a continuous positive mechanism. The reason for the proposition of this process is to stress a process from ecological characteristics of behavior to ecological types of social organizations. Technology is a crucial component connecting ecology and society. Technology is important, for it can increase the availability of an environment and determine people's economic targets. In addition, it can cause some pressure among social relations through economic targets, so that economic targets can be converted into requests in social relations, promoting a specific social structure. Therefore, an ecological environment can form an ecological type of social organization, especially production organizations, through corresponding technology types.

Income partition and its partition forms involved in previous economic research on production relations are related to technical requirements and stimulate social organizations, especially production organizations. Its function is to offer a main form of stimulation systems that can realize necessary activities regulated by technology. As a result, (1) it can create a regulatory agency that can realize necessary activities regulated by technology, where labor supply relations and the supply process are determined by making specific people subordinate to enterprises. (2) By meeting production requirements of modern technology, it also determines social separation between investment and labor and income on investment and salary, which finally makes property ownership, investment, relations between profit and salary, etc., become the core of social production. In terms of production relations, there are three subjects: claim structure of income and resources, how to utilize these requests to promote decision-making and things needed to be done in a regulatory agency controlling resources and the overall structure resulting from income and product flows.

Obviously, there are relatively covert but understandable relations between current economic organizations, which were mentioned above and known as production relations before, and the usage of ecological resources. From this perspective, we even can say: so-called economic organizations or production relations involve resource utilization and institutionalization of economic behavior. They can be divided into three independent aspects, and the combination of these three aspects forms a production system. The so-called property right system offers a right of social security to decision-making on resource utilization and allows owners of property to generate profit by establishing a resource management system. This management system and its relations with legal order resulting from the property system are the first basic economic aspect. The second basic aspect of a production system is its labor markets with equivalent effects, which mainly provide a proper form of labor supply. If a legal organization of resource control and decision-making plans to complete necessary work, it must control proper types and quantity of labor force. The standard core of economic organizations is authority over people and combination of property rights of resources. As the third basic aspect, profit sharing and distribution can be regarded as a return system guiding resource utilization and motivating people. "Basic energy of economic group centers around trends of its return system, namely status of profit division. The normal order of an economic organization is constituted by property rights and authority and profit division is the energy for normal operations of machines".[13]

In addition, Figure 2.2 indicates the requirements and restrictions of production organization modes for other organization modes of social life. As this process is well known, a relevant detailed description is avoided in this chapter.

Finally, there are some adaptations in the process shown in Figure 2.2.

First, it is likely that people's dependence on regional resources and regional ecological environments is changed through regulation of social organizations and change of technology application. Furthermore, in order to either utilize resources effectively or alleviate dependence on environments, people carry out organized social adjustment and self-conscious technological change. Obviously, technology can alleviate people's dependence on environments, and it is the most common method of alleviating people's dependence on environments. In addition, people always enter other resource environments or merge themselves into a larger resource environment through migration or via markets, etc., to change the limitations of a specific resource

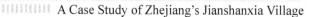

environment to people's activities. However, the latter mode is impacted by transport costs and other non-economic factors, such as possibility of acceptance of newcomers in other environments and patterns of acceptance. Influences of power and tradition (such as division defined by the state, traditional contact modes between different districts and settlement tradition of resource usage) on resource allocation are obvious. Clearly, the constraint implies the influences of macroscopic social organizations on the relationship between people and resource environments in specific regions.

Moreover, social organizations in specific regions also have important influences on modes of production organization and technology application. However, we will discuss this issue later.

Second, Figure 2.2 is conducive to interpreting problems.

Figure 2.2 also demonstrates a concept: the ubiquitous imbalanced regional development in reality is primarily related to imbalanced regional ecological environments. Both economy and society in a large region or a small area, such as a village, are limited by the ecological environment, leading to dominant or recessive ecological characteristics. Hence, a continuous interactive process with regional characteristics can be formed in any region because of traits of ecological resources, utilization of ecological environments, people's operation modes and units (the production organization process), and adaptive change of social organization and life. In the analysis and developmental research of the economic and social status of a region, ecological analysis of behavior and type analysis of social organization should be continuous and consistent.[14]

Obviously, the ecological concept of nature in an economic society shows the continuous effects of ecological environments on productive processes, economic organizations and social organizations and life; also, limitations of ecological resources for HR application should be taken into account.[15] Thus, economic sociology expresses a theoretical ambition relating to ecology, technology, economic organization and people's interrelationships in organization structure.

Unfortunately, in the face of complicated empirical facts and high complexity of regional economic and social development, the established research framework and logic in economic sociology is not perfect. Now it is confronted with the following two problems.

The first problem is about how to explain unbalanced economic development and social change in similar environments and also similar economic development and social change in different environments. Obviously, interpretations of this problem from the perspectives of empirical facts and economic sociology show discrepant accounts, with the interpretation based on economic sociology being deficient. This may be because of simplification of complex factors in the reproduction process of economic relations and social systems in economic sociology.

The second problem is that it is impacted by achievements in other subjects (such as cultural transmission, social control and social anthropology[16]). For instance, in terms of organizational sociology, even though people apply the same type of technology in the same production process, it is possible for them to choose different organizational units and structures, especially in grassroots organizations or small social production organizations, where technology is not closely related to ecological adaptability. Clearly, this is an important challenge against the concepts depicted in Figure 2.2.[17]

2.4　Industrialization and Getting Rid of Natural Resource Constraints of the Village

Anyway, the research on economic sociology done above reminds us to study rural industrialization and reestablishment of rural organizations from the angle of organizational change in ecological resource utilization.

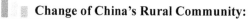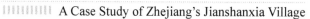
As can be seen from Figure 2.2, we can reinterpret the transformation of the commune system and its influences on Jianshanxia Village: before termination of the People's Commune, although the village resource environment had impacts on village organization, the effects of the state's enforcement intervention were far greater than those of the village resource environment.[18] In this process, the state played a role in controlling village resources, intervening in the village production organizations and other social organizations, and monitoring the process of organization and operation. In addition, the country automatically directly restricted the technology of resource utilization in villages to allow small changes only by controlling urban and rural mobility. Against this background, the most significant change caused by transformation of the commune system is the weakening of national action factors. The national role is maintained by sustaining village division and the boundaries of regional resources. Traditional influence mainly affects the village in the following ways: commune heritage, including existence of village communities, continuously raising the status of villages as rural organizations, weakening of clan organizations, disappearance of clan culture, convention of activity depending on village collective and demonstration of city units, organization modes and welfare of urban enterprises, etc. Thus, in addition to commune heritage, constraints of village resource environments on village change constitute a primary element affecting village economic and social change after termination of the People's Commune. That is to say, as the country gave up direct supervision over village production organizations and social organizations, more technology of resource utilization and change of production organizations adapting to resource characteristics of each village were applied.

Of course, it means that the characteristics of village resources came top among factors affecting village organization. At least its direct action was more powerful than that of the country. This is the basis of differentiation of change modes of each village after termination of the People's Commune.

After termination of the People's Commune, influences of village resource characteristics on village production and modes of production organization became significant immediately in Jianshanxia Village. Broadly speaking, there are some environmental elements, namely land shortage, labor surplus and no optional change of village resource boundary, in terms of resource characteristics of Jianshanxia Village. In addition, there are some special environmental elements, such as low capital accumulation and high transport costs to enter other resource environments. Obviously, with respect to probability of technology of resource utilization, the former elements caused difficulties in developing traditional agriculture in Jianshanxia Village, while the latter ones resulted in difficulties in developing individual or household industry in the village.

We can now study Jianshanxia Village's ecological environment and economic issues one by one.

In terms of the ecological environment and economic types of Jianshanxia Village, according to general resource standards in rural areas, there is a sharp contrast between development after termination of the People's Commune and the state of resources in Jianshanxia Village. The resource conditions of this village were poor. Even today, in view of its conditions, it is still not suitable for economic development and community building of a modern village.

First of all, Jianshanxia Village is short of land resources. As mentioned before, the village occupies a strip of land. The natural villages of Shangmen, Jianshanxia, Hongtanqiao and Changpantian lie in a long narrow valley successively where Lingxi Brook forms the center line. The valley is 1,800 meters long from south to north, and its widest part from east to west is no more than 200 meters. The valley is surrounded by continuous mountains and steep hills. Even the gentile hills have an incline of 20–28 degrees here. Obviously, the geography and topographic features in this region lead to many problems related to people's livelihood and production. These problems include the following: (1) The occupation ratio of arable land in the village was extremely low. There was 5,382 mu non-arable mountain forests (including 3,124 mu wooded mountains) and only 40-mu of valley floor in this village. After 1969, due to Xiaoshan Land Reclamation, the village obtained 132 mu new arable land in the Qiantang River (including a 36 mu fishpond and 50 mu bamboo fields). However, the newly obtained land was not large enough and was more than 80 kilometers away from the village, which was quite far for villagers in Xiaoshan in the 1980s. In addition, there were no convenient means of transportation for the village labor force to commute between the village and the land in the county. (2) Conditions for farming were extremely poor. The soil of mountain forests in the village are made of a natural yellow mud with a thin solum, so it is only proper for the growth of forest trees, where coniferous forests, bamboo forests and commercial theropencedrymion dominate. Sandy soil covers the steep slopes and mountaintops, and so these areas are basically barren. As the mountains are steep, production and utilization of trees are not convenient. Now the village has 40 mu valley floor scattered in 10- to 20-meter-wide areas on both sides of Lingxi Brook with high terrain, where the ground elevation is generally higher than 9 meters. As for the characteristics and fertility of the soil, this one was developed from weathering of residual soil, accumulation and flood alluvial deposit of various types of rocks; so, the land has been reclaimed for use as tea fields and dry land based on the properties and fertility of soil and has been included into the unified planning land of the village collective. Soil improvement of the reclaimed land in the Qiantang River has been conducted through reduction of soil alkalinity and water-logged compost by pig raising for years, and houses and agricultural workshops have been built in this region. However, the living facilities are simple and crude and the transportation between the land and the village is poor. (3) Other available natural resources are ordinary and the village has no unique advantage. For example, as regards water resources, underground water is not abundant; domestic water is scarce in summer (especially after the establishment of Xiangtianling Reservoir in the upper reaches of Lingxi Brook) and the water contains many mineral substances; as for the climate, Jianshanxia Village generally has a northern subtropical monsoon climate. However, according to meteorological data from 1954 to 1992 provided by Xiaoshan Weather Bureau and my own observations, sunlight, temperature and rainfall in this village are quite different from those in northern and middle parts of Xiaoshan. The duration of day in this village is about two hours shorter than in the northern riverside area of Xiaoshan, which is bad for the growth of general crops. With respect to wildlife resources, though there are numerous varieties of wild animals and plants (including nearly 300 varieties of wild medicinal plants), the number of these wild animals and plants is too small to generate profits.

As a result, during the development of the rural industry, Jianshanxia Village has no abundant local raw material. In addition, it has much difficulty in development of agriculture and sideline production and even cannot produce sufficient food for its villagers. Since 1953, grain rations of villagers have been supplied by the state. In recent years, the food supply of villagers is realized by purchasing agricultural and sideline products in grain-producing areas nearby. Due to the low yield and few types of grain, oil plants, meat and poultry, vegetables, etc., produced by arable land in the village and reclaimed land in the Qiantang River, they can only play a supplementary role or be distributed among villagers as material benefits.

Second, Jianshanxia Village is remote, with poor transport infrastructure. Improvement of local transportation requires heavy investment. As mentioned before, villagers once hid in this village to avoid wars during the post, and it was a guerrilla area before the founding of the PRC. For a long time, the village was accessible to the outside world via mountain paths only. After the completion of the Jinhua–Xiaoshan highway in March 1960, the nearest site with transport service was still 8 kilometers away from the village. The county highway connecting to its adjacent village, Fangjiantang, wasn't opened until 1981. In addition, before the 1970s, all roads in Jianshanxia Village were 1-meter-wide roads paved with oval stones, so villagers could only use wheelbarrows or two-wheeled carts. After 1977, the village started to repair its roads, at a cost of more than a million yuan. Theoretically, a region with poor natural resources can be improved by having access to other resources. However, two costs must be considered in this process. Under conditions of proper transportation and other reasonable social conditions, the transportation cost should be calculated. If road conditions are poor, the cost for road repair should also be considered. Therefore, for a long time, it was difficult for Jianshanxia Village to access the larger ecological environment and resources in other areas and carry out exchange of products and information.[19] For example, inadequate transportation restricts development of local industry and it is quite difficult to develop individual or household industry, which was particularly suitable for other rural regions, here. In addition, lack of bidirectional flows of HR shows poor conditions of resource sharing and exchange. In other words, the village is not attractive because of scarcity of resources and poverty. Hence, senior technical and managerial talent is urgently required for economic development and community construction of the village. However, it is difficult to attract these talents, and villagers with specialized secondary education and above continue to move out of the village. According to statistics, from 1949 to 1995, there were nearly 50 graduates with specialized secondary education and above (including a few senior intellectuals). However, none of them worked in the village after graduation, except that some of them returned to the village after retirement.[20]

Obviously, this situation led to decisive factors affecting the relationship between society and environment of Jianshanxia Village technically. According to the food chain theory put forward by Stinchcombe, the natural topographic features of this village have effects on the food supply of this village. As land becomes increasingly rare, it cannot be a superior resource of the village. In other words, under current technical conditions of land utilization, land within this village cannot produce enough food for its villagers in any way. Hence, in consideration of food supply, which is a basic issue for survival, this village has to have access to other environments and resources in other regions. As a result, conditions of geography and the transportation economy of this village are critical for its survival and development. In other words, the relationship between this village and the external environment is a decisive factor for the survival and development of the village.

The external environment and a village itself are equally important for a proper relationship between the village and its external environment. Therefore, approaches, including technological means and organization forms, applied by this village to create proper relations naturally become decisive factors affecting the survival and development of the village.

In terms of relations between the village and external environment, under the resource conditions above, there are several objective possibilities for Jianshanxia Village. The first possibility is the villagers and even the whole village move to a good environment with sufficient land and other resources. However, the surrounding areas of the village have been developed one after another and the state has implemented a strict policy of division management since 1949. It is almost impossible for the village to move unless the country needs to move it for the sake of water conservancy construction. The second possibility is that villagers go out for work to cope with land shortage and labor surplus of the village and obtain labor remuneration as supply of external resources. The third possibility is local industrialization in the village, where villagers access a larger environment through commodity exchange of industrial products in the market. The fourth possibility involves methods of entering other environments, including by intervillage cooperation and village mergence organized by the government and application of other technologies of land resource utilization in the future, etc. Among the four approaches mentioned, the first and fourth ones are least impossible, while the third one is the most effective.

Confronted with a crisis, people often make a smart choice. At least, the remote feature of Jianshanxia Village did not stop the villagers from improving their life. The villagers developed the handicraft industry, namely Chinese rural industry, a long time back to deal with land shortage, which basically formed a special tradition of production and operation in this village. According to records of this village:

> As Jianshanxia Village is surrounded by mountains and its entrance faces a bamboo forest, sideline production of handmade paper made of green bamboo is its traditional industry. In the past, "seven shuidui and one road" was used to describe the village (shuidui is a wooden plate driven by waterpower). It reflected that the village only had one road and villagers relied on the paper industry only.

> According to legend, the paper industry in this village started in the Qing Dynasty and has an industrial history of 300 years. During the Grain in Ear season, villagers cut down tender bamboos and chopped them into short pieces. After removing the skin and flesh of bamboos and mixing the rest of bamboos with lime, the mixture is steamed till it becomes sticky. After that, the mixture is rinsed with clean water and then fermented with urine. It is dried under reduced pressure and put in a stone mortar, mashed with shuidui and poured into a groove. The paper substance is filtered from

the groove with a bamboo screen. After drying, the paper substance turns into handmade paper.

By the early period of the Republic of China, there were 18 groove households and 36 grooves in Jianshanxia Village. Generally, 10,000 pieces of paper were produced every year. The price of one piece of Yuanshu paper made from good raw material was equal to the price of two *dan* of rice, and the price of one piece of Basihuang paper and Haifang paper made from slightly inferior raw material was equal to the price of one *dou* of rice (*dou* is a Chinese unit of measurement, one *dou* of rice is equal to 6.25 kilograms of rice). Villagers worked for business owners and only earned in exchange 1–2 *sheng* of rice every day (*sheng* is a Chinese unit of measurement, one *sheng* rice is equal to 0.75 kilogram of rice).

From the 1920s to 1949, due to frequent wars, the output and price of handmade paper were not stable. During the Chinese People's War of Resistance against Japanese Aggression, business owners even stopped production. However, the villagers could only rely on more than 30 paper grooves in the village. After 1949, the situation in the rural society increasingly went against development of rural industry. However, due to shortage of resources and the industry tradition in Jianshanxia Village, both the government and villagers actively improved the papermaking industry, instead of focusing on expansion of land and food supply, which were obviously impossible. According to the records of the village:

After the founding of the People's Republic of China, in order to encourage villagers to develop productive forces, the county government organized groove households for production in Changtan Township, set up the committee of papermaking improvement and loaned groove households in financial or material difficulties rice. The supply and marketing cooperatives set up a post in Yongxingqiao to purchase and sell handmade paper and unclog marketing channels in the North. Merchants from Shanghai and northern Jiangsu came to buy a great quantity of Basihuang paper and Haifang paper. In 1951, the village had 32 groove shovels, 15 pihuo and seven shuidui and produced more than 8,000 pieces of handmade paper with an annual output value of 80,000 yuan, where the price of one piece of Basihuang was 10 yuan.

In 1952, the government started a plant of handmade paper improvement in Daicun to reform tools of papermaking and help papermaking masters improve paper quality. Afterwards more than ten types of paper, including Yuanshu, Haifang, Siliuping, Changsan, Baijian and various Huangjians as well as various types of newspapers, were developed, with the output of Siliuping being the highest. The price of one piece of green or white newspaper was 24 yuan. Since 1952, the supply and marketing cooperative started to sell handmade paper, issue loans and pay earnest money for handmade paper. Due to stable price of handmade paper, the production of handmade paper gradually recovered. The village basically supplied green bamboos, the raw material of papermaking. When there was poor harvest of bamboos, the village had to buy bamboos from adjacent counties, such as Fuyang and Zhuji. In 1956, during the period of advanced agricultural producers' cooperative, there were 30 paper grooves. At the same time, in order to develop production, villagers went to Yuhang, Fuyang, Zhuji and even Jiangle and Shunchang of Fujian to purchase raw material for papermaking, accounting for about 50% of total raw material. There were 470 able-bodied people in the village and they produced about 210,000 pieces of paper every year. As forests were damaged during the "Great Leap Forward" in 1958, raw material became more insufficient after 1959. In the 1960s, there were eight production teams in the village. Each production team only used one paper groove, and the annual output of paper reduced to 5,000 pieces. Moreover, during the "Great Cultural Revolution", the production was impacted seriously. A villager made about only three jiao on each workday, and the village became one of the poorest in the county. After 1975, village factories for production of filter paper, papermaking and mosquito-repellent incense were completed successively. With the development of mechanical papermaking, the production of handmade paper gradually disappeared. In 1992, the village only had six grooves and three pihuo used for private sideline production of toilet paper. In the same year, the output of handmade paper was 2,060 pieces with output value of 80,000 yuan, accounting for 0.3% of total village output value of industry and agriculture.

In fact, the industry of handmade paper gradually shrank. One reason for it is that limited green bamboos in this village failed to support mass production. Another reason is that, after 1956, the market of raw material required by the rural handicraft industry and crude industry was not sound and could even not exist legally. Therefore, it was not a long-term policy for the village to conduct rough processing of low technical added value with local forest resources. The industry lasted for more than 100 years. Especially after 1949, due to support from the country, the village industry of papermaking trained some professionals in production, operation and raw material purchase and developed a trend of sideline production. As a result, when the industry gradually shrank after 1958, villagers neither managed to seek raw material nor gave up their sideline production. They only changed product types immediately. Since the 1960s, papermaking was gradually replaced by production of bambooware in the village. According to records of the village:

> Jianshanxia Village cut down about 870 thousand kg of mao bamboo every year. The production of bamboo ware is mainly conducted by foreigners. Villagers also sell original bamboo.

Since 1962, the production brigade invited Xu Zhongfu, a maker of bamboo ware, to teach six commune members how to produce bamboo ware, which was the first step of production of bamboo ware in the village. Afterward villagers, including Bao Xingqiao, Yang Yongchun, Jiang Xunquan and Yang Yongqiao, etc., learned making of various types of bamboo ware from foreigners successively. In 1967, a bamboo-mat maker from Magu Village, Zhongtan came to this village to give instructions about production of bamboo mats. At that time, there were eight production teams in the village and 2–4 members of each team learned how to make bamboo mats. Bamboo products were purchased by the supply and marketing cooperative. The village produced 8,000 bamboo mats every year with output value of 120 thousand yuan.

In the second half of 1969, the plant of bamboo ware was founded with about 50 workers. Products included bamboo mats, pigu, potscouring brushes and bamboo boards, etc. Bamboo products were preferentially supplied to villagers and the rest of them were purchased by the supply and marketing cooperative and other units. Afterwards due to bad management, the plant was shut down in 1976. From 1969 to 1975, the annual income of bamboo products was 50 to 100 thousand yuan.

In 1983, after the agricultural contract system was implemented, specialized households of production of bamboo with economic vitality ware appeared in the village. In 1992, there were three specialized households that mainly produced bamboo boards, bamboo chairs, and bamboo ladders, etc., with annual income of 40 thousand yuan.[21]

It indicated that the resource status of Jianshanxia Village forced villagers to seek means of livelihood excluding agricultural development with land resources. Hence, under good conditions of capital and markets, villagers are willing to introduce various profitable non-agricultural production projects and technology and realize market exchange of non-agricultural products. After villagers were trained during original rural industry for more than 10 years, relying on intuition and common sense, villagers without knowledge of economics were able to understand that industrial development and massive machinery production can make the village survive effectively, which lead to a consensus among villagers for a long time. However, there are two major difficulties in developing an industry in a village. The first one is with regard to capital, product selection and production technology, talents, as well as markets and marketing talents, which are slightly obscure but more important, and permission of the state for market circulation of rural industrial products. The second one is that a mode of production organization and corresponding distribution structure, accepted by villagers and meeting the needs of production technology, are necessary during the development of the industry.

Irritated by these difficulties, the village collective organization tried its best to seize opportunities of developing the new industry and transforming the old rural industry probably because of obvious pressure of the resource environment. In 1974, confronted with bad management of the village factory of bambooware, the village set up a dyehouse in the original position of the Yangs' ancestral hall, but the economic benefits of the dyehouse were poor. In March of the next year, an accident created an opportunity for villagers to overcome the first difficulty. The villagers met a warm-hearted master worker whose surname was Ding. Master Ding had been engaged in the industry of filter paper for years and had business contacts with large national oil fields, such as Daqing, Shengli and Datong. He gave advice to the village party branch to build a factory for oil filter paper in the village. Dramatically, a factory in Haining mistakenly remitted 5,000 yuan for dying to Jianshanxia Village, as there was a dyehouse in the village. The village party branch decided to borrow the 5,000 yuan and 15,000 yuan from adjacent villages as the initial capital for setting up the Jianshan Factory of Oil Filter Paper. The factory was located in the Jiangs' ancestral hall. Via interpersonal relationships, the village quietly got in touch with two retired workers of Suzhou Hongguang Paper Factory and hired them for technical guidance. Cotton pulp, the raw material for oil filter paper, was purchased from Haiyan, Zhejiang. With the help of Master Ding as the go-between, oil filter paper was sold to oil fields, such as Daqing, Shengli and Datong. Thus, all elements required to set up a factory, including projects, technology, capital, a production site, raw material, markets, etc., were ready. All the villagers were very enthusiastic about this event. After six months, the factory was completed. The factory was poorly equipped. It only had two beaters, one oil press and other reconstructive facilities from the traditional papermaking plant with fixed assets worth 105,000 yuan. However, the factory was put into production and achieved an output value of 198,000 yuan in the same year, and the sales volume of its products gradually increased. In October 1976, in order to expand production, Jianshan Factory of Oil Filter Paper was renamed as Xiaoshan Factory of Oil Filter Paper. The factory moved to the former position of the dyehouse covering 129,000 square meters and achieved an output value of 202,000 yuan in the same year. In 1977, its output value doubled and reached 467,000 yuan.

Since then, early industrialization of Jianshanxia Village started quietly.

The performance of the factory delighted the villagers. However, they soon found out that the significance of the factory lay in its central role in developing the village industry. After depending on this factory, the village set up Xiaoshan Paper Factory and a paper box workshop in succession, and the factory also expanded its scale and product types in around a decade. Xiaoshan Paper Factory was built in 1980 in the former Yangs' ancestral hall, covering 3,490 square meters. The factory shared its staff with Xiaoshan Factory of Oil Filter Paper, and both factories were known as Xiaoshan Paper Factory to the outside world. In 1981, 100,000 yuan was invested to purchase automatic paper machines, rotary spherical digesters, boilers, cutter bars, automatic conveyors, weighbridge, etc., which were mainly used for the production of corrugated paper and cardboard paper. During this period, as the production of state-owned enterprises within the industry recovered, problems, including stockpiling, shortage of funds and losing production, came up in the factory because of competition. After the management of the factory changed in 1983, its production took a turn for the better and its annual output value and profit reached 4797,000 yuan and 733,000 yuan, respectively. The paper box workshop of Xiaoshan Paper Factory was founded in 1983 to develop coordinated production. It was located in Shangmen Shadi and covered 3,575 square meters. It mainly produced various paper boxes and was a subordinate to Xiaoshan Paper Factory.

Table 2.4 indicates that by setting up a small factory in 1975, Jianshanxia Village turned to a new page in its history and at least developed new economic types in the village, for Jianshanxia Village started to enter a larger resource environment and get rid of restriction of village ecological resources. Of course, the processing industry of handmade paper and bambooware helped the village overcome the shortage of land previously so that the village exchanged external resources in a rough way. However, the industry of handmade paper and bambooware is of a low technological level and used raw material from the village, which, basically, is a form of extensive utilization of village resources. Though raw material was purchased from other regions because of expansion of production later on, both the village and these regions were not rich in resources or economically developed. As a result, the industry of handmade paper and bamboo ware could not bring considerable economic benefits to the village or change the form of resource utilization and economic types of the village. However, the new factory changed everything. Apparently, the income coming from the factory was a result of machine production. In fact, the major cause for the income was that there were exchanges between both raw material and product commercialization and the developed market environment outside the village. In the new exchange process, economic benefits of the village depended on funds, transportation, product technology and quality, information, marketing and modes of production organization instead of types of village ecological resources, which was the real start of getting rid of restrictions of village ecological resources. Consequently, after 1975, the village (brigade) set up a factory with simple products and low technology. According to economic theory, it is a collective economy with unclear property rights. However, Figure 2.4 shows that, through new technology of resource utilization allowing access to resource environments outside the village, the factory indeed brought benefits to villagers. Since then, at least the village collective had capital sources for expanded reproduction; as each household had members who worked in the factory; they started to have gradually increasing fixed currency income to ensure abundant supply of food and articles for daily use.

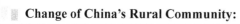

Table 2.4. Statistics of the basic conditions in Jianshanxia village in 1957–1996.

Year	Hou.	Pop.	Ind.	Ind. & Agr.	Pro.	Agr. & Sid.	Per. & Inc	Num.	Emp.	Per. & Gra.
1957	187	814	14.1			14.1	104			
1958	210	807	8.6			8.6	67			
1959	203	868	12.5			12.5	78			
1960	205	864	8.6			8.6	59			
1961	220	865	9.7			9.7	75			
1962	233	941	20.1			20.1	145			344
1963	231	989	17.3			17.3	114			331
1964	227	1,092	23.6			23.6	103			280
1965	229	1,075	16.9			16.9	110			275
1966	229	1,093	18.5			18.5	79			446
1967	237	1,128	19.2			19.2	87			409
1968	244	1,166	16.8			16.8	75			405
1969	249	1,188	14.1			14.1	73			416
1970	254	1,185	11.9			11.9	66			408
1971	249	1,180	19.0			19.0	100			465
1972	247	1,198	17.2			17.2	65			500
1973	257	1,202	17.5			17.5	82			508
1974	266	1,236	21.5			21.5	85			482
1975	272	1,250	18.5	2.0	10.8	16.5	87	50	400.0	473
1976	298	1,272	38.1	20.2	53.0	17.9	100	62	762.9	493
1977	307	1,282	60.2	46.7	77.6	13.5	116	65	843.0	494
1978	327	1,285	50.0	37.3	74.6	12.7	120	79	940.5	534

Table 2.4.   (*Continued*)

Year	Hou.	Pop.	Ind.	Ind. & Agr.	Pro.	Agr. & Sid.	Per. & Inc	Num.	Emp.	Per. & Gra.
1979	319	1,275	32.4	22.4	69.1	10.0	129	95	413.7	600
1980	321	1,271	36.5	25.7	70.4	10.8	141	48	397.9	554
1981	311	1,303	43.5	31.7	72.9	11.8	170	98	575.5	554
1982	316	1,347	64.7	55.5	85.8	9.2	122	135	523.0	517
1983	348	1,356	79.6	69.1	85.6	11.5	256	136	406.6	447
1984	355	1,358	138.7	127.7	92.1	11.0	372	209	489.0	485
1985	361	1,364	225.7	209.0	92.6	16.7	458	227	691.6	473
1986	374	1,368	250.7	219.0	87.4	31.7	547	260	871.2	455
1987	392	1,380	574.4	519.0	90.4	55.4	765	354	1,040.7	502
1988	388	1,384	1,098.3	1,010.0	92.0	88.3	944	517	2,230.2	484
1989	425	1,392	1,490.9	1,380.0	92.6	110.9	1,068	576	1,493.1	475
1990	410	1,391	1,504.8	1,400.0	93.0	104.8	1,219	583	1,835.3	418
1991	417	1,395	2,689.0	2,586.0	96.2	103.0	1,527	711	2,391.0	391
1992	396	1,381	2,434.8	2,315.4	95.1	119.4	1,812	650	2,415.4	500
1993	396	1,378	3,254.9	3,132.1	96.2	122.7	2,592	682	3,138.0	Since 1993, our country has delegated the grain pricing right to corporation.
1994	380	1,367	4,190.9	4,002.2	95.5	188.6	2,970	702	4,040.0	
1995	380	1,368	8,971.0	8,366.7	93.3	604.3	3,804	671	5,735.0	
1996	376	1,357	7,200.7	5,562.0	376.0	1,357.0	7,200.7	5,562	376.0	

Notes: Hou. = Household; Pop. = Population; Ind. & Agr. = Industry and agriculture gross output value (10,000 RMB); Ind. = Industry gross output value (10,000 yuan); Pro. = Proportion in industry and agriculture gross output value (10,000 yuan); Agr. & Sid. Agriculture and sideline gross output value (10,000 yuan); Per. & inc. = Per capita annual income (yuan); Num. = Number of employees; Emp. = Employee annual income (yuan); Per. & Gra. = Per capita annual grain (jin).

It is worth noting that it was the village brigade that played a leading role in setting up the factory, resulting in unprecedented benefits, which were directly felt by villagers. It seemed that the existence of the village brigade was unprecedentedly important and attractive for villagers. No villager would act like an economist to think about the causal relationship between the existence of the village brigade and the factory. Options that could bring benefits to villagers are obvious: (1) Output value and profits could be increased by expanding production. (2) The village could add new types of products or start a new factory producing popular products. For villagers, what is urgent is to meet needs relating to capital, equipment, technology, raw materials and sales staff, instead of changing the brigade (village) mode. This situation was similar to the early stage of township enterprises appearing later on. However, since Jianshanxia Village set up the factory in 1975, the pattern of industrial development characterized by mass production and extensive expansion was obviously profitable in more than a decade in China because of shortage economy. As a result, the villagers' idea seems simple, reasonable and practical.

Consequently, the major change of the rural political pattern, namely replacement of communes by villages, in 1984 didn't show great impacts on Jianshanxia Village as it did in other adjacent villages. After termination of the People's Commune, as the resource boundary of the village didn't change, it is still true that only factories could make the village survive. Though termination of the People's Commune made various approaches of industrialization become possible objectively, villagers might only realize that the brigade was renamed as a village. There is no doubt for them that they should continue to work in factories. Importantly, there is also no doubt that the form of village collective factories should be retained, as there is no other feasible way for the village.

As a result, after termination of the People's Commune, the village paid more attention to development of factories, leading to rapid growth of industrial enterprises.

2.5 Technology, Social Capital and Types of Organization

After 1984, the industrial economy of Jianshanxia Village rapidly grew. The basic information is as follows:

(1) The village set up Hangzhou Jiangnan Factory of Electric Mosquito-Repellent Incense. According to the records of the village, "in March 1998, the cooperation intention was negotiated between Jianshanxia Village and Guangzhou and Shanghai offices of Sumitomo Chemical via Zhongshan Xiaolan Switch Factory of Zhongshan and they signed a contract of technical cooperation. In October of the same year, Hangzhou Jiangnan Factory of Electric Mosquito-Repellent Incense was built with a 2 million yuan investment and came into use. The factory was in Shangmen Shadi and covered 7,200 square meters (10.8 mu) with floorage of 1,872 square meters. In 1989, the factory introduced two automatic assembly lines made in Japan and produced 4 million boxes of mosquitocide tablets and 1 million electric mosquito killers every year. It produced the Langchao™ series of mosquito eradication products, winning high praise from Sumitomo Chemical and the trust of domestic and foreign consumers and was selling well in more than 20 regions in China. In 1990, the factory had fixed assets worth 8,849,000 yuan and 219 employees. Its annual value of production, profit and tax were 4.5856 million yuan, 3,044,000 yuan and 2,575,000 yuan, respectively".

(2) The village started the Hangzhou Langchao Dinuo Hygienic Product Co., Ltd. "In May 1992, the cooperation intention was negotiated between the village and Italy's Cardillo Company via Zhejiang Papermaking Group. On October 23, approved by Hangzhou Administration for Industry and Commerce, the village established Hangzhou Langchao Dinuo Hygienic Product Co., Ltd, which was a Chinese–foreign joint venture with registered capital of 1 million US dollars (0.67 million from the Chinese side and 0.33 million from the Italian side). The company could produce 30 million medical

mattresses every year. The company and covered 3,125 square meters (4.7 mu) with floorage of 1,250 square meters. Medical mattresses were its main products. According to the contract, 50% of products were sold by the Italian side overseas, while the other 50% was sold by the village".

(3) The village created Hangzhou Langchao Industrial Company. After 1984, original factories of filter paper and papermaking and the workshop for paper boxes grew. For example, by 1990, workers in the filter paper factory increased from 40 to 350; almost all facilities in the factory had been updated; fixed assets of the factory were worth 1.4543 million yuan. In addition to oil filter paper, the factory also produced thick paper, plaster paper, filter paper, chemical paste and mosquito eradication paper, etc., which were sold to the Daqing Oil Field and the Third Pharmaceutical Factory of Shanghai. In the same year, the output value of the factory was 8.1 million yuan and its tax and profit was 8884,000 yuan, increasing by 16.3 and 5.14 times those in 1977, respectively.

On June 1, 1991, Jianshanxia Village applied for establishment of Hangzhou Langchao Industrial Company, which was approved by No. 124 document of Hangzhou Planning Committee (1991). It was a group-type village enterprise that mainly produced mosquito eradication products and subordinated Xiaoshan Factory of Filter Paper, Xiaoshan Factory of Papermaking (including the paper box workshop), Hangzhou Jiangnan Factory of Electric Mosquito-Repellent Incense, agricultural workshops and village forest teams. The company covered 354.93 million square meters (53.2 mu) with floorage of 9,824 square meters. By 1992, the company had fixed assets worth 5.52 million yuan and 650 employees, including 1 economic engineer and 50 professional technicians (including 15 technicians with a technical title). Its value of annual industrial output, profit and tax were 23.1537 million yuan, 1.0501 million yuan and 1.35 million yuan, respectively (where employees and economic indicators of agricultural workshops and village forest teams were not involved).

(4) Transportation and power. Village factories required good transportation and power. Before the 1980s, transportation and power of Jianshanxia Village were poor. In the 1970s, roads in the village were narrow, and people could only transport materials by hands, which was quite inefficient. In the 1950s, wheelbarrows were the main means of transport in the village. Due to narrow and bumpy roads, a few people were often needed to transport long objects, such as mao bamboo, on slopes. Before road repair, manual steel-wire two-wheelers gradually replaced wheelbarrows. In 1974, the village collective bought the first walking tractor in the village. In 1983, the village bought the first Jiefang 5-ton goods vehicle. Since then, manual vehicles were gradually replaced by transport machines. By 1992, there were three 5-ton goods vehicles, one 1.5-ton good vehicle, a minibus and a car in the village; the villagers bought 14 motor tricycles and more than ten motorcycles and walking tractors.

With respect to electric power facilities, after the village was electrified in 1969, power was mainly used for illumination in nearly 10 years with a variable voltage of 50 kVA. After the village set up factories, electricity consumption gradually increased. In 1985, the village invested 100,000 yuan to purchase one small diesel generating set with installed capacity of 248 kW to make up for power supplied by the country. In 1987, the village spent 40,000 yuan for reconstruction of 5.5 kilometers low lines. In 1991, the village established Hangzhou Langchao Industrial Company and purchased two diesel generating sets with installed capacity of 616 kW, so the total installed capacity reached 864 kW. In 1992, the village consumed 58.33 kWh, of which 51.13 kWh was supplied by the municipal power supply bureau and 72,000 kWh by the village; 518,400 kWh was consumed by the village industry and public utilities and 64,900 kWh was consumed by families.

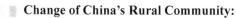
(5) Business management. Village factories always attached great importance to product quality and corporate reputation. However, the village figured out how to manage enterprises when it developed new enterprises. According to records of the village: "Since 1985, enterprises of this village have been rated as high-integrity units by Xiaoshan Administrative Bureau for Industry and Commerce all the time. Meanwhile, since 1983, by implementing the contract system, the enterprise strengthened its management and perfected its rules and regulations. In 1987, Xiaoshan Factory of Papermaking was rated as an advanced unit in the township; in 1988, it was rated as a first-class industrial enterprise by the municipal people's government of Xiaoshan. However, in 1989, on the basis of three established enterprises, the factory of electric mosquito-repellent incense came into use, which brought pressure to Xiaoshan Factory of Papermaking. As a result, the management foundation of the factory was impacted, resulting in a large loss, interruption of production and reduction of production for three months in 1989 and 1990. In order to change this situation, in March 1990, the factory applied an internal responsibility system based on raw material, salary, fees, production, and marketing after repeated discussion and demonstration. As internal contract management of the enterprise was strengthened through the internal responsibility system, reduction of economic benefits was well controlled and economic benefits were improved two months later. In 1991, after the foundation of Hangzhou Langchao Industrial Company, business management gradually became standard". In June of the same year, the company created a leading group for accounting inspections and a leading group for standardization, measurement and comprehensive quality control. At the end of the year, the company passed the acceptance inspection for comprehensive quality control conducted by the economic committee and the quality management association of Hangzhou, the acceptance inspection for enterprise standardization by Zhejiang Bureau of Standard Measurement and the acceptance inspection for seven items of foundational management by Zhejiang Bureau of Township Enterprises.

In the same year, the company was rated as a first-class industrial enterprise by the municipal people's government of Xiaoshan. The next year, it was rated as a key township enterprise of Hangzhou by the municipal people's government of Hangzhou.[22]

Thus it can be seen that the village collective developed factories by expanding their scale. In 1992, the industrial economy of this village reached its golden age and turned into the foundation of the village economy (see the column showing 1992 figures in Table 2.4). In the eyes of most villagers, it seemed that as long as they continued this pattern of development, the rapid growth of industrial economy and continuous improvement of villagers' life in this village would not be impacted regardless of even some minor setbacks to operation and management.

However, this is not true. In fact, the "internal responsibility system" has shown that not all problems arising during the gradual expansion of industrial economy could be solved without any controversy or difficulty. In fact, an important change had appeared quietly. The village was dogged by at least two problems: the first one was on how to develop the village industry. Initially, the biggest difficulty in factory management might be selection of a proper product or project and obtaining of capital and technology; how to manage a factory; how to determine departments, positions and staff of an enterprise; how to unify rights and obligations; and how to regulate and implement systems of employment, salary, and rewards and punishments. The second one was about objectives of village enterprises, especially profit flows of village enterprises. For instance, though enterprises were set up by the village (brigade) collective and belonged to the village collective, should they be managed by the village collective all the time? Should corporate profits be directly managed by the village collective or shared by the enterprise and the village? Should expanded reproduction of established enterprises be determined by these enterprises or the village organization? According to economic sociology, these two problems actually refer to the following: first, industrial technology should be strengthened in enterprises to establish authority relationship, activity structure and distribution relationship. In other words, to meet the technical requirements of projects requires proper patterns of organization. Second, the village should establish authority relationship, activity structure and distribution relationship for these enterprises. The former one mainly involves internal relations of enterprises, while the latter is about relations between the village and enterprises.

Objectively, due to the extremely limited ecological resources available for agricultural development, most villagers of Jianshanxia Village agree to develop non-agricultural industries, such as village industry. However, they have a divergence of views on how to manage these enterprises. After termination of the People's Commune, though the village set up factories, they had few choices for factory management. Especially, in terms of relations between enterprises and the village collective, neither the collective nor the villagers had legal autonomy. During the early period in the 1970s, most People's Communes were regular in Xiaoshan. Within the commune system, both private factories and contract were permitted. As mentioned before, only communes and groups were allowed to start factories to make up for the lack in agricultural economy. Therefore, these factories were used to make up for the low agricultural production of the village. In terms of personnel, the main leaders of the brigade naturally took charge of the factories. As for the staff of these factories, each household can recommend their members to work in the factories in accordance with their needs, and the brigade then chose the staff members on the basis of family balance. Funds needed by factories were offered by the collective. The collective raised funds among villagers allocated some funds and applied for a loan from national banks or borrowed some money from adjacent villagers. The land for factories is state-owned and managed by the village. In the past, the land was public land for ancestral halls or clan activity. Taking a part of profit paid to the state, the remaining profit was divided into three parts, with the major one used for the collective activity of the village (such as construction of village public facilities), the second part for wages and benefits of workers, and the minor part for expanded reproduction. To sum up, though factories do not belong under the traditional agriculture and forestry of the village, they were collective projects of the village. Hence, these factories should be managed in accordance with legal collective ownership. The only difference was that labor organization of factories could not be the same as other large collective activities of the communes and groups. Due to the standard of technology, division of labor should be conducted in line with factory methods. Factory management involved division of work types and shifts; a factory should have departments for production, selling, finance, inspection, etc.; and staff should include a factory director, accountants, technicians, suppliers, etc. However, the management was not the same as that of general urban factories. Though the wage level of village factories was similar to that of state-owned enterprises and large collective enterprises in Xiaoshan, village factories were not strong enough to offer a labor security system, socialized medicine system or housing distribution system to their staff as state-owned enterprises and large collective enterprises did. As the leaders of factories and the village were the same, the owner of factory profit was unclear between an enterprise and the village.

Of course, the development pattern is extensive, and it was popular until the transformation of the People's Commune. In 1983, responding to the call of the Xiaoshan government, Jianshanxia Village implemented the family contract responsibility system for agriculture and forestry. Compared with the period of the People's Commune, the autonomy of the village to business activities was expanded. In fact, the village didn't play an active role in the operation of the village business. As for the private economy, the legality of household business in agriculture, forestry and sideline production was confirmed. Production teams between the village and households had no effect. However, due to limited resources and poor transportation, nearly 400 households in the village could not meet their basic needs through agriculture, forestry and sideline production, let alone set up family factories as households in some other regions did. They still took the income of family members from village factories as their major income. In addition, village factories, regarded as the backbone industry by most villagers, were still at the stage of early accumulation. At least, as can be seen from Table 2.4, before the rapid expansion of the industry in 1988, the economic benefit of village factories was not high. Though more than one member of one family worked for the industry, their wage level was low. Also, enterprises didn't have much profit left for welfare redistribution among villagers. As a result, villagers expected the village to start more factories, especially large factories, for more job opportunities and to enable worker to earn more wages, instead of changing the collective ownership of village factories.

On May 1984, the commune system was officially ended in Xiaoshan. The original office of the Yunshi People's Commune became the office of the people's government of Yunshi Township and the Jianshanxia Brigade turned to Jianshanxia Village. The change reminded the elders in the village of the rural pattern after the land reform. Of course, the change was not fruitless. For many villages in Xiaoshan, including villages near Jianshanxia Village, to recover the organizational system of townships and villages and set up villagers' committees as rural grassroots organizations meant to further confirm and expand the management autonomy of families. In addition, the CPC Central Committee started to clearly encourage the development of township enterprises.[23] Households were allowed to conduct businesses independently or jointly as long as they had enough capital and other necessary conditions. They could hire workers privately as long as they were able to afford them. Unlike economists and party officials in cities, they didn't have to be particular about the capitalistic nature of hiring labor. Therefore, in the process of industrial economic growth in these regions, township, village, joint and individual business appeared at the same time, which came to be known as township business collectively. Their common ground is that all of them were created by farmers and were thus different from state-owned, large collectively owned and private enterprises. In Jianshanxia Village, the inhabitants might not cherish the village collective economy, but they got used to family oriented life like villagers in other villages. They expected clear ownership of family property and absolute autonomy for family property, even to figure out their shares and possession forms of previously collectively owned property. They hoped to get rid of unnecessary public property and forms as well as corresponding forms of collective labor as far as possible. However, it seemed that due to various elements, villagers in Jianshanxia Village thought that they could not find a way to replace the village industry formed during the commune period.

This may be because of the convention of economic activity of this village. As mentioned before, village history has shown that all village factories were managed by the village collective. An obvious change after the commune system was expansion of village industrial economy, leading to the increase of income of the staff. Generally, this indicates that the convention of collective activity was formed during the development of village industry. Furthermore, the convention should be related to some covert or direct factors, avoiding other possible forms and types of mass production and development of industrial enterprises.

The first restriction was limited village resources and poor transportation. Land in Jianshanxia Village was rare. After setting up several village enterprises, the last more than 40 mu land in the village was used for housing and public facilities. In fact, land for new enterprises or extension of original plants after 1992 was purchased from adjacent villages via the township government. Therefore, it is almost impossible for the village to allot villagers land for household businesses. All villagers understood that, after the construction of roads providing access to the outside world, the development of village non-agricultural economy depended on smooth transportation of goods. Factory profit was affected by timely arrival of raw material, transportation costs and delivery of products. Though the raw material for bambooware was obtained in the village, the finished products had to be transported to the outside for selling. Owners of about seven grocery stores in the village

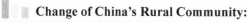

understood that goods bought wholesale in Linpu Town or Chengxiang Town, which were thousands of meters away from the village, were more profitable. As for villagers who bought diesel minibuses for passenger transport and tractors for freight transport, they lived off this transport. However, villagers knew that it was not easy for individuals to solve transportation problems by themselves, as the village was not near traffic arteries. Only the village could solve problems related to road facilities and vehicles. The average economic status of each household was low. A household was unable to afford various aspects of running a business. As for poor transportation blocking marketing information, this is a factor that cannot be improved by individuals. As a result, although China's macroeconomy might attract individuals to run a business after the termination of the People's Commune, most families did not have sufficient economic strength to run a family business. Even though there were few family factories in this village after termination of the People's Commune, it is still possible that households divided the village industry or transformed collective ownership into other systems, such as the stockholding system, to actually possess enterprise assets.[24]

Admittedly, although many family factories in Jianshanxia Village might not spring up after People's Commune, it does not mean that households could not separate village collective factories as usual or convert the collective ownership of village factories to shareholding system or other systems like in other villages to clarify the corporate assets possession of each household. However, this was not even theoretically possible for Jianshanxia Village at that time. Theoretical discussion and reform practice on the property rights system of publicly owned enterprises and township collective enterprises wasn't carried out until the mid-1990s. Before that, villagers never thought that they can have shares of village enterprises. Villagers thought that operating machinery equipment and fixed assets of factories were valuable as a whole and no one should take them apart. In addition, the expanding village industry brought more job opportunities and income to villagers.

Objectively, the technological types of village industry didn't support change with regard to industrial production and profit distribution. Especially since the 1970s, the production of all factories relied on machines and more than 10 million yuan was invested to purchase mechanical equipment and build plants, etc. In addition, lots of funds were spent in expanding the market and for other expenses during production. The capital invested in factories mainly has three sources: funds accumulated by the village collective (primarily through industrial industry), funds raised among villagers and funds from a state loan, which was the major source. The hosts of fund-raising were first the village party branch and the village committee, and then the Langchao Industrial Company. All three sources supported the activity conducted by the village as a unit. (2) The village industry didn't require detailed knowledge and technology of HR. Machinery used in the village industry can be divided into two types. The first one is supermatic installations, such as the small assembly line for production of mosquito-repellent incense, which can be easily operated by workers. The second one is semi-automatic installations, such as machines for filter paper production, which require high physical power and are of low complexity. In terms of packaging, the assembly line method was adopted, where workers only took charge of fixed links without difficulty. There were only three complex links in enterprises. The first one is core technology, including equipment installation, debugging and capital repair, which were mainly conducted by equipment manufacturers or regular external experts. The second one is marketing, requiring a few staff members with a certain amount of marketing ability and relations, but most villagers thought they were not qualified. The third one is senior management of enterprises. Due to the process and nature of village industry, the main leaders of the village party branch and the village committee held a concurrent post in the village enterprises. In general, these three links only needed a few staff members (during the period of prosperity, there were about 100 staff members on the management and in the various departments of village enterprises). Although the content of different types of work was completely different, only a few types of work required strong physical power. General people

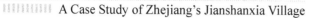
can adapt to most types of work in the village industry. Though there is income difference between different types of workers, it was mainly caused by the different amount of work done rather than work types. As a result, the income difference among workers was small. So, rapid polarization related to income and the status of villagers didn't occur.

Meanwhile, there were restrictions caused by non-economic factors, beyond conditions related to resources and technology. Due to these factors, villagers still regarded unitization in regard to production organization as the first choice for a long time after the commune system. The first factor in the village organization was the leadership. Leaders of the village organization thought that it was correct and proper to develop a village industry, made up of the village labor force and leading to village welfare. This idea might originate from examples of urban factories. In the initial stage of the village industry, leaders of the village (brigade) learned from the village papermaking which had a history of more than 100 years and from the examples of urban factories. However, the first difference between handmade papermaking and the making of filter paper is that the latter requires large mechanical equipment. In addition, their places of origin and purchase as well as the transport of raw material, such as cotton pulp, were different. Hence, the latter was more important, while the former was just a reference material for village leaders. At that time, village leaders simply wanted to copy the pattern of factories seen in the cities. It seemed reasonable, as due to the urban–rural dual system since the 1950s cities became so advanced that rural people, especially villagers of poor Jianshanxia Village, looked forward to an urban life. As a result, urban units, including factories, became good examples for rural people. During the early stage of the village industry, as factory markets could not be opened to the village industry legally, the village had to cope with material purchase and production marketing flexibly and reduce the welfare and salary of workers. As a result, these village enterprises were once more highly compared with flexible state-owned enterprises in the market. Initially, it was regarded as an involuntary means for the sake of survival, reflecting the entry level of factories. Due to limited conditions, the village cannot do whatever it pleases. As a result, the village tried its best to balance manpower utilization among village households and copy the welfare mode of urban factories for a long time. In fact, villagers also supported the urban lifestyle in examples of city units.[25]

Before villagers gradually became wealthy since 1992, similar to villagers of other villages, the residents of Jianshanxia Village thought that compared with rural people's life, life of those living in urban units was much better, for they had money to pay basic necessities of life, they didn't have to make most articles for daily use by themselves, they had living security — especially retirement pension and medical insurance, their children could enjoy good education in cities, they could enjoy many cultural and recreational facilities and activities in cities, their social status was high, etc. Before the great change of the urban unit system took place in China in the mid-1990s, it was hard for villagers to imagine and understand that people can have a stable income with social aged and medical insurance under a non-unit system, education opportunities dependent on levels of urbanization and education popularization, and content and forms of amusement that are related to the development of media. Of course, the urban welfare points that villagers noticed were related to units. In the eyes of most villagers, disadvantages as a member of urban units included the small living space, lack of freedom caused by fixed working hours, high expenditure, the one-child policy, etc. However, after the collective labor system from 1956 to 1980, villagers were not afraid of the factory system and unitization. The best choice for villagers was to set up factories in the village, as they could enjoy most benefits of urban workers and have a large living space at the same time. As a result, with the development of village industry after the commune system, villagers felt that their living standard was gradually getting close to that of the cities.

Interestingly, after the termination of the People's Commune, the state always supported and encouraged village unitization.

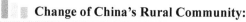

Correspondingly, both the municipal government and the township government attached great importance to the development of economy, especially collective economy, of poor villages, such as Jianshanxia Village, and greatly commended the development performance of the village collective industry. In addition, the unexpected achievements with regard to industry and construction of a village with poor ecological resources especially can show the excellent performance of the local government and set a good example to other villages. People often associated the collective property with socialism in rural areas. At least there is no political risk to strongly support the village. Hence, in the process of development of the village industry, the local government was often in favor of the village in terms of preferential policy, loan projects and evaluation, and even directly affirmed unitization of this village. Since the mid-1980s, the village has been cited many times. In 1992, the village was rated as a model village of Xiaoshan and listed in the developed villages of Xiaoshan with 40 other administrative villages. These titles were retained until 1996.[28]

The village collective promoted the village industry from the perspective of social structure. Continuous expansion of the collective industry made possible the development from villages to urban units. As a result, after the termination of the People's Commune, the changes in Jianshanxia Village were characterized by village industry, continuous expansion of collective industry and improvement of public utilities and welfare, and development of villagers' life toward urban life. Naturally, the so-called village unitization occurred.

These changes were mentioned in *Chronicles of Jianshanxia Village* published in 1993.[27] Before 1996, the organization mode and the social pattern of Jianshanxia Village impressed visitors very much. It is worth noting that most able-bodied villagers were staff members of village enterprises and enjoyed old-age subsidies, employee pensions, medical security, nine-year compulsory education and reward of higher education, public utilities and the infrastructure of the village. Among a series of written systems of unit operation established by the village and enterprises, important ones include the following:

The Assessment System of Advanced Party Branches (1987, party branch), the Assessment Rules of Excellent Party Members (1987, party branch), the Contact System Between Party Members and Farmers (1987, party branch), the Management System of Party Members Going Out (1987, party branch);

Rules and Regulations of Safety Utilization of Electric Power (1987, party branch and village committee);

Detailed Rules and Regulations of Village Construction Planning and Management Policy (1988, party branch, group of land policy and village committee);

Basic Conditions of Family of Spiritual and Material Civilization, Five-virtue Family and Patriotic and Law-abiding Family (1990, village committee);

The System of Mountain Forests (1991, village committee);

Constitution of Village Cooperative Foundation (1991, village committee);

The Decision on Establishment of the System of Rural Labour Accumulation (1991, party branch, village committee, Langchao Industrial Company);

The System of Financial Management (1991, village committee);

Stipulations and Regulations on Cooperative Medical Care (1991, party branch, village committee);

The Management System of Cable Televisions (1991, village committee);

The Management System of Hangzhou Langchao Industrial Company (1991–1992, Langchao Industrial Company; contents include systems of recruitment, retired workers, worker management, corporate finance, year-end bonus allocation, labor protection appliance and welfare treatment);

Rules of the Eighth Five-Year Plan of Jianshanxia Village (1990, party branch, village committee, including rules of development of village industrial and agricultural economy and per capita income, projects of social development, family planning, population control, construction of the Party and the masses, social security, mountain forest production, investment planning, etc.).

After 1992, the village further added and revised some systems of unitization management. These are as follows:

The Constitution of Association of Aged People of Jianshanxia Village (1992, Village Association of Aged People);

The Responsibility System of Land Management of Jianshanxia Village (1993, village committee);

The Constitution and Related Files of the Joint Stock Cooperative System of Hangzhou Langchao Industrial Company (1993, Hangzhou Langchao Industrial Company, the industry office of the people's government of Yuanshi Township, Xiaoshan, authority of rural industry of Xiaoshan);

The Constitution of Village Committee of Jianshanxia Village (1994, including the working system of village committee, responsibility of each committee, management and systems of village group leaders);

The System of Forest Management of Jianshanxia Village (1994);

Systems of "Shuangzheng" Activity (1995, party branch; including the assessment system of advanced party branches, evaluation rules of excellent Party members, the contact system between Party members and farmers, the management system of Party members going out, the system of inner-party activities, the training system of development objects, the management system of party membership dues);

The Constitution of Village Committee (1995, including the working system of village committee, mediation and security, mountain forest management, science, education and culture, family planning, responsibilities of four committees of civil welfare, the system of village representative assembly, management of village group leaders and the system of making village affairs transparent);

Non-governmental Regulations of Village (1995, village committee);

The Management System of Social Comprehensive Governance (1995, village committee);

The Management System of Mountain Forests (1995, village committee);

The Management and Utilization System of Files (1995, village committee);

The Management System of Safety Utilization of Electric Power (1995, village committee);

The Management System of Village Finance (1995, village committee);

The Ninth Five-Year Plan of Jianshanxia Village (1995, party branch, village committee);

The Notification on Further Improvement of the System for Contracted Responsibility of Mountain Forests (1996, village committee).

In general, these systems are based on the village. According to contents, intensity, goals and scope of application of these systems, Jianshanxia Village has established a basic institutional framework required by village unitization around 1992. The framework basically covers institutional distribution of a unit, including the organization system of party and government and relations between them, production work, relations between a village and its enterprises, core leadership of the Party branch, mass organizations below village committees, employment and wages, and public welfare.

The next section will continue to observe the structure, the roles of people in the structure and their activities.

First, it seems that we should amend the original explanatory paradigm that we applied. In our opinion, the limited ecological resources of Jianshanxia Village only objectively show that to develop an industry is the most economical choice for the village. However, it is the social capital and industrial technology of the village that determines how to make the choice come true. In the early stage of village industry, non-clan village collective, the unit variant and village (brigade) structure formed during the commune system, and the system of public land controlled by the village and convention of collective action for years obviously became necessary social capital to make up for shortage of material capital. After the termination of the People's Commune, the continuous action of the social capital promoted the growth of the village industry in the form of village collective enterprises. As a result, the new industry and its profits attached to the village ensure employment and provide an economic foundation for the development of village unitization. Rural–urban differences and urban units that have been in existence for years set good examples to the village in regard to unitization. As a rural grassroots unit approved by the state, a village should learn that actions and achievements form urban units and thus promote village unitization because of independence of the village in terms of employment, economic calculation, and public welfare.[28]

To sum up, from the perspectives of technology, national politics and social capital, and selection and input of new technology, the state's loose attitude toward entering a large resource environment of villages through market contact, production organization adapting to new production technology, and adaptive change of original social organizations caused by appearance of new production organizations are the most critical factors.[29]

Endnotes

1. Qian Hang conducted a case study and general interpretation. See Qian H and Xie WY. *Rural Clan Patterns in Taihe, Jiangxi*. Shanghai: Shanghai Academy of Social Sciences Press, 1995.

2. See (1) Ma JH. *Today's Xiaoshan*. Hangzhou: Hangzhou University Press, 1994. (2) Indexes of the Third National Top 100 Counties (Zhejiang), *Qianjiang Evening News*, February 13, 1996. (3) Statistical Bulletin of Xiaoshan Statistical Bureau (1994–1996).

3. In 1986, the village party branch and the village committee designated several retirees in the village to compile records of the village. However, due to great difficulty in data collection, the compiling work was finally suspended. Nonetheless, the village never forgets that "records should be complied in the flourishing age to remember the flourishing age". Since the 1980s, great change has taken place in the village during the rural reform. "In the village, there are lots of new houses, clean streams, plants and enterprises and happy laughter and cheerful voices. In today's Jianshanxia Village, people live and work in peace and contentment. Today we are no longer as we have been". As a result, the village is able to compile records emotionally and economically (preface of the *Chronicles*).

4. For instance, the per capita net income of Chinese farmers was 1,220 and 1,578 yuan in 1994 and 1995, respectively. According to the forecast issued by the State Statistics Bureau on December 29, 1999, in 1999, per capita disposable income of urban residents was 5,859 yuan, an increase of 9.2%; per capita net income of farmers were 2,205 yuan, an actual increase of 4% (China's economic objectives this year have been achieved on schedule, *Zhejiang Daily*, front page,

December 30, 1999). According to "The Statistical Bulletin on Economic and Social Development of Zhejiang in 1999 by Zhejiang Statistical Bureau" (February 28, 2000), per capita net income of rural residents in Zhejiang was 3,948 yuan in 1999 (*Zhejiang Daily*, third page, March 9, 2000).

5. In short, in terms of figures, this small village once became one of the main production bases of electric mosquito repellents in China. In 1995, it provided 1.5 billion original paper cards of electric mosquito repellents, accounting for 90% of the total output in China. Except some of which were exported, they accounted for 60%–70% of national market share. In recent years, the total industrial output value of the village has accounted for more than 95% of gross output value of industry and agriculture. According to economic strength, in 1995, collective fixed assets of the village was worth 18.8352 million yuan (including 18.323 million yuan of the village industry), its gross output value of industry and agriculture was 89.71 million yuan, the collective tax was 3.3353 million yuan, the profit of village industry was 1.7735 million yuan, and collective assets from the village were worth 15.6626 million yuan (including 14.4893 million yuan from the village industry). From 1992 to 1997, the total value of village output increased by 39.4 times, an average increase of 28%, where the total industrial output value increased by 48.6 times with an annual average growth rate of 29.7%. Based on the lifestyle and improvement of living standard, in 1994, more than 72% of able-bodied villagers worked in collective enterprises and the per capita net income of villagers was 25.6 times that in 1977. Since the 1980s, about 3/4 of the villagers moved to new two- to three-storey houses with a per capita living space of 40 square meters. Since 1985, the village has been rated as the comprehensive advanced village of Yunshi. In 1986, it became a civilized village unit of Xiaoshan. In 1992, it became one of the more than 40 model villages of Xiaoshan. In 1995, it was listed in top 50 villages of Xiaoshan. The evaluation of model villages involved a set of detailed standards and rigid indexes.

6. After transformation of village enterprises in 1997, the number of employees of these enterprises reduced, and in the annual overview of the village "Enterprises Run by the Village" was changed into "Village Enterprises".

7. See (1) Hong YY. *Chronicles of Jianshanxia Village*. Beijing: Tuanjie Press, 1993. (2) *Jianshanxia Village of Yunshi Township* (Overview) (1993–1995).

8. The term, "village unitization", in this paper originated from impression. By the way, I am not the only person who has such an impression. According to the village secretary, in the early 1990s, an important official of the central government visited this village and called the village the "New Socialist Countryside", which might be related to village unitization and collectivization.

9. The village committee legally undertook some tasks which will be discussed later, including propaganda of national laws and the ruling party; autonomous transactions of the village, such as perfection of systems of the village committee, guarantee of participation of villagers in autonomous activities, economic development, and improvement of public affairs and public welfare; coordination of government work; education of villagers on observing law and discipline, etc. See Wang ZY and Bai YH. *Development of Township Regime and Village Committees*. Beijing: China Society Press, 1996: 91–101.

10. In this sense, it may be a little odd to seek interpretation in economic sociology. Since the derivation of economic sociology from Karl Marx and Max Weber, it is mainly good for research on economic behavior as social behaviour and economic processes as social processes and not good at explaining patterns or mechanisms of regional economy and social development. However, the situation has since changed. Since the 1960s, economic sociology started to pay attention to ecological resources and environments naturally. Meanwhile, it not only absorbs new results of environmental economics but also takes note of the classical origin of environmental economics again. As a result, it seems that the general research of economic sociology tends to adopt a gentler and more practical path. In other words, it started with research on relations between ecology and society and put forward a new theoretical analysis. Since then, economic sociology started to observe regional economy and society and their differences from an ecological basis.

11. Pierce D and Warford J. *No Doomsday: Economics, Environment and Sustainable Development*. Trans. Zhang SQ *et al*. Beijing: China Financial and Economical Publishing House, 1996, pp. 4 and 9.

12. Stinchcombe AL. *Comparative Economic Sociology*. Trans. Yang XD. Hangzhou: Zhejiang People's Publishing House, 1987, pp. 28 and 92. Stinchcombe once attempted to explain the relationship between resources and ecology. He pointed out that "the total biological productivity of a region depends on environmental parameters, such as sunshine, temperature and available water resources. Total output of living matter depends on growth of living beings with these resources and environmental characteristics, where solar energy is transformed into organic compounds in food chains". Other species also depend on the biological matrix, which is the basis of food chains. Each link of a food chain obtains biological matrix from the lower links and consumes it. Meanwhile, it also generates substances shared by lower links or the environment and higher links. Generally speaking, if a species wants to be stable in an environment, the total basic resources needed by a species should be balanced during each stage. Hence, he thought, "we can define resources normally and ecologically. A resource refers to a stable ecological system in a specific environment. The system determines the possible recovery ratio of an environment in specific technical conditions. No other possible recovery ratio can be stable beyond this possible ecological system. Technological change plays a role by adding probability of various ecosystems. As a result, technology broadens change of recovery ratios, making new rates of activity become possible". (*No Doomsday: Economics, Environment and Sustainable development*, pp. 29 and 32.)

13. See Stinchcombe AL. *Comparative Economic Sociology*. Hangzhou: Zhejiang People's Publishing House, 1987, pp. 154–155.

14. Contemporary economic and social development pays less attention to reducing poverty and enhancing the average living standard of people. However, no technical indicator or value criterion is the best to measure various types of economic and social development. Problems of regional unbalanced development, such as differences in terms of degrees of economic development and stability and income inequality, are quite prominent. (Research findings in statistics and econometrics have powerfully demonstrated the unbalanced development, such as Stone R. *Mathematics and Other Papers in Social Sciences*. Beijing: Beijing Institute of Economics Press, 1994.)

China is no exception. Since 1949, China has devoted itself to seeking economic growth and social progress with equality and stability like most developing countries. Chinese leaders paid more attention to problems of guaranteeing the minimum subsistence, narrowing the income gap, improving employment and maintaining monetary, fiscal and price stability than leaders in most other developing countries. As a result, for decades, the most prominent characteristic of Chinese society and economy was to pursue equality and stability. For example, in rural areas, the movement of land reform in the 1950s eliminated the landlord class. As a result, the income of the highest class reduced by 20%, while that of the lowest class increased by about 50% in rural areas. Afterwards the Socialist Transformation further strengthened income equality in rural areas. The income of members of rural society was mainly constituted by labor income (or wages) and the state's redistribution, where property income and rural inequality of income caused by scale and quality of private land was basically removed. The course and results of these social movements surprised some American sinologists (see Wang JL. *Mao Zedong's Idealism and Deng Xiaoping's Realism: An American Scholar's Discussion on China.* Beijing: Current Affairs Press, 1996, pp. 26–35). However, differences and inequality with respect to development and income were apparent, where one major problem was regional differences or regional inequality. Before the reform, this situation was severe in rural areas. For instance, the rural land reform and the socialist transformation narrowed the gap among members of rural society, effectively strengthened equalization among members of society and avoided polarization. However, due to the different labor forces of different rural families, different quantity and quality of land and irrigation conditions resulted in different incomes, leading to serious income inequality in rural areas. To remove the inequality, methods of taxation, investment, migration, etc, were advisable. China's fiscal policy also inhibited or narrowed the gap among provinces. However, it is difficult to evenly benefit various counties and villages by the national fiscal policy. The state only could stress the self-dependence policy and relieve the shortage of food supply and national investment. In terms of urban and rural income, in the 1950s, China gave living cost subsidies, put up the purchasing price of agricultural products and provided more medical and educational professionals to the rural area, which greatly improved the differences between town and country. However, for decades, factors, such as low investment in rural areas, failure of free mobility

of rural population, low price of agricultural products and rapid development of urban services, offset the influences of the state's policy to some extent. It is worth noting that since the reform, due to geographical and policy factors, similar regional differences become increasingly obvious. Both statistical results and case studies show that various regional differences have existed and become increasingly obvious during the course of China's economic and social development in the last 20 years (see (1) Ma H and Sun SQ. *Economic White Paper: China's Economic Situation and Prospect (1995–1996)*. Beijing: China Development Press, 1996, pp. 19, and 249, 251. (2) Jiang L, Lu XY and Shan TL. *Social Blue Book: Analysis and Forecast of China's Social Situation from 1995 to 1996*. Beijing: China Social Sciences Press, 1996, pp. 334–361.) Taking economically developed Zhejiang as an example, according to an evaluation of 20 representative indicators in 1995, the gap between the rapidly and slowly developing regions was more than one time, where general social development indexes of Hangzhou, of the fastest development, and Lishui, of the slowest development, were 73.94 and 21.36, respectively. The gap reflected both rural–urban disparity and the disparity between developed coastal areas and underdeveloped mountainous areas (see Yang JH. Five Contradictions Puzzling the Social Development of Zhejiang. *Zhejiang Social Sciences*. 1998(2):82). It is especially significant in vast rural areas. Some counties (towns) and villages that were developed early in a rapid manner attained a moderately high standard of living, while other regions turned into poor counties, townships and villages because of the difficulty of development, which was quite unsatisfying. Governments at all levels paid more and more attention to how to help rural backward areas get rid of poverty and improve unbalanced economic and social development in rural areas.

That is to say, although national governments have reached a consensus on global integration, regional interdependence, cooperation, etc., the Chinese government have also made great efforts to make domestic rural backward areas free from poverty. However, due to natural, historical and man-made factors, the unbalanced situation is getting worse, leading to a serious contradiction between regional non-independence and regional unbalanced development.

Obviously, if the contradiction cannot be controlled, regional imbalance will become a main cause for social inequality in China.

As the poverty of some poor rural villages and underdeveloped villages in developed regions is mainly related to regional unbalanced development, what is the origin of regional imbalance and can the problem of regional unbalanced development be solved?

For a long time, people generally thought of the above problems from perspectives of natural conditions and policy and usually asked economists and sociologists for help. Naturally, economics and sociology are asked to provide general rules, explain the imbalance and offer related solutions. However, it seems that some theories of economics and sociology are deficient. In addition, economics and sociology are young and immature subjects, while macroeconomics and macrosociology are powerful. In other words, both economics and sociology seek universal coverage, but their logic is congenitally deficient, where induction and abstract processes usually focus on universality but ignore regional particularity. When people expect domain and application sciences in economics and sociology, economics just highlights and fixes its subject nature from research on national economics to "specialization of knowledge and systematization principles". Obviously, it goes against the pattern of studying nature or society via technology formed in natural sciences since modern times. Microeconomics and other branches of economics developed later have not changed this convention yet. Strictly speaking, as a social science, the development of economics gives no cause for much criticism. However, it reflects that growing from modern scientism, economics is overoptimistic about controlling both nature and society and overrates controllability of economic and social development. Accordingly, few scholars pay attention to influences of ecological environments on economy and society during exchange between people (society) and environment or their interacting control and discuss a special stipulation formed by regional special resources. Thus, one important fact is that regional particularity is as important as universality in regional development; the stipulation formed by ecological resources and the environment of a region is the most important characteristic of the region and even lays a foundation for the special development pattern of this region. Due to ignorance of this fact, insight and practical effectiveness of economics are severely weakened in terms of interpretation and settlement of regional imbalance.

Fortunately, two global ecological movements since the late 1960s brought about horizon reform to economics, sociology and even all social sciences. Through research on wasting of resources, environmental pollution and breaking of ecological balance in developed industrial countries caused by high production and high consumption, people understand that their direct control of nature and indirect control of nature via social control are limited and may be limited forever. The natural environment plays a role in restricting population, health, environments, the whole human society and economic development and environments. In other words, nature still plays a role in controlling human beings, and arrangement of economic and social development should take this fact into account. As a result, Leiss William attempted to construct "ecological Marxism". He held that the idea of nature control is the root cause of ecological crisis and that both concepts of nature worship in naturalism and conquest of nature in industrialism should be abandoned and nature control only means control of relations between man and nature (see William L. *Natural Control.* Trans. Yue CL and Li JH. Chongqing: Chongqing Publishing House, 1993). Economists proposed that if the concept and the mode of economic growth are not changed in a timely manner to control wasting of resources effectively, people will be confronted with "the limits to growth" or catastrophic recession of global economy. After the late 1980s, economists put forward sustainable development on this basis, where discussion on the limits to growth caused by traditional economic policy was converted into that on how to realize economic growth in favor of the environment or how to strengthen environmental protection through proper economic growth. For example, David Pierce and Jeremy Warford called discussions on relations between environment and economy from the late 1960s to the early 1970s and from the late 1980s to the early 1990s "two environmental revolutions". In addition, they correctly pointed out that the early economic growth model criticized by both environmental revolutions is capital-oriented and stress that investment in necessary machinery, plants and infrastructure will increase income; afterwards it stresses technical progress, forming the model, "investment of capital construction + technical progress = feasibility of economic growth". However, the practice of developing countries has shown that it is not true that input of free natural resources is as important as capital and technical factors in a traditional mode, in developing countries. The theory of sustainable development in the late 1980s described a process that does not allow deterioration of natural environments and discussed the effects of environmental quality and environmental input on improving real income and quality of life. In addition, it expressed two convictions: correct environmental policy is conductive to economic growth, and the environmental problem is internationalized and its settlement requires international cooperation, especially rich countries helping the poor (see Pierce D and Warford J. *No Doomsday: Economics, Environment and Sustainable Development*. Trans. Zhang SQ *et al*. Beijing: China Financial and Economical Publishing House, 1996, pp. 8–10).

Undoubtedly, this turn continues to raise the status of environmental action. In other words, by stressing temperate utilization of environmental resources, it potentially emphasized people's submissiveness to environments. As a result, a new consensus on ecology is gradually formed and strengthened in both natural and social sciences: in pre-industrial society, people were extremely deferential to nature and thought that they are a part of nature, which is advisable; in industrial society, people regarded themselves as the creator and thought that the meaning of nature was to offer people resources in accordance with people's needs and development capacity, which is haughty, dangerous and unreasonable. Based on the same logic, the theory of sustainable development in the late 1980s held an optimistic attitude, systematically reviewed the theory of economic growth limits in the 1960s and 1970s, and demonstrated the importance and the possibility of coordination between man and environment (see Dasgupta PS and Heal GM. *Economic Theory and Exhaustible Resources*. Cambridge: Cambridge University Press, 1989).

The formation of this consensus has a significant influence. As social sciences start to pay attention to ecology, ecology, which originally studied the relationship between biological organisms and their environments, is no longer the exclusive work of biologists and zoologists. For the sake of harmonious development of humans, societies and environments, social scientists attach great importance to application of ecological principles to research on human societies, population, etc. For example, anthropologists consciously analyzed influences of the survival mode and technology for environmental development of a social or cultural unit

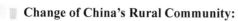

on it social structure and culture. Murphy pointed out, "direct mutual exchange and mutual effects between ecological environments and social systems and the significant effect of technology in this process show that ecology is an important factor for social change and evolution". (Murphy RF. *Culture and Social Anthropology: An Overture*. Trans. Wang ZJ *et al*. Beijing: The Commercial Press, 1991, p. 154.) Sociologists studied the relationship between human groups and their natural environments in the name of human ecology. Sensible economists finally acknowledged a fact that should have been admitted long ago: "though human beings continuously invent new technology, growth is potentially limited"; "as the existence of human beings must depend on extraction, processing and consumption of natural resources, the world economy is closely related to environments. Meanwhile, these resources must comply with the law of indestructibility of matter and law of conservation of energy and finally turn into waste material"; "if the environmental factor is ignored during economic management, economic growth does has its limit". Hence, even economists holding an optimistic attitude toward economic growth think that they should focus on and discuss sustainable development realized through reduction of wasting of resources and environmental pollution. In addition, they should understand that the environment is important for the economy and for the welfare of all people; environment degradation often occurs in an economic process and is especially caused by wrong management styles (economic distortions in government's policy in particular); settlement of environmental problems requires correction of economic distortions and incentives for conservation of resources and reduction of pollution. Only when incentives for conservation of resources and reduction of pollution (including economic incentives) are adopted can sustainable economic and social development be possible; in addition, cooperation and joint action of all countries should be ensured through an incentive mechanism to effectively protect global common resources. (Pierce D and Warford J. *No Doomsday: Economics, Environment and Sustainable Development*. Beijing: China Financial and Economical Publishing House, 1996, pp. 3–5 and 9.)

As people attach great importance to ecological resources and environments, economists, sociologists and even historians have to adopt a pragmatic approach to explain and solve the problem of regional development imbalance and pay significant attention to restrictions of regional resources on regional economy and social development. For example, in *China's Economic Revolution* published by Alexander Eckstein, an American economist and sinologist, in 1977, he put forward a very creative view: "China's economic pattern basically reflects the interaction among scarcity, ideology and institutional frameworks. Harsh facts, such as poverty, shortage of land, capital and technically bridle-wise labor, are caused by resource factors of China. The idea to strongly pursue a strong, self-reliant, egalitarian nation and society appears in modern history and contemporary ideology of China. Systematic utilization of labor force to replace land and capital shows shortage of resources. Methods of mobilization and promotion of labor force reflect function of ideology and institutional frameworks" (Eckstein A. China's Economic Revolution. In: Wang JL (ed.), *Mao Zedong's Idealism and Deng Xiaoping's Realism: An American Scholar's Discussion on China*. Beijing: Current Affairs Press, 1996, p. 1.). According to factors such as resources, technology, organization and ideology mentioned by Eckstein, it can be seen that there are some common methodological features in research on regional economic and social problems from the perspective of regional ecology. In other words, it explains some economic and social characteristics of this region from the angle of regional ecological environments and stresses to explore the most reasonable way and means for economic and social development of a region from the perspective of characteristics of regional environments. That is to say, regional development imbalance may first involve unbalanced regional ecological resource distribution.

In my opinion, this method is not only suitable for observation of development of large regions, such as China, but also for that of small regions, such as a village and a town.

In other words, with regard to interpretation and settlement of regional development imbalance, ecology directly raises two major questions: (1) Is it necessary to consider regional environmental costs during regional economic growth and regional social development? (2) Are there restrictions of regional ecological resources and environments on regional economy and social development? If yes, how to break these restrictions and maintain sustainable development at the same time?

Economic sociology collectively expresses the concepts above.

15. Stinchcombe thought: Theoretically, it technically deepens classical theory on relations among Marx's productive forces, relations of production and superstructure. There are some new Marxist theories in economics and sociology. Its "core of theory, as Marx listed in his work, should be ecology and technology of a society and production activity conducted by enterprises in this society on this basis, namely productivity, and value created by enterprises and claims of right of products and related political support, namely productive relations". He wanted to "summarize and describe economic sociology required for perfecting and unifying new Marxism" (Eckstein A. China's Economic Revolution. In: Wang JL (ed.), *Mao Zedong's Idealism and Deng Xiaoping's Realism: An American Scholar's Discussion on China*. Beijing: Current Affairs Press, 1996, pp. 23–24).

16. Radcliffe-Brown AR. *Method in Social Anthropology: Selected Essays*. Chicago: University of Chicago Press, 1958.

17. In addition, in view of final requests of economic behavior, if all issues relating to underdevelopment can be attributed to unmodifiable resource structure and resource boundary in a region and restrictions of traditional cultural habits and from state, society, politics, etc., people need to consider a difficult problem: how to seek economic and social development of a region with established resource structure and resource boundary. Interestingly, the concept of social capital in economic development was introduced to discuss these problems recently. So, social organization in ecological utilization is the next topic in this book.

18. This may be the first precondition of low efficiency of village economy at that time. In fact, even the state supports to improve village economy, but the state's intervention cannot directly influence the adaption of resource environments of each village. As a result, the state cannot consider productivity requirements of village economy. On the basis of the details given in the last chapter, economic production efficiency of villages is not the main measurement for the country to

consider village organization, if there is a measurement. On the macrolevel, as Eckstein said, government policy and land resources entangle with each other in a peculiar manner. In other words, in an economy with land shortage, only continuous increase of per mu yield can increase agricultural yield, so the use efficiency of land should be increased every year. In an economy with capital shortage, non-capital investment should be enhanced. Therefore, the Chinese government prevented labor transfer from rural areas to urban areas and encouraged labor to return to their hometown. As a result, the economic structure changed, but the labor structure was stable. Meanwhile, the gap between industrial and agricultural labor productivities enlarged.

19. I agree with the opinion in the records of the village and in other material: this village is still "remote and quiet". Transportation in this village is poor. 33 kilometers separates Chengxiang Town of Xiaoshan from Jianshanxia Village via Daicun Town, where an 8-kilometer fourth-class highway connects Jianshanxia Village and Dai Village. Under normal traffic conditions, it usually takes more than 40 minutes to drive from Chengxiang Town to Jianshanxia Village at a speed of 40 kilometers/hour. To take a private minibus is the common means of transportation, which will take nearly one hour to get to the village because of stops. A distance of 33 kilometers is not a long one for modern people. However, a vehicle leaves National Highway 104 in Daicun Town and enters the mountain area. After that, passengers will see more and more hills and less and less fields, people and vehicles. They cannot see busy streets and roads in cities, so they may suspect this place has no contact with the outside world. In addition, during the daytime, there are few people in the village, making the village quiet. From 9:30 to 10 am in the morning on the day after I entered the village, I walked from the village entrance to the end of the village and observed people I met. I found that, except five to six greengrocers in the village, the aged sitting aside houses and one private businessman who was arranging bambooware, there were only six to seven people. I was surprised and asked the villagers the reasons for this situation. Most of them replied that most villagers are workers of factories. At this point, they may have already gone to work or be taking rest at home after coming back from the night shift. If it is not cold, the traditional outdoor activity for villagers is to enjoy the cool temperature on both sides of the village roads after dinner.

20. Due to long-term restrictions of these conditions, the original economic accumulation of Jianshanxia Village, especially its industrial economic base, was poor. For example, the industrial base of communes and groups was weak and primitive accumulation problems of rural industrialization were quite sharp. In addition, the infrastructure of the village was weak and the quality of life poor (such as housing, schools, roads), leading to special difficulties related to accumulation and reproduction.

21. See *Chronicles of Jianshanxia Village*, pp. 84–86.

22. See *Chronicles of Jianshanxia Village*, pp. 91–95.

23. Literature after Chinese Eleventh CPC Central Committee Third Plenary Session shows that the significance of developing township industry was not approved until 1984, and the development directions, layout policy, business scope and sources of funds, etc., of township industry were clearly defined in policy (see Party Documents Research Office of the CPC Central Committee. *Selected Important Documents since the Third Plenary Session* (I and II). Beijing: People's Publishing House, 1982; *Selected Important Documents since the Twelfth National Congress* (I, II and III). Beijing: People's Publishing House, 1987; *Selected Important Documents since the Thirteenth National Congress* (I, II and III). Beijing: People's Publishing House, 1992).

24. In fact, not all families were poor and lacked proper conditions. However, before the mid-1990s, it seemed that the Xiaoshan government didn't encourage private industry. Furthermore, the able-bodied people of this village were recommended as leaders of the village, leading to impossibility of other types of enterprises in this village.

25. In addition, in terms of power control and benefit distribution of village organizations and cadres, in spite of difficulties during observation and discussion, the observer speculates that the village organization understands that to continue, expand and perfect the pattern of village industry means to ensure its absolute control of village affairs. This situation was strengthened after the termination of

the People's Commune. Village cadres can obtain a steady source of income as members of village management in the expansion process of village industry.

26. On December 26, 1996, Jiang Guosong, the first thief of Jianshanxia Village since 1949 was sentenced to death. According to the one-vote negation system, the titles of the "Example Village" and "Civilized Village" of Jianshanxia Village were canceled.

27. With the development of village economy, villagers' life was improved. In 1992, among 812 able-bodied villagers, 80% worked in village enterprises; the per capita income of staff members of village enterprises was 2,415.4 yuan, and that of villagers was 1,812 yuan, which increased by 1.87 and 14.62 times, respectively, compared with those in 1977. Since 1988, Jianshanxia Village was the village with the highest income in Yunshi for five consecutive years. Before 1949, villages' houses had a stonewalling structure, but were crowded and shabby. In the 1980s, housing fever gripped the village. Villagers paid attention to both the internal and external appearance of their houses. In order to protect cultivated land, the village conducted construction planning management since 1990. From 1981 to 1992, 68.2% of farmers moved to new two-to-three-storey houses with a per capita living space of 37.2 square meters. In their houses, TVs, sewing machines, electric fans, bicycles, watches, etc., were common and instruments like refrigerators, washing machines, dual-purpose machines and video recorders were increasingly seen. There were six automobiles, 14 tricycles, 10 motorcycles and six walking tractors in the village. Since 1984, the pension subsidy system has been implemented. Female villages above 55 years of age and male villages above 60 years can obtain 15–50 yuan every month. In 1989, workers in village enterprises started to enjoy the retirement system and retirement pay.

Education, health and culture of the village have been developed. In April 1989, the village invested 300,000 yuan to build a primary school. In the same year, the system of nine-year compulsory education was implemented. Students enjoyed free education from the nursery class to middle school. Since 1992, the village regulated that students who are admitted into a technical secondary school or above will receive 300–800 yuan. Since 1949, more than 50 villagers studied at a technical

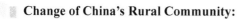

secondary school or above, where there are two doctoral students, one professor and one associate professor. Now there are ten teachers and 211 students in the primary school of Jianshanxia Village. Both the enrollment rate of school-age children and the enrollment rate of pupils are 100%. The village has eradicated illiteracy among young adults. In 1989, the village invested 120,000 yuan to build a satellite ground receiving station and install more than 400 moving-coil loudspeakers for the villagers. Thus, the village became the first village with broadcasting and television transmission in Xiaoshan. Meanwhile, a switchboard covering 100 telephones was installed, and 70 households installed telephones. In the same year, the village built a garden for the aged, a club for the young, and an activity room for women containing newspapers, books, televisions, videos and chess, table tennis tables, basketballs, etc. In September 1991, the cooperative medical care system was recovered through fund-raising among farmers. Health facilities in the village were improved. Now 20.3% of villagers installed flush toilets in their houses. There is no longer an outdoor toilet in the village. Villagers' drinking water is obtained from wells and running water.

Village construction develops rapidly and the appearance of the village greatly changes. Since 1977, the village has invested more than 0.5 million yuan to repair and expand village roads. 1,200-meter bumpy cobblestone roads were replaced by asphalt and cement roads. In addition, there are 600-meter clay-bound macadam roads in the village. The village road is connected to the road of Daicun Town. Meanwhile, there are pine and cypress trees on both sides of roads, many flower beds and stone chairs, 250 streetlights, and one hexagonal pavilion. Jianshanxia Village has been transformed from a poor village into a wealthy village.

Since 1985, the village has been listed in the list of advanced villages of Xiaoshan and Hangzhou. In 1986, the village was rated as the village-level civilization unit in Xiaoshan County; in 1992, it was rated as the model village and civilization village in Xiaoshan City. During the same period, organizations such as village party branch, Youth League Branch, Women's Congress, and Family Planning Association were successively rated as advanced units in Xiaoshan City and Zhejiang City for the outstanding work performance in land management, social security, judicial mediation, militia, and endowment insurance (cited from the Overview of *Chronicles of Jianshanxia Village*).

28. Of course, there are some special factors of the village. (1) Due to shortage of land, this village has no task of grain planting. So the village develops industry without hesitation an due to lack of any alternative. (2) Since the rural reform, China gradually approves and advocates township industry and local consumption of labor force, leading to loose policy related to the rural industry. (3) After wars and political change for years, the original clan pattern significantly declines and clans have been replaced by the village, a legal grassroots unit for foreign exchanges.

29. In this sense, although regional resources are limited, appropriate collocation of resources and proper application of new technology can realize creative development of resources. On the premise of fixed resources, proper combination of technology is crucial. In the unitization process of Jianshanxia Village, introduction of new technology caused adaptive changes of organization modes and its unitization can even be regarded as a new type of technology of resource utilization and operation. She Xiaoye discussed similar issues from the perspective of cooperative behavior in social relations, social capital and rural industrialization. He put forward that, in order to make up for material capital and labor force, villages need cooperative behavior and collective action; the latter requires social capital formed via social relations as its startup foundation; due to non-free mobility or high costs of mobility, traditional administrative organization authority becomes the organizer of collective activity during rural industrialization; with the development of industrialization, it further carries out comprehensive community cooperation and community collective action. His opinion is interesting.

By the way, it reminds me of the disadvantages of the interpretation method in economic sociology. Ultimately, ecological viewpoints in economic sociology usually ignore people's choosing ability, other factors affecting selection and significant differences caused by different choices when they describe direct and indirect restrictions of ecological conditions. As a result, economic sociology reveals the slight fatalism of economic and social development. Even economic sociology stresses the significance of technology and its role in connecting technology with ecology and society, but its fatalism cannot be removed. However, there are various factors affecting social and cultural structure and social change, such as population, ideology, events, cultural innovation, human action (especially social movements), technology, etc. As Parsons said, it is difficult to point out a single crucial factor, and the single-factor theory is just an immature product of economic sociology as one single factor always depends on some other factors. (Parsons T. *Societies: Evolutionary and Comparative Perspectives*. Englewood Cliffs, N.J.: Prentice-Hall, 1966.) Therefore, there are many factors that can affect regional economic and social development. In addition, restrictions of regional environments on economic and social changes in the region are formed through interaction between social and environmental forces. Technology, organization and policy incentives play a critical role at least in the relationship between environments and people.

Hence, the issue can be transformed into an issue about ecological conditions that economic sociology usually ignores. In my opinion, it should be a focus in economic sociology. The transformation may be significant, especially for underdeveloped countries and regions.

Chapter 3

Village Unitization and
Community Transition

3.1　Unitization Linkage: Community Improvement

In brief, the village system transition process of Jianshanxia Village is under the combined actions of ecological resource factors (land resource is inappropriate for the development of agriculture, and transportation cost prohibits the development of family unit industry or other non-agriculture industry), traditional factors (priority in the production of handicraft industry and sideline production), state force-driving factors (restriction on patriarchal clan, coercive provision of village boundary, administrative village as rural grassroots and support for rural collective economy), political organization process factors (village team structure and village team organization with administrative functions and convention of organizing rural collective action), capital and technical factors in favor of the introduction of industry in villages. Subject to the synergistic influence of these factors, village communities unanimously agree with the decision of village team collective to initiate industry in the later period of People's Commune on the whole. Following the termination of People's Commune, the administrative village is affirmed to be rural grassroots by the government once again. As a general rule, the formal organization of the grassroots as the party branch in grassroots organization and the villager committee in villager autonomous organization does not need to take overall production and organization responsibility for villager family and villager group like the relation between the group organization and subordinate production team in the period of People's Commune. But, for the same reason, its economic functions in villages depend on the accessibility to production resources and production department, and especially the control of business enterprises after the execution of family contract responsibility in agriculture and forestry. As a consequence, if permitted, this tendency could propel two major rural leading organizations to maintain or reinforce existing village-run industries. Benefiting from the expansion of village industry economic scale by the expansion of factory under the directive of village collective, Jianshanxia Village earned high profits before 1992 and even 1995. Therefore, this promotion process seemed to be relatively smooth and successful. Village collective enterprises gradually grew stronger and eventually developed to be the overwhelming part of village economy. Enterprises basically overlapped with village grassroots in economy coverage and employment coverage. In this process, village organizations also endeavored to subjectively learn the welfare and other operation systems of city unit to govern villages and enterprises, which led to the comparability between village unit and city unit in the long run.

Admittedly, comparability does not mean equality. City unit refers to the organization which integrates industrial organization unit and basic social organization unit. In his detailed study on the origin of unit system in China in the 1950s, Lu Feng pointed out the prime system relation: (1) The country on the one hand tried to eliminate market relations and take administrative means to control the distribution of resources and on the other hand compulsorily commanded enterprises to undertake laborers' perpetual employment and welfare responsibility, therefore resulting in the full reliance of laborers on the place of employment. In essence, it revealed individual attachment to the country. (2) Limited by the political structure and principles of New China in the national organization process, law did not become the prime means of social governance. Consequently, economic organizations introduced into administrative management organization structure based on public ownership turned to be the direct means of national administrative management organization in social governance. (3) By the same token, when the party organization in the absolute leading position of national political life extended to all basic social organizations, laborers' place of employment also became their prime place of political participation. (4) For individuals, party organization and administrative authority in the place of employment were not only the managers in labor process but also represented the party and the government in political and legal terms. Under the condition of the full control of social life under national administrative power, numerous individual social activities (such as marriage registration, household registration and job transfer) could not proceed without the approval and proof of party authority in the place of employment. "When the organization form in the place of employment contained these systems, basic social organizations turned into 'units'".[1]

The quadruple relation demonstrates how the country successfully actualizes the entire absorption of public ownership of personnel's economic life, political life and social life in the place of employment by means of unit system. However, from this perspective, a unitization village like Jianshanxia Village was not totally identical to mature city unit in the 1960s and 1970s or city unit in the 1950s. To put it simply, unitization village also follows administrative means (including the employment of village administrative authority formed for decades) to control and distribute the foremost economic resources inside villages and tries to undertake the perpetual employment and lifetime welfare of village laborers and all villagers, with the view of facilitating villagers' attachment to villages and enterprises. In the meantime, unitization village naturally promotes the natural penetration of village community party and "political" organizations into village enterprises by way of village collective-funded factories, corporate village collective ownership and appointment of party branch and village committee cadres as village enterprise leaders. But, anyhow, there still exist multiple differences between unitization villages and city units in terms of system foundation, system contents and system orientation. In particular, its origin from village's affinity to or simulation of city enterprise organization, basic organization management system and pattern is not similar to state intention, resource and authority in the construction and control of city unit and city society. Hence, the difference between the two is also evident in practical system relation.

The following are some instances:

(1) In city unit system, since laborers' place of employment could not totally integrate with residence community all the time, unit governance system and neighborhood committee governance system could proceed in parallel. The country classifies overwhelming social roles to be undertaken by individual personnel under public ownership within the scope of unit governance and groups them into the governance scope of neighborhood committee as community members and family members, therefore generally forming the governance pattern in which individuals are governed by the unit and families are governed by neighborhood committee. While in unitization village, both laborers' places of employment and residence community are placed in a relatively small village district and accordingly, the distance between the two is not much, at the same time, villagers have a close connection with families. According to the conventional habits, family remains to be the most important income and consumption unit. Besides, villages still respect the family system and habitually treat individual villagers as members of some families. Therefore, in villager governance practice, it is hard for villages to either totally separate villagers from employees in village enterprises or separate village governance process from family governance process. While viewing villages or employees in village enterprises, people would never forget that he or she is a family member of some village. In other words, in unitization village, enterprise is inseparable from community, individual and family. In reality, villages are more precisely composed by community families instead of individual villagers. In consequence, villagers not only rely on village enterprises as individual employed personnel but also rely on respective families as community members. Unitization villages still find it hard to cross over families to directly control individuals. In this sense, family

is still a major variable in unitization village. Factors such as the change of family economic power often directly affect the relation between individual laborers, villages and village enterprises, or in the same way, the relation between individual laborers and enterprises often represents the relation among families, villages and village enterprises.

The influence of the structure is that even though all forces in the village would rather totally imitate city unit, unitization villages could not easily actualize the overall absorption to individual employed personnel like that. At least, unitization villages will definitely pay a more heavy cost if they plan to realize the overall absorption of employed personnel and their families.

(2) In city unit system, all resources that could be allocated by the units come from public ownership countries, or otherwise, public ownership countries entrust units to specifically allocate and govern resources. Such resource supply with basic guarantee was exactly the gap between unit and village for a long time after the 1950s. Unitization villages are exactly endeavoring to realize the full guarantee for village residents' food, clothing, accommodation and transportation. However, as the result of the shortage of national resource supply, the guarantee degree in unitization villages is totally up to the productivity effect of villages in reality, in particular industry enterprise profits. From this perspective, although the resource supply means in city unit results in the long-term low efficiency of units in production and operation, its low efficiency seemingly does not endanger the survival of units under the guarantee from the country. But, this is not true for unitization village because its control on laborers and specific progress of unitization are more easily directly affected by the productivity effect of village enterprises than city unit. It suggests that the low efficiency encouraged by the unit system and the non-accessibility of unitization village to low efficiency possibly constitute the

unique and sharp contradictions confronted by unitization villages. At this point, the unitization survival basis of unitization village seems to be more vulnerable than the city unit with a history of decades.

(3) For the same reason, in city unit, the unit should share the overall supply and guarantee provided by the country and for compensation, it should simultaneously entirely control unit members. But, unitization villages still lag behind city units in village member resource supply and interest distribution. For instance, employed personnel in village units could not become legal "city residents" no matter what division of labor that they are engaged in because their household register is still agricultural registered residence and their social status is still farmer. Even so, their medical treatment, retirement and salary welfare are less regular or guaranteed. In addition, nothing could guarantee the permanent survival of these. Likewise, in city units, employed personnel did not confront unemployment risks before reformation and even enjoy the protection of national re-employment mechanism after reformation. Unitization village basically does not take the unemployed's re-employment and job transfer problems into account. Admittedly, members of unitization villages could not benefit from the housing policies implemented by the country in city unit at any period. There are many other similar cases.

Now that unitization villages could not match with city units in the guarantee for village members, it suggests that unitization villages usually fail to completely control village members and additionally fail to imitate all measures executed by city units to entirely control village members. To be exact, social control in unitization villages would still follow some other conventional practices in rural society for a long time.[2]

As proved by the above data, all sorts of differences between unitization villages and city units in specific rules and regulations might not indicate the differences in degree.

The following sections mainly emphasize the point that village unitization has still been an unprecedented and formidable social transition throughout the history of Jianshanxia Village, or at least an unprecedented approach, means and process for villages to get close to basic city organization pattern and city life throughout further description. Therefore, village unitization practically generates multiple revolutionary influences on basic village organizations such as village communities and other village organizations. The principle seems to be rather evident: now that the village enterprises in Jianshanxia Village incorporate overwhelming labor force, village collective industrial economy takes up over 95% shares in village economy. Then, village organizations' unitization management for enterprises and continuous expansion of such unitization management to overall villages imply that the overall village community has been incorporated into a new organization process and organization system. Modern resources contained by unitization usually give rise to diverse reformation in villages and even unconsciously trigger certain revolutionary transitions of village social organizations and social life. It could be generally acknowledged to be the overall integration of village social organizations and social life based on the transition of economic production process. Certainly, such transition is more possibly incurred by the factory system (organization means and labor process) included by unitization. However, because the unit system has been combined with industrial organization, administrative organization and social organizations for decades, or say, it is the previous factory form of China prior to the formation of market economy's leading status, transition of villages might be stimulated by modern resources in unit system as usual. From the perspective of observers, such transition is very interesting and observation of such transition often propels people to reflect over past rural society analysis and peasant theories (in particular those traditional theories that preach the incongruence between peasants and modern society). Without a doubt, the thing also has another side. The difference between unitization villages and city units stated above has indicated that from the perspective of city unit

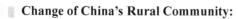

system, unitization village is still an underdeveloped unit. Logically speaking, it certainly means that unitization villages still preserve some traditional customs of villages, probably referred to as rural resources in general cases. The combination of these resources with modern resources in unit system frequently turns village unitization transition momentum and causes the process to become more complicated. For instance, some changes inside the villages seem to be related to rural traditions. But, in reality, they might be more related to the technology type of village economic production. The most typical example is that villagers tend to have common life experience and value preference in many aspects in village life, but these do not belong to the so-called homogeneous social phenomena. Instead, they are connected with the enterprise goal of full villager employment, failure of technical division of labor condition in promotion of high professionalism and failure of employee income and status in high stratification in village unitization process. On the contrary, some changes seem to be ascribed to the modern resources in village unitization process. This demands further observation and discrimination in reality. For instance, villager autonomy, direct democracy and village affairs transparency executed in villages ought to benefit from the introduction of modern political system in villages. However, the undeniable fact is that villagers often comprehend and accept village grassroots autonomy and direct democracy in accordance with traditional majority principle. While observing such phenomena, observers habitually wonder whether such phenomena imply that village is in the transitional state from rural society to legal society, or whether such phenomena suggest unit system's natural affinity to some traditional resources in rural society in reality. This problem is worth pondering.

3.2 The Interaction between Unitization and Community Environment

It is uncertain whether village unitization indicates the transition of village organization means, all the more in addition to the introduction of industrial economy to village. In the study on the community transition of Jianshanxia Village, researchers hold that although the unitization process has changed some factors in the community, the most remarkable change is not the increase or decrease of general community environment factors, but the matching mode and mutual effects of these factors, or say, the structural relation inside community instead. It seems to be the basic transition feature of village community in unitization process.

The research first starts from two aspects to probe into the transition in community environment.

First of all, community is regarded as a residential place in general cases. As the residential district, community naturally represents the adaptation of a group of people to natural environment. Therefore, community in this sense contains the natural residence characteristics shaped by ecological environment (including location, form, size, superficial characteristics, climate, natural resources, communication with outside community and transportation route) and human adaption to natural characteristics (artificial lifestyle or culture). Apparently, the unitization process of Jianshanxia Village rarely changes the residence characteristics shaped by natural environment as stated in the last chapter. Unitization is essentially a method to adapt to residential environment, and in particular, industrial production technology adopted by village in unitization process indeed provides a brand new resource utilization means. But, in a strict sense, it provides technologies for resources outside the villages. As for the village itself, it primarily provides a chance to utilize rural labor force and other social resources. Since both production of raw materials and product market are outside the village, it does not offer any new method to use rural natural resources. Consequently, the village unitization process of Jianshanxia Village leaves insignificant functions in the transition of residence limitations caused by natural environment. This phenomenon deserves special attention. The reason is that sustained environment and residence characteristics usually mean the continuity of some interaction relations inside the community caused by natural factors. But, whether such sustained interaction relations could match with the transition caused by the introduction of village unitization will be another interesting problem. After all, this does not mean that unitization would not lead to any transition of community environment. At least, it always reflects a new interaction relation and function process inside the village and suggests the transition of human adaptation to natural environment.

The following six phenomena demand more elaborate description for further research.

(1) **The boundary of community:** Sometimes, community researchers would hesitate in the demarcation of community boundary. It is not simply because community residents' social interaction relation and process always get rid of community geographical boundary. Another reason is that there exist two kinds of different community boundary demarcation standards objectively, namely, the statutory community (city, county and village boundary prescribed by the government according to legal proceedings) and the natural community. After all, it is not a big problem for Jianshanxia Village to define its community boundary as the statutory community. The history of Jianshanxia Village already proves that state force gives priority to respect for existing natural community pattern in the construction of village organization. After 1949, the country even basically classified administrative villages by the distribution habit of natural community. Owing to the gradual growth of the village population and architecture over decades, the four natural villages inside the administrative village already connect together. As a result, the statutory community and natural community become an entirety in Jianshanxia Village.

As a matter of fact, such conditions in Jianshanxia Village are very commonplace in Xiaoshan City. The specialty of Jianshanxia Village is possibly that its village unitization process seems to specially reinforce the boundary of statutory community. Prior to unitization, Jianshanxia Village also had a prominent boundary of statutory community like other villages in the very beginning, which could be proved by its prohibition of random land transfer among villages, free appropriation of capital or change of household. While unitization even lists statutory community as the demarcation boundary, the over 30 written regulations under the framework of village unitization system stated in the last chapter are all drawn up by village organizations. These regulations all take village as the applicable boundary. One of the core contents of village unitization welfare employment and welfare distribution, including villager cooperative medical service, pension insurance system and education investment all exclusively target native rural residents. The regulations explicitly stipulate that villagers from other villages working in enterprises shall not enjoy such welfare nor corporate dividend as employees. This regulation even specifically states that married women from other villages could still enjoy welfare, but married women who leave the village shall not enjoy the original welfare.[3] In this way, village unitization is always a collective action inside the village from beginning to end and the outcome of village unitization seems to clarify the village boundary all the time.

Either inside or outside the village, either government departments above village level or the masses below village level, no one would consider such regulation which strictly differentiates local natives from external outsiders abnormal. For the government, as of the disintegration of People's Commune (actually after the attack against "equalitarianism and indiscriminate transfer of resources" advocated by People's Commune in the early stage), it does not have any interests, energy or legitimacy to seize profits from villages. For the villagers, now that the government has prescribed village boundary in land, forestry and other scarce resources appropriation and use, household register governance and village autonomous organization setting, various kinds of benefits created by village unitization have no reason to be randomly given to outsiders from other villages. This is also true for other villages. As it is, all allocation and welfare in city unit also exclude people outside the unit. From the perspective of observers, the reinforcement of village unitization on the boundary of statutory community is indeed a very natural process and villagers have good reason to agree with such reinforcement. At least, before market economy gradually obtained legitimacy in the 1990s, numerous administrative, production and welfare procedures more or less, explicitly or implicitly, confirmed the boundary of closure. In the city, socialist system often implements the unit socialism which takes unit as the boundary. In the village, the internal protection functions of villages such as Jianshanxia Village in history have been apparently reinforced by resource village appropriation stipulated and supported by the government. Eventually, unit closure in village unitization process is further consolidated. In consideration of the limitation of village resources, especially scarce resources, it seems that there is no reason to pin hope on the creativity of any single village. A more reasonable choice is to invite outsiders from other villages to share welfare here.

Interestingly, although the welfare requirements contained by the village unit demand administrative village to be the boundary, industrial production and organization process contained by unitization gradually demand breakthroughs in the boundary of legitimate communities such as administrative village. For instance, enterprises have growing demands for high-standard and stable technicians, accountants and marketing personnel. Since people who have received education above technical secondary school inside the village do not return to the village for work, it is hard to choose the above-stated talents from native villagers and the village could only invite talents from outside villages by all means (including high income and welfare). On the contrary, since local land resources are basically used up, enterprises need to expand reproduction factory to outside villages through purchasing land from neighboring villages or formulating supporting labor force employment solutions. However, in the present stage, the free access of outsiders to the village and factory is still regarded as the sharing of internal village profits in the eyes of villagers in Jianshanxia Village.

For this reason, centering around the boundary of administrative village legitimate community, village unitization also contains the force of reinforcement and the force of disintegration, while the two often trigger tension inside the community.

(2) **Community center:** The community always builds up certain fixed centers to offer economic (business), professional (medical care) and agency (school and local government) services to residents. While the social interaction process inside the community often comes into being around the services in this center, according to the discrepancy in service capabilities and categories in the center, all sorts of communities could be even grouped into several types, such as Saunders' so-called self-contained community (isolated village), town community (open village), city community (small- and medium-sized city district), metropolitan community (small community inside the metropolis) and so forth. For the village community, there used to be a causal statement. This statement generally classifies villages like Jianshanxia Village as some self-contained small-peasant economic society. From the perspective of community classification, it is akin to certain autonomous communities. In fact, the research of Shi Jianya concerning village, city and town networks indicates that quite a few villages in China have been totally classified as isolated autonomous communities a long time ago, among which the most common one should be town community in connection with village market network. Along with the construction of roads, transportation commuting and popularity of communication instruments, village communities have more and more exchange with the outside world, and especially contact with surrounding cities and towns. Villagers usually need to visit government departments, buy production materials and life necessities, go to the credit cooperatives, take a bus or even watch operas or films in these places. Villagers consider that they need to overcome the insufficient village community services. On the part of community, village has entered a town-centered larger community, namely, the so-called town community, no matter whether people have realized or acknowledged this point.

Jianshanxia Village also belonged to this type before unitization. For solving the shortcomings of the village in business and education services, villagers need to obtain daily services from the neighboring village several miles away or Daicun Town 8 kilometers away. For instance, if villagers want to take a bus destined for the city, they need to first go to the neighboring Fangjiatang Village; and if villagers want to go to the middle school or credit cooperative, they need to first visit Yunshi Town. Larger business facilities are mostly located in remote Daicun, Linpu or farther towns and Hangzhou downtown. However, villagers feel rather inconvenienced when they need to retrieve services from these places. Accordingly, village unitization process naturally has the intention and action to provide more convenient welfare and services for residents. It invokes some major changes inside the community. In particular, it brings about the initial differentiation of all central points inside the community. Large factory turns out to be the center of resident labor, basketball court and few other recreational facilities inside the factory become the activity center of young employees, village organization workplaces such as village party branch and village committee inside the factory become the office and management center of the village; medical treatment room inside the factory becomes the clinic of residents. The interesting thing is that because most families in the village do not till land, they need to buy grain, vegetables and subsidiary food. At time passes, there spring up a batch of vegetable growers and vendors who specifically serve Jianshanxia Village from surrounding villages. They place over 10 vegetable stalls with a length of around 20 meters in the middle of the village road. This ultra-small vegetable market and nearby timekeeper maintenance, tailoring and hairdressing stalls act as daily service center of the community. Additionally, Secondary Village Committee also sets up the assembly hall next to the vegetable market as village elderly activity room, home of militia and TV projection room. Regardless of the small customer flow, these architectures still act as the public activity center of the community objectively. In addition, after the foundation of the assembly hall in the 1950s and the foundation of factory in the 1970s, four ancient ancestral halls of the village altogether vanished. It signals the disappearance of ancient ancestral activity center. It brings about another problem objectively, namely, the absence of large assembly venue inside the community. As a result, as a natural replacement, the open space next to the brook and the open space left between the road and villager houses become resident leisure and face-to-face exchange center after renovation. Primary school is absolutely the education center of the village which allows children to receive education and join in activity and allows adults to wipe out illiteracy. In some cases, the playground of the primary school could also act as the assembly center. In daily life, other important notices will be released to villagers by broadcasting, village cadres' or villager group leaders' door-to-door visit, enterprise workshop wallpaper, road signs and wall slogans along the main road. Therefore, information communication inside the community is not that difficult.[4]

The appearance and differentiation of the above-mentioned central points do not necessarily provide some evidence for the general theory of community ecology, but might objectively testify that the service demands of community residents have changed in village unitization process. In addition, these new demands could be only comprehensively satisfied in town community. Some obvious demands could not be satisfied by corresponding services in the community as usual. For instance, "farmers' market" is informal and small in scale. In addition to the limited product variety, product price is even higher than other villages. Most unmarried young people feel that the village lacks recreational facilities and "cultural life" here is rather monotonous. There are simply seven grocery stores in the village. Without any restaurant, the village could not provide normal living and accommodation services for outsiders. Such inconvenience is deemed as the undeveloped expression of the village by villagers inside and outside the village. It propels common community members and Secondary Village Committee to move forward toward township in the village community construction process. Therefore, "the Eighth Five-Year Plan" (1991–1995) and "the Ninth Five-Year Plan" (1996–2000) enacted and issued by Secondary Village Committee specifically list

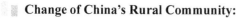
the part of "social development planning project", spare no efforts to improve village environment, gradually develop in the direction of village urbanization construction, create village civilization town and elaborately plan park, farmer's market, village-level restaurant, recreational city center, enterprise shopping mall, village nursery, village office building, school supporting facilities and other major projects.[5] Since 1990, some projects have been implemented, but facilities such as hotel and recreational center could not be implemented yet because of financial difficulties. The reason is that overall community construction mechanism basically complies with the convention of village unitization to rely on the financial power of village collective and especially village enterprises, but village enterprises could hardly offer powerful financial support in the stage of investment and production expansion. Insufficient services provided by community collective naturally create opportunities for some community families to engage in paid service industry. Accordingly, the seven privately owned small grocery stores keep stable operation all the time and the declaratory income is calculated by the owner himself. Generally, the income is slightly higher than the average level of village enterprise employees. Considering such services compensate for the shortcomings of village collective service functions and share a part of taxation work from town, principal leaders in "two village committees" still tolerate and support the legitimate operation of such private (family) business in spite of the difference from village collective. After all, such family operation does not possess the capacity of fast growth without exception and subjectively, the seven privately owned stores never project to open larger shopping malls in the future. It means that it always preserves complementary and low-level service functions inside the community.

In this sense, within village boundary, unitization tends to introduce township and most possibly provides township services required by community residents.[6] However, the actualization of township is up to collective economic productivity during the unitization process. After all, this point is not always guaranteed.

(3) **Size of community:** The size of community indicates the size of resident activity space and population density. As a general rule, larger community size means larger resident activity space and smaller familiar population proportion inside the community. Therefore, there is full reason for community research to closely connect community size with resident interaction relation type.[7]

Unitization in Jianshanxia Village proceeds on the premise of the approval for statutory community boundary. Now that it takes place in statutory community, this problem is basically non-related to the change of community size. Or to be more specific, unitization might possibly have direct influence on community population density. In fact, community exactly effectively controls the growth of population inside the community and accordingly controls the growth of population density by potent unitization management in family planning and basic balance between resident immigration and emigration (see Table 3.1). However, with respect to the expansion of community space, unitization obviously does not come into effect. Accordingly, in the process of unitization, the size of community remains unchanged. Theoretically, it probably means resident familiarity relative to the size of village community before unitization. Maybe there are no major changes in the unitization process and many interpersonal contact dimensions could be consequently preserved. For instance, residents, in particular household heads and peers, are very familiar with one another; people are accustomed to keeping the role relationship in the village in face-to-face communication; behavioral regulation for community residents often resorts to discussion and persuasion for face-saving considerations; villagers are very sensitive to outsiders and so forth. Actually, such conditions not only exist in Jianshanxia Village but could also find verification via observation at any time.[8]

Unchanged community size just reflects its benefit to the maintenance of traditional community interaction, but not necessarily implies that such traditions have been entirely preserved. For this reason, it does not suggest that community resident interaction does not change during

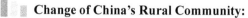
unitization process. On the contrary, around 7 and 800 residents from Jianshanxia Village participate in factory production process and corporate bureaucracy management process. All of these change the time, form and contents of interaction among residents, especially when resident face-to-face communication has reduced to a large extent. As for community social control, enterprise management and village management do not simply rely on discussion and persuasion, but relatively formal written laws instead. While mediating interests and contradictions, giving rewards or punishment for resident behaviors, more and more economic calculation dimensions and treating methods have been introduced.

In this way, community size almost becomes one of the most difficult integrated environmental factors of unitization. In condition of unchanged community size, the process of unitization means community member interaction contains two kinds of gravitational forces in two directions. Since traditional means of interaction have been greatly preserved, community interaction under unitization could be contained, but unit rules have been already introduced to the community throughout the recommendation of formal community organizations. Accordingly, two rules inevitably tangle with each other.

(4) **Population isolation degree:** Under normal circumstances, population isolation degree (namely, the gathering degree of community population collective—including some units, teams or groups—in some place) caused by race, culture (such as language and religion) and occupation discrepancy would immediately influence the formation of community social network. Apparently, greater population isolation degree causes more impediments to the consensus of important community controversies. In Jianshanxia Village, there is no isolation shaped by language and occupation factors all the time. Before unitization, the most typical isolation was shaped by clan and family name. For instance, Anle Hall, Sizhi Hall, Cilü Hall and Zhixian Hall built by Shao, Yang, Jiang and Bao Family used to be the residence of

four clans in the village in history. After the 1950s, the four ancestral halls were successively used for other purposes and their identity as the central place of religious activities did not legally exist anymore. However, centralized residence condition of different family names was not changed for a time. Afterwards, commune structure and village team action of People's Commune and state suppression of religion and culture made for the disintegration of religious isolation. After all, such a shock was not supposed to be profound at the psychological level at least. In the memory of elder villagers, until the period of "the Cultural Revolution", different factions related to family names inside the village often got involved in all sorts of fights from time to time.[9] Interestingly, if the Yang Family invited the theatrical troupe to perform "Generals of the Yang Family" to celebrate festivals, other families would order "Defeat of the Yang Family in Jinshatan".[10] It is possibly a kind of verification.

After the mid-1980s, Jianshanxia Village underwent two rounds of resident housing construction and corporate factory construction fever, which totally broke through the original centralized residential pattern of the same family in the village. The "two village committees" and land management group first implement unified planning and unified dispatch in land use. Newly built houses are usually separate from original centralized residence of the same family. Next, the "two village committees" retain external designers, organize unified construction and grant large subsidy to release two plots of residential joint households. In consequence, the centralized residential pattern of the same family inside the village is basically reserved. Additionally, during unitization process, most adult labor force of the village engages in similar occupations with identical salary and welfare. It adds some kind of mutual sense of identity among residents. Females of the marriageable age in the village start to be attracted by rural economic conditions. Due to the reduction of "out-married" proportion, there appear more rural marriage connections. It encourages community residents to forget their original family name conventions.

As a result, village unitization is generally a process in favor of relieving traditional population isolation conditions. At least, it does not intensify the degree of community population isolation. But, it is worth noticing here that it seemingly could not be used to suggest the fact that unitization naturally offers a new fixed way to reach community consensus.[11]

(5) **Spatial competition:** Like any other community, Jianshanxia Village also confronts competition in land use purpose (proportion of land use for industry, business, institution, agriculture and residence) and residential place. Due to the scarcity of village land, such competition seems to be more inevitable. Even the community strictly prevents outsiders from arbitrarily dwelling in the village to relieve spatial competition; it could not eradicate internal community competition. Two kinds of competition are rather commonplace. One kind of competition could be seen from the forests contracted by residents. Residents often bother about the quality of their own contracted forest resources and some of them even quarrel with each other for the boundary. Another kind of competition could be seen from the allocation of resident building plots. Residents have specific judgment and expectation over the quality of residence and the social identity represented by the plot and usually desire to seek ideal residence.

In many village communities, such type of competition severely affects community unity sometimes, but for Jianshanxia Village, unitization almost effectively restricts spatial competition. In line with unitization management mode, the village takes village collective "unified" planning and unified dimension to, on the one hand, regulate village collective factory land priority in land arrangement. On the other hand, it especially establishes land management group as the professional functional organization in charge of issuing management systems, approving land and mediating disputes pursuant to relevant articles. During this process, the land management group shall not make decisions with individual or family preferences and pay close attention to the publicity of the implementation process. In the end, community spatial competition among residents is suppressed. Grievous or ferocious fight does not appear for a long time.[12] "Two village committees" compulsorily stipulate that remaining land should be used under unified planning by the collective. Especially, resident disputes in land allocation rarely take place after the construction of joint household architecture. Even in some years, there are no mediation disputes submitted to the village committee.

(6) **Community environmental quality:** Due to the relation between product category and production technique, the industrial development process during Jianshanxia Village unitization does not result in severe industrial pollution or reduce environmental quality in local community in most cases.[13] The community needs to improve environmental quality. The first concern is water. Because mineral contents in village brook and surface water do not conform to health requirements, the village needs to replace it with deep well water or tap water. The second concern is fecal treatment. Besides, I observe that resident domestic rubbish disposal should be the foremost concern to be solved by the village now. The village collective specifically arranges several formal cleaner positions in charge of daily cleaning work in factory, road and other public activity regions. Therefore, these regions are cleaner. But, comparatively speaking, resident domestic rubbish disposal is still a tough problem. As explained by the director of village committee, residents tend to choose landfill method in rubbish disposal on Maozhu Mountain. Throughout the field investigation, I find that some rubbish has been obviously discarded in the brook, some drifts downstream and some rests in the shallow ford. In other interviews, I verified the inaccuracy in the speech of the director of village committee.

Probably for fear of disclosing embarrassing secrets to the outside world, the director of village committee distorts his negative attitudes toward civilized domestic rubbish disposal mode. In reality, if the village wants to solve this problem with existing technology, the routine is to draw lessons from urban management and resort to professional environmental protection institutions and equipment or landfill sites. However, it might exceed the economic bearing capacity of the village itself. In local governments or urban environmental protection institutions, it is not classified as their own responsibility.

In my opinion, this case seemingly proves that once principal village leaders have relatively intense environmental protection awareness, unitization administrative-led institution could usually offer them a convenient social mobilization mode. However, village unitization alone fails to solve the technical and financial support required by environmental quality. For this reason, village unitization alone accordingly fails to improve village community environmental quality. Many problems maybe demand proper service connection between city and village.

Following the observation on location stated above, the research starts from the perspective of community population to probe into the interaction between village unitization and community environment. The reason is that community is not only a place but also gathers a group of residents. In a broad sense, resident population structure has demographic significance and meanwhile offers some important background knowledge concerning community social structure, social momentum and attitude. For instance, it often demonstrates community social attitudes and social systems by fertility and economic and social transition by population transition. While there also exists some obvious connection among labor force, population structure and social organization, obviously, it is hard to observe.

In general, existing materials and observation results hardly figure out the interaction between population structure and village unitization process in the village. However, owing to the restriction of population structure, village unitization silently affects population structure. This finding has been proved by observation results, for instance the following:

(1) **Population increase and decrease:** Table 3.1 implies that natural population growth in the community since 1985 has been relatively slow. In addition to some years, the growth rate is below 0.7%, while absolute population size and natural growth rate after 1992 present declining tendency and even negative growth tendency. In terms of immigration, emigration slightly outnumbers immigration in a balanced state. Such changes might be less related to or not related to village unitization process. For instance, after 1991, male population size inside the village stably reduced, but female population size greatly reduced. This could be ascribed to the increase of marriageable females, the high out-married proportion above internal village marriage, young females studying in technical secondary schools and higher learning institutions and their change of residence registration or some other uncertain reasons (including residents' immigration to Xiaoshan municipal location, their economic income, house-buying ability in the city, employment location, marriage and other complicated factors). But, some conditions were possibly related to village unitization process. For instance, village fertility rate had been effectively controlled and annual newborns were controlled to between 10 and 20. According to the above assumptions, this was closely connected with forceful family-planning work via unified channel and system during unitization process. Besides, balanced community population migration situation never showed forceful external "driving force". It was likely connected with some kind of attraction generated by village economic growth and welfare guarantee during unitization process.

Table 3.1.   1993–1997 Population change situation in Jianshanxia village.

Year	Hou.	Pop. sum	M	F	Fer. sum	M	F	Mor. sum	M	F	Imm. Ins. sum	Imm. Ins. XS	Imm. Out.	Emi. Out. sum	Emi. Out. XS	Emi. Out.	Tra. Imm.	Tra. Emi.
1993	369	1,378	660	718	12	5	7	9	3	6	3	1	1	8	4	1	2	3
1994	380	1,367	654	713	15	6	9	8	7	1	1		2	14	6	1		6
1995	380	1,368	651	717	10	5	5	8	6	2	3		2	10	9		4	
1996	376	1,338	651	706	12	9	3	9	6	3	6	6	2	17	17	4	5	
1997	368	1,333	655	698	15	8	7	11	3	8	1	1	1	9	4	2	2	1

Notes: Pop. = Population; Fer. = Fertility; Mor. = Mortality; Imm. = Immigration; Emi. = Emigration; Tra. = Transfer inside village and town; Hou. = Household; M = Male; F = Female; Ins. = Inside the province; Out. = Outside the province; XS = Xiaoshan.
Source: 1993–1997 annual overview.

(2) **Population composition:** Unitization process obviously could not affect various factors of community population composition, such as gender proportion, age composition, family name composition, marriageable age, language, education achievement, urban–rural distribution, occupation variety and so forth. Likewise, these factors would not leave any immediate influence on the unitization process one after another. However, the mutual influence between unitization and population composition is obviously more remarkable than the influence of unitization on population increase and decrease.

For instance, since the elders have a relatively high proportion in the village, the growth rate of the elders is above the growth rate of the total population. Till 1993, there were 215 elder people (males aged above 60 and females aged above 55) which accounted for 15.6% of the total population.[14] Pursuant to general standards, the village now has entered the aging society. Such background easily propels the village to take local governments' suggestions for enhancing rural elder work during the unitization process and concentrates on the welfare of the elders. Many practices directly imitate city units and neighborhood committee, including the foundation of aging organization (in 1989, Village Association of Aged People was established in response to Provisions on the Protection of the Legal Rights and Interests of the Elder in Zhejiang Province and principle of "looking after the elderly, providing the elder with opportunities to enjoy themselves and learn by themselves and doing something in their old age"), the establishment of security system (including the setting and implementation of pension system, staff retirement system and "five guarantees" system for elderly persons with no family), the provision of activity space (around 400-square meter elder activity center), the handling of social old-age insurance[15] and relatively fixed relief work in festivals. From the perspective of staff mobilization and capital arrangement, such work mostly depends on the unitization operation of the village. As of 1992, the village transferred 60,000 yuan from village collective fund per year for pension subsidy; as of 1997, the work expenditures of Village Association of Aged People totaled 98,000 yuan (including 60,000 yuan old-age pension allowance). Consequently, similar to city unit, this village also lists the elder problem as a work in need of long-term devotion during the unitization process. Moreover, once the village deviates from the unitization process, elderly community work will confront rather tough transition problems with regard to staff equipment and capital supply.

To be sure, it is difficult to clearly see or judge the role of village unitization in the change of aging population. What is more distinct should be the influence of village unitization on female occupation composition. In Jianshanxia Village, females account for 50% in population gender proportion and labor force composition. In 1992, gender proportion was 92.2 (male): 100 (female); and around 400 female labor force accounted for above 48.2% of the total labor force. The village unitization process provides new employment channels and occupations for the female labor force. Till 1992, around 80% of the female labor force worked in village collective enterprises. When community "half the sky" state expanded from population gender composition and labor force composition to occupation composition, community social pattern, especially female status and family relation in the community naturally demanded corresponding adjustment.

A similar situation could be also seen from community population cultural composition. After 1949, under the advocacy of government departments, the village held large-scale illiteracy education activities in 1954, 1974 and 1979, and gradually diverted the focus of illiteracy education to young adults, party and league members. During the unitization process, the village takes the improvement of residents' education degree as a key task and especially executes more forceful measures to elevate population literacy rate. In addition, the village also strengthens staff training. It founded staff technical school in 1988 which trained altogether 175 staff till 1992 and founded infant parent school in the same year which held five sessions until 1991. Under strenuous efforts, there were 1,013 villagers with primary school and middle school education degree which accounted for 73.4% of total population, and 100% teenagers, young people and young adults became literate in 1992. Furthermore, the village continually invested capital to offer preschool and primary education infrastructure to villagers and successively built village kindergarten and primary school teaching building. These actions not only help enhance community population education degree but also activate residents' education needs. Admittedly, another problem also deserves attention. For instance, resident education degree is inversely proportional to resident age. Limited by economic power and schooling procedures, the village could only offer preschool and primary education and therefore, those villagers who want to receive education above middle school have to go outside. However, villagers who receive much longer education outside and obtain higher education degree tend to be reluctant to return to the village. In particular, no villagers who have received technical secondary school and above education have returned to the village for work. As a result, the role of village in education investment and population culture composition during the unitization process seems to add to the outflow possibility of highly educated residents. It indeed brings about some special difficulties to resident supplement outside the village.

3.3 The Community System in Unitization Process

The observation of community environmental transition during the village unitization process ought to consider the cultural characteristics or cultural traditions in community environment. Regardless of the importance and interests of this problem, it is still hard to figure out yet. Therefore, the research does not dive into the problem in detail.

Compared with the transition of community environment factors as stated above, the interaction among unitization, various community factor structures and factor relations in Jianshanxia Village appears to be more explicit or overt. The interesting fact is that the research on community social system or social structure usually emphasizes how the community should maintain previous social systems and organization modes, focus on its continuity, the formation and maintenance of community unanimous behaviors as well as the mutual dependence of all social units inside the community apart from the description of general community relation and activity social network. However, the unitization process in Jianshanxia Village seemingly offers a counterexample to some degree. It often proves to observers that a community social system could rest in a stable transition process.

The research plans to explain from three aspects by reference to Sanders' community system observation framework.

3.3.1   Village-level organization-centered community system mode

As a rule, community contains a series of subsystems as a social system. As certain geo-relation "unit" in ordinary meaning, the community is always composed of some organization units.[16] Indeed, Jianshanxia Village is still made up of multiple subordinate

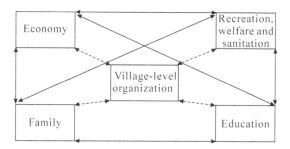

Figure 3.1.   Mutual correlation of general community system.

organization units in view of its identity as a unitization village. In the sense of community, these community components could be still incorporated into five main parts or departments including village-level organization, economic organization, family, education, and recreation, welfare and sanitation. The five departments all exist in common village communities, and the mutual interaction relation among them is as shown in Figure 3.1.[17]

But, the unitization process in Jianshanxia Village produces significant major influence on community social system. First of all, as stated in following sections, the village collective organization under the lead of "two village committees" universally covers principal economic departments, most recreation, welfare and sanitation departments and education departments in the village. Accordingly, community relation paradigm of the village could be modified partially according to Figure 3.2 which highlights the direct control right of village-level organization under the lead of "two village committees" on most village economic departments, and welfare, sanitation and recreation departments. As for the interaction inside Jianshanxia Village community system, sanitation and recreation departments mostly exist as the subordinate departments of village collective organization instead of the independent units relative to village "administrative units". Inside the village, only the family unit possesses organization unit meaning relative to the village collective. In summary, in spite of the interaction

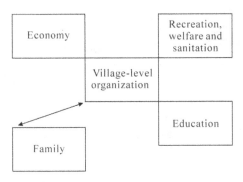

Figure 3.2.   Mutual correlation of community system in Jianshanxia village.

between family and other composition units inside the community system, it could be still realized by the connection with village-level organization.

Second, concerning the promoting role of community components in the operation of community system, Jianshanxia Village also presents some interesting characteristics under the rules of unitization. The basic situations are as shown in Table 3.2.

Table 3.2.   Community system operation characteristics.

Community system operation process	Operation characteristics
New residents	Immigrants by fertility or marriage (most of them are females); rare residents are introduced by technology.
Socialization	Training residents' ability for community participation by corporate work flow and work system besides household life and face-to-face communication.
Communication	Face-to-face contact and public opinions formed by the exchange of ideas; organized communication channels such as broadcasting, television or written notice.
Vocational differentiation and status distribution	Agriculture and forestry production becomes auxiliary economy component; most residents deviate from agricultural production, but they do not have high degree of differentiation in terms of labor division, status and role professionalization; it restricts community service functions, but makes for the improvement of female status.

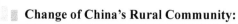
Table 3.2.   (*Continued*)

Community system operation process	Operation characteristics
Distribution of articles and services	Products are basically used for exchange with the outside world; life necessities should be procured outside of the community; the community tries to provide all sorts of services, but it still depends on the outside world in reality.
Social control	The community more and more relies on village-level organization and village companies, and tends to provide criteria and maintain social order by statutory institutions and economic scales; the community also refers to and respects villager's interpersonal contact habits and corrects any bias of motivation or behavior. But, there also are some conflicts between the two kinds of scales.
Reputation distribution	As for the arrangement criteria of social reputation, power, wealth, ability, justice or public affinity and personality should precede clan family name and qualification.
Power distribution	Consistent with reputation distribution, power distribution adheres to the election system and majority principle in form and respects production organization authority and community coordination management authority in nature.
Social mobility	There exists transverse flow of young and middle-aged residents caused by employment, education or immigration between the community and the outside world. Without class differentiation, there basically is no cross-class longitudinal flow. However, there exists longitudinal flow from general employees to the management layer inside village companies. Limited by the unit system and village scale, it is rare to see the downward flow from the management layer.
Coordination and integration	Subject to the decisive influence of village company production conditions; primary integration by village-level organization.

3.3.2   Village organization and family: Two cores in institution combination

The above circumstances indicate that Jianshanxia Village after unitization is not a pure rural society or homogeneous society anymore, which could be more apparently manifested by community institution combination and activity characteristics.

1. *Unitization means the full-functional tendency of village-level organization*

Composition structure of Jianshanxia Village as village-level organization is as shown in Figure 1.1 of the book. The "two village committees" composed by village party branch and villager committee take the leading status in village-level organization. After the implementation of village self-governance and village committee direct election system, many "two village committees" get rid of the support of state authority during People's Commune period and execute rural responsibility system in agriculture. This directly reduces organization capacity and influence, while the unitization of Jianshanxia Village in turn intensifies the leading status of "two village committees" in organization process, economic support and system framework, and even results in village-level organization full-functional tendency to some degree.

First of all, supported by the legitimacy of the ruling party, village party branch maximizes the power of village party branch and party organization throughout the full leadership in village affairs. The relation between party and "politics" is originally a very interesting link during contemporary political process of China (the village committee is habitually referred to as the village-level "politics" although it is expressly stipulated as villager autonomous organization). It is totally simplified as the leading and being led relation in unitization society and unit. Therefore, the unitization process in Jianshanxia Village seemingly means that the party branch increasingly realizes comprehensive leadership and concrete management in community affairs. There are generally two realization means. First, Central and Local Party Committees at all levels clearly proclaim village party branch to "exert the leading role in taking the masses to push forward common prosperity and collective progress".[18] Village party branch in Jianshanxia Village illustrates the regulation as an important village affair in immediate leadership and administration. In system setting, the two Objective Assessment Systems of Building Advanced Party Branch enacted by the party branch in 1987 and 1995 clearly regulate the specific tasks and indicators in "implementation policy", "community spiritual civilization and public welfare cause construction" and "economic construction" and behave as the full-functional tendency apart from the proposal of leading group construction, organization construction and other party construction objectives. In most cases, all major written rules in the community are formulated by the party branch and village committee. Even the community management provisions issued by village committee clearly state that all major work should apply for the approval from the party branch.[19] After 1995, although village committee more frequently issues community management provisions alone, important written systems including village regulations and non-government agreements, community integrated governance, forestry systems, power utilization systems and financial systems come into effect from the date of approval by full party members and villager representative assembly. The status and authority of "full party members" inside the community nearly equal that of villager representative assembly. As for the allocation and use of leaders in community departments, the "two village committees" execute cross-equipment akin to city unit. Among these community leaders, principals in party branch take charge of village enterprises, principals in village committee take charge of secondary leadership in party branch and enterprise, and principals in party branch enjoy higher authority and power as the main representatives of the party organization. Party branch and principals in party branch enjoy legitimate authority in practical actions including major community decisions and enterprise operation. Villagers are accustomed to the situation. Accordingly, in daily life, villagers tend to seek help from professional departments like Mediation Committee and Family Planning Association to solve specific community affairs (such as family disputes and family-planning indicators), but directly appeal to principals in party branch for major affairs (such as school facility investment, recruitment and transfer). The second means is generally the teamwork of two committees or other departments under the lead of party branch. Party branch clearly puts forward in its own working system that it shall cooperate with the two committees at work and "give play to the mass organization role of the Communist Youth League and Female Congress". Especially after 1993, party branch focuses on the consistency with national political reformation progress. In general, professional regulation formulation and management work in the village are the responsibility of the village committee. Party branch puts more energy in village enterprise operation and party organization construction in form.

From this point, it indicates that the party branch-centered pattern of Jianshanxia Village during the unitization process is not inferior to the leadership structure of general units during mature unitization period. Besides, Jianshanxia Village is as improved as and even more improved than general city units in some aspects (such as party member–peasant household connection system and outward management system).

By the same token, since collective activities presided by the "two village committees" or organized by the village committee cover most social public life spheres, "two village committees" actually permeate into every aspect and level of the community. Inside the village, the "two village committees" actually undertake the responsibility of overall management and providing more and more social services and welfare. Apart from the organization and working rules in party branch and village committee, special management work implemented by village committee leaders contains power supply, forestry, village land and house building, community custom and family civilization management, labor accumulation and public welfare programs, unified finance, social security, state policy, family planning, public facility management, public information collection and management, internal financing subsidy and social development planning. Relatively speaking, apart from above management work, the village committee also holds responsibility for offering welfare return to community residents, providing village enterprise employment opportunities, old pension, preferential compensation, education and medical treatment. Once comparing these regulations with village committee function and task principles in Organization Law of Village Committee of People's Republic of China in 1987 and 1999 revision editions, it could be found out that under the framework of villager self-management, self-education and self-service, above-mentioned written rules formulated or implemented by Jianshanxia Village Committee elaborated all functions and operation practices according to practical village situations and in the meantime greatly expanded function scope in the direction of villager self-management, self-education and self-service.

As long as village enterprise-led village collective economy could offer financial support by virtue of the continuous economic growth, the community always takes delight in accepting the benefits brought about by such changes and the function expansion of "two village committees". At least no villagers agree with ineffectual and irresponsible village committee.

Although such changes in village grassroots democracy and autonomy are often praised by residents, they actually reflect village collective enterprise and village collective community working process in Jianshanxia Village. Besides, either "two village committees" in charge of community management or common community residents basically view it as the practice in proximity to city unit and community. Without any doubt, in the eyes of observers, although such changes belong to the expression and outcomes of village unitization, some involved crucial methods and development potentials are not totally unitized or non-unitized. It could be explained by two examples. First of all, while implementing significant management community measures, the "two village committees" complied with the majority principle and public opinion inclination of the village, stressed publicity and openness and even executed "public affairs publicity system" (October, 1995) much earlier than most villages across the country.[20] Its form and force are rather rare to see in common city units. Second, the "two village committees" are likely to take one economic measure rather than regular unit administrative directive measure to carry out various rewards and punishment management. It seems that villagers have already become accustomed to these measures.[21] As observers, although it is hard to examine whether the majority principle and economic dimension generated from villagers have been accepted and implemented by the "two village committees" or whether the "two village committees" have introduced these principles into the community and exerted special training effects on community residents, it is certain that the intrinsic value priorities contained by such measures do not totally abide by typical unitization system. Hence, it invisibly fabricates some contradictory dimensions in community actions. Especially, after the intensification of economic dimensions, it facilitates the tension of interests among individuals, families and village collectives, and more importantly, aggravates the potential contradictions between village collective and village enterprise collective. Because the former prefers unitization, the latter has to take enterprise operation mode into account.

In addition, the increase of the power of the "two village committees" during the unitization process could also be seen from the formal connection between community represented by the "two village committees" and "superior" organization. In general circumstances, the village itself is at the intermediary level between the government and the peasant family. At the end of People's Commune system, local governments at all levels simply keep formal connection with village-level organizations, but not have any direct communication with peasant households. While the unitization process in Jianshanxia

Village further consolidates the status of the "two village committees" and subordinate village-level organization as village representatives, the "two village committees" hold high consciousness for this. For this reason, the village notices the internal development of village community public cause, and the external implementation of diverse policies and laws as "superior" local party and government. The party branch pays special attention to the practice of political and ideological requirements by means of party affairs system in overall work. The "two village committees" jointly lead special village organizations, and put state laws, regulations and policies for citizens into practice, including Land Management Law, Conscription Law, Marriage Law, Public Security Administration Regulation, family planning and other policy tasks.[22] Now that unitization pattern has executed full power to "two village committees" objectively, Jianshanxia Village appears to be more effective in implementation than common villages.

Unquestionably, implementation of these provisions conforms to state willpower (assessment demonstration standards).[23] For the sake of compensation, it could surely seek appreciation and support for unitization from local government. Therefore, village unitization process is actually subject to the support or guidance or even reward from village government and municipal government.[24] Benefits accompanied by such rewards in reserve contribute to maintaining the status of the "two village committees".

At this point, village unitization forcefully makes for the function of state power in grassroots like the overall unitization system.

2. Continuity and change of family system

In fact, power reinforcement of village unitization for village-level organization suggests interesting changes in community family organization mode, status and behavioral customs.

First, as shown in Figure 3.2, although the village-level organization in Jianshanxia Village during the unitization process successfully covers most part of village economy, welfare, sanitation and education departments, family is still a respected and prominent unit with economic settlement meaning. Even though the village-level organization allocates individual community residents' party affairs, staff income and welfare distribution according to routine unit management standards, it is still used to organizing villager group, considering enterprise employment, collecting public welfare fund and summarizing annual income according to the unit of the household. As for forestry allocation and housing building plot, the village first takes household as the basic unit and subsequently calculates population in each household. So obviously, family could neither be hardly integrated nor show full absorption like individuals in city unit during village unitization process. Expect for village-level organization system, family system turns to be a real part with "subsystem" meaning in village community.

Logically, it is on the one hand caused by the inability of unitization village in offering individual employment welfare guarantee conditions like city unit, and on the other hand caused by family identity as kinship unit, income and consumption settlement unit and its undertaking of remarkable social functions.[25] When it comes to the influence of family, the status of family in village apparently contradicts individuals' full absorption of the "unit" and thereby, allows village social relations to preserve various family contact means and factors. Then, some non-unitized phenomena could be often discovered in observation. For instance, villagers still like face-to-face communication in both daily life and work.[26] Villagers generally value the stability of family and marriage.[27] A typical example is that during the daily management process, even though village enterprises have enacted multiple unit management provisions, they often flexibly deal with affairs with sentiments in practice.[28] Such flexibility is not deemed as good practice by villagers and enterprise management layer. People often complain that familiarity among neighbors affects the reward and punishment rules and the implementation of enterprise management systems. But, the management layer holds the opinion that leaders could hardly refute the request of acquaintances, but could only turn a blind eye. Therefore, although some enterprises in developed industrial countries in recent decades often try to introduce so-called emotional contact and family work practices in traditional department management flow, the observer still believes that the measures taken by Jianshanxia Village do not draw lessons from enterprises in developed countries, but basically submit to community family system and contact habits.

Even so, the observer could still see that unitization indicates the change of village family system as usual.

What would be seen in the first place is that family structure is prone to small core family structure. Growth rate of village household is far above village population growth rate. During the 30 years from 1967 to 1997, the population size increased from 1,128 to 1,333. In 1991, the number even increased to 1395 at peak, and the corresponding number of households increased from 237 to 368. The growth tendency was especially distinct after 1983. The number of households even totaled 417 till 1991. The average number of population in each household was 4.76 in 1967, 3.90 in 1983, 3.35 in 1991 and 3.62 in 1997. Such changes could be attributable to several causes. One of the explicit causes is that males in Jianshanxia Village tend to separate from original large family after adulthood like many other surrounding villages. At the same time, after the completion of People's Commune system, the village takes household as the cardinal number to calculate population or labor force in forestry, building plot and recruitment quota. Such a habit usually boosts villagers' preference to live alone. Another relatively implicit cause is that during the unitization process, villagers stably increase their income and gradually improve welfare conditions. Due to the implementation of old-age guarantee terms and measures within the community, the aged could find life guarantee and do not encounter any misgivings or resistance in their small family life. Additionally, during the unitization process, village enterprises recruit younger villagers as managers and staff cadres. Those young villagers have higher influences and status now than that in the period of Peoples' Commune. If permitted, many young villagers would like to make decisions on their own, independently manage their own small family life and expect to keep a close but less intrusive and loose relation with parents in the small community space.

Family miniaturization surely affects family relation and behaviors. I have mentioned the benefits of independent living for young adults of different ages and genders many times in the interview. Since villagers in two generations would have more freedom and fewer contradictions, there are rare disputes among family members. Now that the village is rather small, family members could still visit and help each other at their convenience.

In essence, against the background of village unitization, the influence of family miniaturization tendency on every aspect of family relation is not limited by this point perceived by villagers. The observer also discovers that first, as the result of the small size of core family, adults in most families need to undertake more social roles. Consequently, small core family mode characterized by overlapping roles starts to influence the relation and value orientation of family roles. For instance, female labor force mostly works in village enterprises and obtains similar working mode, income and working time like male employees. In most circumstances, most female labor force first undertakes their rights and obligations in the community as employees. Such new habits are conducive to elevating the status of females in the family. Hence, in every family, in particular new derived families since the 1980s, rural male chauvinism could be rarely seen.[29] Second, industrial operation-centered working mode contained by village unitization process also triggers numerous changes of villagers' daily behaviors and habits through family miniaturization. Generally, young families have higher working couple proportion and various family behaviors increasingly imitate city customs.

For instance, I inquired that peasant buildings in Xiaoshan region preserve some traditional structure. To be specific, with focus on structure symmetry, these buildings have bright space and average compartments. Peasants would place the old-fashioned square table in the main bedroom in the ground floor; separate a kitchen and a utility room for piling farm tools, grain and dried firewood on two sides, and separate additional bedrooms in equal sizes upstairs. Jianshanxia Village also followed such housing structure before the 1980s. However, the housing built after the 1990s all followed independent building or joint building design and independent villa or joint villa appearance pattern like city community. No two buildings are repetitive. As for the internal design, the housing values small family household and leisure functions and removes traditional utility room. Or otherwise, the utility room does not pile farm tools like before. Besides, internal decorative materials and pattern also bear similarity to city housing. As a whole, village housing attaches great importance to personality, asymmetry, private family space and so forth. Together with the architecture in the period of the Republic of China, the architecture before the 1970s and the architecture in the 1980s, these new architectures record the changes of villagers' judgment for housing functions and housing aesthetics and architecture structure. The village also invites city and community planning professionals to arrange future overall planning and architecture style in village community. This planning stresses the utilization of mountain, river and natural terrain and personality styles of all sorts of architecture. If the village follows such architecture pattern arrangement in the future, the architecture style and housing functions in the community should totally bid farewell to the style of traditional village community. In accordance with my analysis, the change of villager housing is directly shaped by the unified employment of city architecture designers. Another implicit cause is that villagers have basically deviated from traditional agriculture and forestry industry in working mode and they naturally do not need to consider any design related to agriculture and forestry in housing design.[30]

There are numerous examples. Although the research could not ascertain whether such examples could be used to prove the radical changes in village production and operation means and organization assembly means could totally alter the details of villagers' life, it is sure that such changes in daily life actually unconsciously suggest that peasant habit description, peasant conservatism and other existing peasant theories which advocate the contradiction between peasant and modern country or modern progress all need verification and revision in real village transition.

3.3.3   Dilemma of unit boundary and staff supplement

In theory, the transition of community system in Jianshanxia Village during the unitization process could be also observed from the perspective of community staff supplement, community labor division and communication and community adaptation to internal and external pressures and integration. The thesis merely further investigates community staff supplement problems.

On a regular basis, any type of community always needs to supplement new residents, and trains and controls these new residents by means of socialization, persuasion, suggestion or constraint. This also constitutes an important aspect of community system and operation. Community staff supplement primarily proceeds by three means, namely, natural population growth caused by high fertility rate in excess of death rate, mechanical population growth caused by high immigration rate in excess of emigration rate and population growth caused by the merging with other places or units of various causes. Taking the situation in Jianshanxia Village, for example, the third means does not exist at all. Moreover, it is impossible for Jianshanxia Village to merge into other villages or incorporate other villages. Therefore, the research will not further talk about the third means. The first means indeed exists, but as stated above, there is no direct connection between village unitization process and community population growth in some aspects and more seriously, the relation between the two remains uncertain in some other aspects. Naturally, the research will not expound the first means. In comparison, the influence of unitization process on community population migration is more direct.

In the eyes of the observer, if village unitization process does not always propel the community to successfully transfer with universal standards of "progress" (some cases might force the community to fall into a dilemma sometimes), then community staff supplement problem might be certain evidence. As can be seen clearly from the above statement, first, during the unitization process of Jianshanxia Village, emigration population is far greater immigration population. In light of the statistics in Table 3.1, total immigration population was 196 and total emigration population was 323 from 1971 to 1977. The proportion between immigration and emigration population was 1:1.65. During 1984–1992, there were 58 immigrants and 120 emigrants at the proportion of 1:2.07. During 1993–1997, there were 14 immigrants and 58 emigrants at the proportion of 1:4.14. Second, the quality of emigrants might be much higher than that of immigrants on the whole. Among emigrants, some of them were out-married females, some chose to dwell in the city after receiving technical secondary school education and above, and some wealthy villagers migrated to city for settlement, opening factory or seeking jobs. Among immigrants, most of them were out-married females, and few of them were elders who originally worked outside and later returned to the native place after retirement. Therefore, in spite of mechanical population reduction problem caused by immigration and emigration, the research could now judge that although the village objectively needs more and more professional technicians, superior enterprise managers, financial accountants and marketing personnel to supplement each department of village enterprise, village population immigration and emigration could not attract such talents.

It is hard not to connect such conditions with the basic background of village unitization. Because village unitization views affirmed village boundary as the premise and further reinforces village boundary in interest distribution and villager psychology, villagers do not welcome other outsiders to dwell in this place and enjoy all sorts of welfare and public services besides out-married villagers. As far as native villagers are concerned, existing conditions are all created by them under strenuous efforts, and village forestry and village positions are limited. In this sense, they have no reason to allow outsiders to share such benefits by settlement. During the village unitization process, numerous villagers often argue that the practice of principal leaders in "two village committees" and principals in village enterprises to recruit neighboring villagers in native village enterprises will transfer local benefits to other outsiders. Many middle managers in village enterprises hold high vigilance toward introducing external professional managers.[31] Although the principals in "two village committees" and village enterprises perceive increasingly greater competitive pressures and have the plan of introducing various operation managers, they could not afford high housing, income and transportation welfare to retain such talents. On the contrary, under village interest protection pressures, the village could only take some alternatives to ask for help for a short time, such as keeping on good terms with technicians and managers by personal charm. In general, in the early stage of village unitization, villagers had obvious repellent emotions against outsiders.[32] Along with the evolution of unitization, villagers gradually relieve their repellent actions, but common middle managers aggravate their repellent actions instead. The villager and village enterprise decision makers hold positive attitudes toward the introduction of external managers, but they could not find a satisfactory method yet. The observer accordingly considers that factory production mode and the possible resulting need for external talents during village unitization process could not eradicate possible interest closure requirements for all.[33] It is indeed a dilemma for the village to develop enterprises and heighten enterprise market competitiveness

and in the meantime stick to village boundary in staff use during the unitization process.

3.4   Effects in Other Aspects: Several Examples

To some extent, the dilemma in village resident supplement reflects that although village unitization would promote some unexpected transition in some of the most difficult revolutionary levels, its effects in community transition could not be simplified as habitual "progress" all the time. This is possibly because village unitization transition means the dual incorporation and integration of modern resources and village land resources. Moreover, the matching of two resources in village community would inevitably result in all sorts of fantastic results.

To be specific, establishing factory and distributing welfare in the long run universally mark the progress of imitating the city, facilitating civilization and implementing socialism. The civilization recognized by villagers or expected by the government might be accepted with varying degrees. But, in this aspect, administrative implementation mechanism of unitization, village-level organization system and the tradition of the village to listen to government instructions and norms more easily prompt the implementation of this progress course in the community. So, while village unitization will distinctly bring about or urge the widespread revolution and transition of community, it is not compulsorily or purposefully constructed by the government as the spontaneous move of the village. Without the guarantee and support given by the country for city unit, now that the village could not temporarily give entire and sufficient welfare guarantee to villagers based on existing economic standards, it is hard to gain complete control on villagers.

More importantly, the main target of village unitization remains community family unit, rather than single employee in city unit. Either in emotion or economy, villagers greatly depend on the family unit or naturally, family is still the calculation unit of income and consumption in all aspects. It could be said that there are actually two sorts of relations, namely, the relation between city unit and individual and the relation between neighborhood committee and resident during village unitization process. Similarly, unitization villages could hardly cross the family to realize the comprehensive absorption of individual villagers. Therefore, the intention for unitization village to have civilization reformation or transition would meet all kinds of setbacks from time to time. Diverse traditions inside the community could be hardly simply integrated by the unitization process. Therefore, unitization produces a kind of interesting effect in the community. Likewise, numerous behaviors and habits in the village frequently present peculiar mixed or transitional characteristics.

In order to prove this point, the research here illustrates three examples.

Example 1: Old-fashioned ritual in free marriage

During village unitization process, marital autonomy is encouraged. Objectively, the young generation of the right age in the village usually has higher income than the elder generation and higher social status in village enterprises. Such circumstances increasingly enlarge the life autonomy of the young generation of the right age and accordingly improve their martial autonomy rights. Village-level organizations also advocate the marital autonomy of the young. The responsibility assumed by "two village committees" in response to "publicity policy" and "execution policy" includes arranged marriage and mercenary marriage. Therefore, during village unitization process, residents' opinions and practices about marriage gradually undergo drastic changes. In the opinion of general villagers, the responsibility of the elder generation is to provide or help provide the houses and betrothal gifts for their children (their sons in most cases), rather than to choose the mate of marriage. Sometimes, parents also look for proper mates for their children, but this is also up to the demands of their children. This suggests that parents would still respect the decisions of their children in the selection of marital partner. In either the elder generation or the young generation, nearly no one agrees that parents have the final say in children's marriage.

But, on the contrary, village-level organizations could not decide or intervene in the expenses or means of wedding ceremony. Likewise, the "two village committees" in principle only demand that villagers not "waste money for a high-profile wedding ceremony and the expense spent for wedding ceremony should be below the local average level". The so-called "local average level" for males here was around thousands of yuan in 1990 and 50,000 yuan (excluding housing) in 1995. Under such circumstances, young males of marital age could not independently cover the expense with their own savings. Instead, young males and their elder generation together assume the huge expenses. Consequently, family here plays a role of the indispensable supporter and protector for family members once again.

Families provide necessary protection for personal marriage and parents still need to offer necessary financial support to children. As a result, most people intend to take parents' advice in wedding ceremony or adhere to the rules in the village.

Many links seem to be very "local". For instance, in around 1995, males had to give 20,000 and few hundreds of yuan as the betrothal gift to females after establishing the marital relationship, while females had to take a set of household appliances and golden vessels as the dowry. In general, males had to wrap two "wedding bags" to send the betrothal gifts. When one wedding bag was sent to females, they had to put the few hundreds of yuan inside the wedding bag and return it to males. Both males and their parents did not personally send the betrothal gifts. Instead, the introducer did this job. Even if the females and males were in the same village and they loved each other of their own will, they would still seek a "fake" introducer. It is called "seeking the matchmaker". When they get married, they should also send gifts to their matchmaker to perform the ritual of "thank the matchmaker". As a general rule, a wedding ceremony is usually held between October and December in lunar calendar. Villagers generally believe that the traditional wedding time is relatively auspicious. In other aspects besides the wedding ceremony, villagers also try to adhere to rules and hold prudent attitudes. However, traditional ritual is still ignored during the unitization process. Such two circumstances would even produce some drastic scenes in some cases.[34]

Therefore, the young generation of marital age in the village chooses partners on their own and holds the wedding ceremony according to the conventions of the elder generation. The will of the two generations is integrated together. Probably outsiders feel strange about it, but inside the village, both the young and elder would deem it as a natural thing.

Example 2: Difficulty in funeral revolution

Village unitization could not integrate or potently integrate fields, affairs and things in other aspects. Funeral revolution in the village community is also a good example.

I have written an article to initially describe and analyze the macroscopic funeral revolution conditions inside Xiaoshan district since rural reformation. It means that since the reformation, Xiaoshan villages and some developed rural areas in Zhejiang Province all renewed ancient funeral ceremonies such as ground burial ceremony and elaborate funeral ceremony. In addition to the normalization and vintage rituals of funeral, the scale of the funeral also rapidly grew. It proves that villages still inherit traditional funeral ceremony attitudes, concepts and methods after the revolution for decades. The emergence of this phenomenon is not caused by backward non-agricultural economy or uncivilized social atmosphere and invalid government reformation. On the one hand, in most places which renew funerals, non-agricultural economy grows fast; when farmers increase their economic income, they seem to have more intense will to hold the funeral. On the other hand, from the perspective of the country, after 1949, out of the considerations for saving cultivated land and transforming social traditions, governments at all levels have repeatedly advocated to crack down on superstition, reform funeral and implement cremation via news media, administrative channels or against-capitalism mass movement. However, these moves simply prohibit the scale of village funeral, but do not fundamentally reform their funeral rituals essentially.

I predict that villagers' "antique" attitudes, concepts and rituals for funeral ceremony or the reason why villagers make choices different from city residents and put a large part of income in funeral ceremony brought about by economic growth is that they believe that their financial and human power investment in funeral ceremony is not an invalid expense. I also observe that funeral ceremony is used by villagers to promote the normalization of community actions and reinforce community sense of identity. Additionally, it also represents villagers' unique explanation for death and the dead. Such explanation not only includes certain Confucian attitudes characterized by "death is alive" but also contains the reincarnation doctrine preached by Buddhism and other folk divinatory legends. On the whole, villagers hold firm belief in the opinion of "the deceased have spirit". This generally suggests that villagers are accustomed to seeking a sense of life above death so as to find the value basis for their own life and labor. Simultaneously, in the face of all sorts of uncertainties in life, villagers tend to seek mysterious protection from their dead relatives. In this sense, governments reduce their functions in rural social field since the reform and opening-up. The reduction of grassroots government in village affairs naturally creates convenience for the renaissance of village funeral ceremony, but it is not a factor in promotion of funeral renaissance in nature.[35]

Specifically in Jianshanxia Village, villagers do not have different opinions about the funeral ceremony from other places in Xiaoshan. What village unitization could change is at most uniform policy planning and implementation in funeral intervention, but could rarely change the thoughts of villagers about the funeral ceremony. As advanced party branch and leading villagers acknowledged by the municipal Party Committee and municipal government, "two village committees" never really pay much attention to funeral ceremony reformation, although they respond to the call of local party committee and local government in the transformation of ground burial funeral to cremation. Simultaneously, they never obtain the response from villagers. Therefore, during the unitization process, villagers basically follow old funeral rituals.[36]

As long as local governments do not rigorously cease traditional funeral rituals in policy or legal terms, "two village committees" would still regard funeral rituals as family conventions, not rigidly intervene nor have enough motive to advocate reformation inside the village. In reality, "two village committees" could only raise some principled or peripheral limitations before 1997. The party branch regulates that party members shall not join in feudal superstition activities or act as sorcerers. In principle, the village committee demands villagers to "be civilized, establish new ethos, be diligent and thrifty, and oppose extravagant wedding ceremony and funeral ceremony, and feudal superstition". Besides, village committee also limits the scale of ground burial funeral in land policy.[37]

In 1997, the situation drastically changed. Provincial and municipal governments finally make up their mind to propel funeral reformation in villages and specifically enact district management provisions. "Two village committees" in Jianshanxia Village start to enact and execute Jianshanxia Village Funeral Reformation System under this background. Surrounding the removal of ground burial funeral and the promotion of economic funeral, the system explicitly regulates the implementation objects, implementation timetable and implementation means. This major move admittedly indicates that village unitization is an organization framework which helps follow state will or government policies. After all, whether the coercive reformation could last forever and whether villagers' expectation for funeral ceremony is gradually and even eventually changed compulsorily demand further verification.

Example 3: Village unitization, villager self-governance and village politics

In the end of the chapter, the research talks about village unitization, villager self-governance and village democracy interaction.

It is naturally two independent procedures. The latter involves the legal source of public rights, public participation and supervision on public rights, while the former involves community interaction mode, including village community composition, relation between residents and community and so forth. However, both the procedures take place in Jianshanxia Village after all. Moreover, they relate to village organization process in contents. Because villager self-governance at least involves the framework and operation of village political community, the two procedures still mutually affect each other. Some problems might seem to be very interesting. For instance, from the perspective of institutional standard orientation, unitization attempts to guide unit full incorporation to individuals, while villager self-governance system (including its self-governance scope, election system and village affairs publicity system) possibly results in the division between public sphere and private sphere. Obviously, it is hard to judge the consistency between the two orientations.

Considering the proposition of the research, the following sections will not elaborate or evaluate village democracy system and operation,[38] but simply imply two phenomena that affect village democracy system during unitization process.

(1) Village unitization possibly contributes to the implementation of "township government" in "village governance". Implementation of

villager self-governance system shapes township government system pattern. The country does not undertake village grassroots social affairs and economic affairs. However, with respect to macroscopic social control and economic regulation, the state still manages to control village grassroots. It naturally means that in township government political pattern, the country has to examine how government rights take effect in villages. According to the Organic Law of Village Committee (trial), there does not exist any administrative membership relation between villager self-governance organizations and village and township governments, but the so-called guiding and being guided relation. In real life, how to process such relation at the operation level could not find detailed and concrete norms from written systems. Consequently, the contradiction between township administrative right and villager self-governance right is inevitable. Township management represents national rights and interests. The country incorporates town into the scope of administrative management and gradually adopts tenure objective responsibilities system. Whether economic index, taxation expense mission, population control and grain plantation index could be completed is the rigid benchmark in grassroots government performance evaluation and cadre promotion. For finishing the tasks assigned by superiors, township management tends to reinforce the administrative control on villages or directly maintains administrative intervention. Even though villager self-governance right legitimacy originates from the common support of national laws, specific villager self-governance rights benefit from the identity of villagers. Therefore, it primarily represents the interests and will of village collective and villagers and protects the legal rights and interests of the village. In addition, the reduction or rejection of all sorts of social affairs and economic affairs in the village comes from the administrative intervention of township government. It does not mean that township government solely implements the control on village according to old-fashioned administrative mode or township government tries to escape township management. On the contrary, two "self-governance village committees" in the village often expect to seek support from township government. If the township government does not need to implement the task indexes appointed by the superiors, township government might not be willing to take administrative intervention measures to intervene in village affairs. To be specific, the problem is about the legal pattern of township governance. How to implement national right and policy in village governance under township government still lacks the support of written laws, or acknowledged norms.

Besides, in general villages, after the implementation of the household contract responsibility system in agriculture and forestry industry, peasant household first becomes the basic unit in rural socio-economic operation. The relation between peasants and village-level organizations is not simply the leading and being led relation anymore. This also suggests that whenever national power and policy need to be implemented in village grassroots, even though village-level organizations positively respond to and match with township government management, they should still analyze how to further permeate from village-level organizations to village families and villagers.

After all, the thing is totally different in Jianshanxia Village. Village party and government feel proud of the economic and social development performance in Jianshanxia Village, but feel anxious about the dilemma in village development. Moreover, village party and government leaders are very familiar with the main situations in the village and are more concerned with the village in daily work. The voice of village party and government could always be smoothly conveyed in the village, and all sorts of taxation and family-planning indicators issued by superiors could always be successfully implemented. The village-level organization in Jianshanxia Village often actively seeks help from village party and government. In case of any difficulties and major events, principals in the "two village committees" would request village party and government leaders to intervene or solve these problems. In some cases, the support given by village party and government to village-level organization is of vital importance. For instance, events such as village enterprises' successful election in cadre enterprises in Xiaoshan city, application for tens of millions of technical transformation programs and state taxation reduction allowances, and appropriation of land in neighboring villages for the development of village enterprises all exert prominent influences on village enterprise development and village unitization process in Jianshanxia Village. Village party and government departments spare no efforts to persuade superior parties and governments. Without their help, it is nearly impossible to finish these tasks. But, sometimes, the work processed by the village is not within the duties of village party and government (for instance, village enterprises determine larger investment programs and discuss joint venture cooperation with foreign merchants). However, at the request of "two village committees" or village enterprises, village party and government leaders would participate in every link of work on invitation. Some trivial work inside the village does not actually require the assistance of village party and government departments. For instance, village enterprises' product trademark and package design planning selection and corporate CIS proposal authentication are all operation management businesses, whereas village enterprises focus on the participation of village party and government leaders in the decision-making process, and the invitees hold prudent attitudes at work and do not bother about whether the work is the duty of village party and government leaders.

The friendly relation between Jianshanxia Village and village party and government should be partially attributed to the cooperation of town and village leaders in personal disposition. However, a more important reason is the special village economy of Jianshanxia Village. Since the village does not need to care about how to implement the plantation task issued by the superior government every year, the friction between village government and village governance continually reduces.[39] Town organization and village organization coexist in harmony all the way. For this reason, village government could easily conduct work in other places. Although the village government deploys index in family planning, conscription and taxation in Jianshanxia Village, the two former indexes do not target overall peasant households. Therefore, this policy is more easily accepted. Concerning taxation imposition, because village enterprises boost economic power and obtain tax reduction and exemption returns from village party and government, there is no problem in implementation. After all, the foremost reason is still the role of village unitization process. Because the unitization in Jianshanxia Village continues the tradition of employing administrative power to manage the community in the village, the implementation of state policies among peasants often relies on village unitization mechanism. Invisibly, village-level organization shares some work in village party and government departments. At the same time, village unitization mechanism also facilitates some potential conditions of village party and government administrative leaders in processing the relation between village governance and village government. As long as village party and government do not intervene in the operation of unitization village, or such intervention does not cause any loss to village economy and village welfare, unitization village could more easily accept the administrative leading and being led relation between this administrative unit and superior administrative unit like city unit.

(2) Unitization's support for the parallel layout of party and government at village-level organization might provide evidence for the separation of powers in village grassroots in China. After implementing villager self-governance system, village-level organization forms party branch and village committee parallel layout as stated above. Therefore, consistent with overall national political system, how to process the relation of "two village committees" becomes a universal problem at village-level organization. In theory and system framework, it is not

problematic to determine the core leading status of village party branch in the village. It could obtain support from three aspects at least. First of all, both national constitution and party constitution of the Communist Party of China (CPC) explicitly announce that the Communist Party of China is the leading core of the socialist cause of China. In village-level organization system, village party branch is also granted the core leading status by the ruling party. Village party organization could propose decision-making suggestions for village affairs by rule, or implement party's policies and guidelines via villager self-governance organization. Villager self-governance organizations are requested to legally conduct all work under the lead of party organization. Adhering to institutional orientation, village committee ought to conduct work under the leadership of party branch. Second, in terms of personnel composition, principals in village committee are often assumed by party members in general conditions. This is possibly because the ruling party always engaged in village party construction work after 1949. Lots of village "elites" would be incorporated by the party in each period. Following the implementation of villager self-governance system, villagers with high reputation and strong administrative abilities are cultivated as party members in general conditions. Even party members assume the post of leaders in village committee; it does not simply mean that individuals need to accept the leadership and constraint of party organization. Additionally, local party government and village party branch also have great influence on village committee election. Local village and town party government would guide the change or adjustment of office term in "two village committees", and village party branch also does corresponding planning. Generally, authoritative persons in the village are usually arranged to be the candidates of village party branch secretary. Although the village committee is directly selected by villagers, superior party government and village branch would use all means to choose the candidates and exert influences on election via party members, party organization or other means.

These conditions often result in the supreme authority and power of village party branch above village committee inside the village. However, "two village committees" would not find evidence from written norms in processing relations in daily work. How to process such work is often decided by specific personnel, in particular the authority and interpersonal relation, or the regulation of superior party organization and local government, of main principals in "two village committees".[40] As a rule, branch secretary will have high social status due to his competence and high reputation; and similarly, Village Committee director will have greater power due to his competence and high reputation. Therefore, in general cases, two village committees still hardly avoid constraints and restrictions and totally avoid the low working efficiency of village-level organization in status identity, working authority and working process.[41] Targeted at such conditions, village-level organizations and village politics researchers often express criticism or worries. But, objectively speaking, low efficiency is not the real deficiency of non-modern public politics. At least, in public politics sphere, low efficiency caused by the implication of authority departments often means low risk.[42] As a result, some critics for village grassroots democratic system indeed ignore this point. If the village does not have multiple political parties and political organizations, the dual-committee system in village-level organization actually represents the power separation of grassroots public politics with Chinese characteristics. What is more important and realistic is not the criticism or cancellation of dual-committee system, but trying to seek the legal evidence and clarifying respective responsibility and mutual restraining mechanism.

In Jianshanxia Village, although the relation between "two village committees" is occasionally subtle, the core leading status of party branch is very distinct. Moreover, the "two village committees" do not fall into any grave conflicts in village unitization process. The party branch explicitly announces to coordinate the work of "two village committees" and exert the role of other village organizations.

Correspondingly, the village committee follows the lead of party organization and principals in village committee also would like to act as the assistant to the village secretary in branch and enterprise. Therefore, even the subtle problem at work in "two village committees" would not be easily perceived by foreign observers. Either villagers or "two village committees" and village party and government departments, they all give high assessment on cooperation. Observers accordingly predict that the formation of the layout is directly related to the favorable interpersonal relation in "two village committees". Simultaneously, main principals in village branch good at corporate operation would act as village enterprise principals and managers of village collective economy in the long run. This also guarantees the core status of village party branch in economy.

Apart from it, from the perspective of institutional construction, observers might presuppose that village unitization more easily accepts unitization party government setting mode. Considering the transition of overall village organization mode, it could be said that "two village committees" naturally continue a variant party governance parallel institution during People's Commune period and an administrative labor division responsibility system under the lead of party organization after village reformation. Compared with common villages, Jianshanxia Village would more easily accept some legacy during People's Commune period as unitization village, including the inclination to the maintenance and protection of village-level organization party "governance" framework.

In this sense, village unitization unquestionably forms constraints on villager self-governance system.

In short, the above phenomena during the village unitization process are very interesting for the observer. However, the observer finds the difficulty in seeking brief explanation for such phenomena logically. Especially, the observer in this chapter tends to believe that village unitization not only includes the spontaneous proximity of the village to industrialization and urbanization but also includes the organization of village industrialization and urbanization like the city unit. Since this process is developed against city urbanization's gradually declining background and lacks national support of city unit, the target of village unitization integration is numerous families inside the community. Therefore, village unitization could not totally absorb employees like real city unit and naturally preserves some social relations and social interaction means as in past village society. This proposition objectively indicates that such phenomena should be explained by insufficient village unitization. Accordingly, they will be quickly changed by further process of unitization.

But, this might not be the case.

Chapter 4 will set forth the main contradictions stimulated by village unitization inside the village. Maybe these contradictions promote the unique transition free from the control of unitization inside the village and even terminate the village unitization process in the end.

Endnotes

1. Lu F. Origin and Formation of the Unit System in China. *Chinese Social Sciences Quarterly*. 1993(5):77.

2. One last point should be mentioned. When Jianshanxia Village tries to develop village enterprises and realize unitization, the overall Chinese society is gradually entering market economy age. Under this background, city unit system starts to be viewed as the product and characteristic of Chinese socialist planned economy by people and progressively enters the reformation and disintegration process. This is a very interesting time difference which actually poses an adverse background for the operation of village unitization.

3. For instance, Relevant Policy Concerning the Implementation of Joint Stock Cooperative System in Hangzhou Langchao Industrial Company states that in "the provision of enjoying shadow shares", 70% shadow shares should be quantified to individuals according to the actual working age of registered employees (including married female employees) in the factory.

4. In September 1995, when I visited the village, the World Conference on Women was held in Jiao County of Beijing. I claimed that World Conference on Women was non-relevant with this village, but accidentally discovered that "two village committees" dispatched tens of posters on mountains, telegraph poles and walls from village entrance to village end. These posters promoted the slogan of the World Conference on Women. I randomly inquired passersby how they knew about the World Conference on Women. According to the research, they learned about this event from TV news, slogans, or chat. I cannot help exclaiming about this.

5. This refers to the Eighth Five-Year Plan in Jianshanxia Village and the Ninth Five-Year Plan in Jianshanxia Village.

6. Village unitization always tends to provide more rich service categories than common villages. If permitted by finance, it would indeed affect service category and urbanization level inside the community. Taking education service, for example, surrounding regions of Jianshanxia Village generally focus on the education degree of children, but only Jianshanxia Village itself resorts to the unitization process to significantly improve village primary school education. According to my research, teaching staff and income of village primary school are all managed by village government, but new school dormitories and new equipment are all procured by village collective, in particular village enterprises, for hundreds of thousands of yuan. To be specific, school phone is installed by the village; half of the income of cooking staff in the school and firewood are funded by village collective; during Teachers' Day or other major festivals, main principals of "two village committees" would visit teachers, join in the conference and exchange opinions with the school according to routine. Therefore, although the school is under the control of government education ministry according to relevant regulations, village primary school is actually controlled by the government and village collective. Generally

speaking, the school knows well the advantages and disadvantages of village collective and village enterprises and appreciates the support given by the village. Accordingly, the village primary school has perfect resource allocation and good teaching quality and leaves tremendous impact on children. For instance, I find that although most villagers speak dialects other than Mandarin, the universal language on campus is still Mandarin. Children read textbooks in Mandarin, and also chat with visitors in Mandarin. Moreover, as proved by the statistics, since 1992, the school has set up 8 classes and more than 10 teachers per year. It is a complete primary school arranged by the village. In addition to local children, tens of children from outside villages including Chuanshan Village, Luo Village, Shishan Village and Dingshan Village also attend school here. The enrollment rate and consolidation rate of children of schooling age in the full village are all 100%. In 1994, Chinese in Grade Two, Nature in Grade Four and Mathematics in Grade Six obtained the second excellent rating in the town, and Mathematics in Grade Five obtained the first excellent rating in the town, and a male child Yang in Grade Six obtained the third place in national primary school mathematics competition (interview notes).

By the way, it is normally acknowledged that the normal transition orientation is from isolated community to open village and town community, city community and municipal community. But, the reality is that such linear "progressive" views could hardly explain the present situations of small community under the background of urbanization and complexity of community transition process. Hence, the so-called conception of small-town construction in China seems to more consider the town community and functions below small city. The reason is that considerable villages can hardly be integrated into city community. The more feasible thing is the village urbanization matched with small-scale urbanization.

7. Saunders divides community size into size of area and population density. The size of area proposition emphasizes that "in larger communities, individuals will have fewer acquaintances, and greater inclination for anonymity and non-personal relation. Moreover, personal contact also has the inclination for specialty, occupation or other social groups, instead of adjoining neighborhood district. On the other hand, larger communities tend to have greater service utility, richer cultural services and higher education and economy specialization degree". The population

density proposition states that density discrepancy would also lead to more discrepancy. Generally, "in regions with high density, artificial environment (culture) is influential, and even irresistible sometimes; in regions with low density, people would have more chances to interact with the natural environment (residence)" (see Saunders. *On the Community*. Trans. Xu Z. Taipei: Liming Cultural Enterprise Co., Ltd, 1982, p. 57).

8. For instance, I once walked from the old factory to the village entrance with Village League Branch Secretary Jiang and encountered over 10 villagers during the 200-meter walking distance. Secretary Jiang amicably greeted them. I asked him whether he knew everyone in the village. He answered that he knew those elder villagers and some children (interview notes).

I arrived at the village in the afternoon during the first visit. At dusk, I went for a walk on the avenue of the village. On my way, most villagers had known that I was "from Hangzhou Zhejiang University for social investigation". At that time, I was surprised at the speed of news communication and villagers' focus on foreign visitors (interview notes).

9. Interview notes.

10. Interview recording.

11. Instead, unitization layout might promote false "consistency of unit" in theory. See the statement about unit superficial consistency, politeness and reality section structure and action in *Unit System in China*, co-authored by Zhou Yihu and Yang Xiaoming.

12. Competition motive comes from economy, race, society and other aspects. Therefore, apart from the competition in this plane space, there is also longitudinal space competition. Like many other villages in Jiangnan, Jianshanxia Village also believes in geomancy. Villagers here think that geomancy will flow to those higher houses. Then, villagers always try to heighten their own houses, even one or half a foot and keep an eye on their neighbors for fear of this. Neighboring villagers often quarrel and even fight with each other.

I once asked village committee director whether such conflicts took place inside the village, and how the village organization managed this. The director answered that most villagers now did not believe in this tradition anymore. Nowadays, because villagers needed to build their houses row by row alongside the mountain, houses in the rear were always higher than houses in the front. After all, the height of houses in the same row was regulated by the village (Interview recording).

13. Light pollution brought about by factory is primarily the coal soot. I once consulted a temporary senior engineer from Beijing to instruct filter paper production equipment modulation and industrial water pollution. The senior engineer said that wastewater discharged by the factory only had non-toxic filter paper crude fiber and would not pollute the water and environment.

14. There were a total of 221 villagers in 1994 with the proportion of 16%; 220 villagers in 1995 with the proportion of 16.07%; 228 villagers in 1996 with the proportion of 16.8%; 229 villagers in 1997 with the proportion of 16.86%.

15. In 1996, altogether 741 villagers joined in social old-age insurance, including 491 corporate employees, 69 disabled villagers (17 outsiders from other villages) and 181 peasants. The policy was as follows: (1) Employee annual cardinal number was 200 yuan, out of which 20% was assumed by the collective and 20% was assumed by employees according to their working age. (2) Peasant annual cardinal number was 100 yuan, out of which 40% was assumed by the collective; annual cardinal number was 200 yuan, out of which 30% was assumed by the collective.

16. Poplin DE. *Communities: A Survey of Theories and Methods of Research*. New York: Macmillan, 1972.

17. Saunders. *On the Community*, p. 150.

18. See the *Notice of Reinforcing Village Grassroots Organization Construction* issued by the CPC Central Committee in November 1994.

19. For instance, Chapter Six of *Financial Management System* in 1991 regulates that the Village Secretary should conduct work under the lead of "two village committees". Chapter Four regulates that large amount of cash disbursement should be discussed by "two village committees". In 1993, Chapter Two of *Association of Aged People Article in Jianshanxia Village* regulated that "Village Association of Aged People is the mass organization established under the lead of village party branch and village committee and the instruction of superior elder working committee". Chapter Three regulates that the first basic task of Village Association of Aged People is to "assist party branch and village committee to promote Provisions on the Protection of Elder Legal Rights and Interests in Zhejiang Province and Provisions on Communist Party and National Cadres' Adherence to Respect and Provide for the Elder, advocate the traditional virtue of respecting and providing for the elder, negotiate maintenance disputes, execute and supervise the signature and implementation of 'family maintenance protocol'". Article 2 of *Village Committee Charter in Jianshanxia Village* in 1994 regulates that "Village committee should conduct all work under the lead of village party branch". *Village Committee Charter* in 1995 affirms once again in "villager representative conference system" that villager representative election system should be "audited by village party branch and village committee" and "villager group management" should "timely submit villagers' opinions and requirements to village party branch, village committee and superior government".

20. Typical cases also include the implementation of "five disclosure" systems in land management and housing construction by Village Committee as of 1988. Till 1993, the system was expanded to "five-disclosure and one-supervision" system. Till 1995, the system was expanded to "five-disclosure, four-presence and one-supervision" system, namely, house building index, house building population, house building site, house building area, house building property disclosure; site selection, sampling, construction, field investigation during construction, public supervision and so forth.

21. Apart from corporate regulations on overtime-leisure wage deduction, the community has precisely enacted fine and reward rules in electricity, forestry, television and broadcasting equipment management. In labor force, the community

formulates the rule of "cash for labor" (40 yuan for male labor force per year and 30 yuan for female labor force per year). One tactful decision is that village committee demands the two parties in forestry disputes to, respectively, pay 100 yuan deposit (conciliation fees) before field investigation. It is said that in practical conciliation, the deposit paid by the unreasonable party will be preserved as the conciliation fees and the deposit paid by another party will be refunded.

22. The sole specialty is that Jianshanxia Village does not need to assume the plantation task under the directive of local government due to limited land resources.

23. Organic Law of Village Committee explicitly stipulates that village committee has the duty to propel socialist spiritual civilization construction and legal construction. In legal construction, village committee should promote the constitution, laws and regulations and national policies and monitor villagers to perform all sorts of duties. In 1990, the CPC Central Committee once endorsed Forum Summary for National Village-level Organization Work, deploying villager self-governance demonstration activities in few or tens of villages in each county nationwide. Ministry of Civil Affairs in charge of this work enacted The Notice of Implementing Villager Self-governance Demonstration Activities in National Villages in the same year and relevant evaluation scoring criteria for demonstration of county (city) and village (town), among which the "quantitative scoring method for villager self-governance demonstration village evaluation inspection" could be divided into six types and 28 items. The sixth type (seven points) is that "villagers should perform citizen obligations according to law and fully complete all sorts of tasks designated by the country", including "timely completing grain, cotton and coil and other procurement tasks and taxation tasks" (three points), "completing conscription tasks, prohibiting legal marriage and ensuring 100% family planning rate" (four points) (see Wang ZY and Bai YH. *Town Regime and Village Committee Construction*. Beijing: China Society Press, 1996, p. 109).

24. There are three means of reward. The first one is the honor reward. Local government grants tens of major rewards to Jianshanxia Village, village enterprises, major village organizations and village principals, including Biaobing Village and other 50 strong villages in Xiaoshan City. The second one is tax reduction

support. The country and local government develop collective industry and sino-foreign joint venture factory and grant all sorts of taxation preference to Jianshanxia Village as the old revolutionary base area and primitive poor village. Until 1993, the government reduced 2,428,404 yuan in taxation. The third one is for local party and government to intervene in major work in village and village enterprises and help solve contradictions. According to me, when most villages, especially village enterprises, need to implement loans, investment in projects, reform shareholding system and construct major public welfare causes, the village party committee secretary and branch industrial township head are often invited to join in the discussion, research and decision of the village. Village party and government feel proud of the performance of Jianshanxia Village and feel anxious about the dilemma in the village.

25. Based on previous experience, the so-called families inside the rural village before industrialization are thought to be homogeneous families. Family often undertakes most training, protection and service functions required by individuals. Families also take clan as the means of contact and do not have any relation with other government organizations outside clan or village. On the contrary, families in developed communities after industrialization often have some other characteristics. In the discussion about American families, Sanders considers that American families have the following few characteristics, including monogamy, small family size, limited relatives, possibility for divorce and remarriage, reduction of family members and functions, increase of family member individualization, proximity to equality between husband and wife, emphasis on the importance of children, divinity of marriage and lots of secular components. Actually, these characteristics are probably possessed by families in developed industrial society. What needs special attention is that even in the last type, family still has irreplaceable functions. For instance, in economy, it is not more important than before as the production unit, but it is still a basic consumption unit; in protection, family still effectively expresses the concerns for personal welfare; in recreation, family is revitalizing; in education, family researches and cultivates children by way of the cooperation between parents and teachers. In a word, family remains the sole source of individual security. Additionally, family also has a basic function, namely, the metabolism of population. Some community researchers also tend to believe that

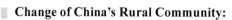

families with young people could further help parents, care for the society and take part in society. Concerning the relation between family and social control, if family does not have strong control as the main community system, controllable social opinions about juvenile crime, truancy and abandonment will collapse.

26. It seems that villagers are used to visiting each other at home and talk about or communicate information in face-to-face chat. When the village builds more and more isolated houses, villagers in turn add more and more face-to-face communication activities. Accordingly, the village specifically sets up public activity spaces like The Aged Activity Center and Home of Militia, repairs avenues, installs street lamp, stone chairs, pavilions and flower beds along the road and villagers also have fixed space for chat in leisure time. In summer without rain, villagers would move out their deck chairs, bamboo beds along the road for coolness, playing cards or chatting from 5:00 pm until 11:00 pm in the night. It is a scene from the village. Although the climate is not hot, and villagers have TV sets at home, they still like such outdoor cooling activities and free chat communication means. I have repeatedly gone outside to observe the scene and find over 3 and 400 villagers there. Most of them are middle-aged and young people.

27. Villagers seem to feel proud of family harmony, including young villagers and employees. Although they have learned diverse fashion styles in city life via TV and other media and tend to get close to city style in housing design, catering, clothing, education and transportation instrument, they are still conservative or stable in family and marital relations. As of 1949, the village still had two divorce cases. I once chatted with two directors of Village Women Conference and some villagers about this. These insiders expressed that the two cases were understandable and they held the opinion that maybe divorce was the best choice for them (interview notes).

28. For instance, different from the equal pay for men and women in city unit, the village always believes that female labor force is inferior to male labor force. During People's Commune in the past, females' income would be reduced. In the process of unitization, most female labor force in the village works in village enterprises and does not suffer from any discrimination in employment and occupation. Moreover, females obviously elevate their family status. However, the

income of females of the same occupation is 20% less than that of males. Females do not complain about this.

In order to assure villagers at work, village collective opens the kindergarten. Limited by capital, teaching staff and location, the kindergarten only recruits preschool children aged over five in the local village. After all, there are many employed couple families inside the village and their younger children could not study in the kindergarten. Moreover, they could not entrust their children to their elders (for other reasons). In such cases, the couple could only change shift to spare more time to take care of children or directly take their children to the factory.

Although corporate management layer clearly states that employees shall not take their children to work, it will not bother about this in reality. In case of any major activity days such as municipal leader visit or foreign guest visit, it will temporarily notify employees not to take their children. Villagers also cooperate with the decision without any hesitation.

29. Females in the village often get off work late at night and go home in groups. Males are used to such life and do not compel females to indulge in household duties. Instead, middle-aged males in small families often buy vegetables and cook meals on their own. In particular, during the peak season of production every year, employed couples or female employees would work in three shifts at the workshop. At this point, villagers who first arrive at home would cook meals for the family. After a long time, males did not feel shamed for cooking anymore and they kept calm while talking to me in the interview. It does not mean that villagers totally abandon traditional gender labor division criteria (for instance, doing the laundry is always thought to be the work of females), and instead, the role relation has been drastically changed in the village.

30. Similar changes also take place in villagers' life habits. For instance, how to remove outdoors toilet is a major problem in the village. Although the local government would repeatedly promote sanitation and even dispatch professional manpower to remove such toilets within the term, since there is a lack of professional municipal environmental sanitation service department in the village, or peasants still prefer outdoors toilet, this problem could not be easily fixed in

the short run. In many counties, village local government often views how many outdoor toilets it has removed as an important political performance. In Xiaoshan, the municipal government has conducted manpower research in environmental sanitation and anti-epidemic department, and finally introduced a sanitation processing method. By way of this method, peasants could take attenuation, hydration, deep ground filtration and disintegration measures to rebuild flush toilets. The sole disadvantage of such new craft is that out of the employment of deep ground filtration and disintegration measures, peasants could not apply artificial fertilizer. In recent years, it does not obtain full promotion in Xiaoshan, excluding Jianshanxia Village. Moreover, the village does not have any outdoors toilet. According to my analysis, it is naturally related to the uniform community action and consumers' proximity to city life inside Jianshanxia Village. But, what is more important is that most families do not till the land anymore and they would like to accept such cheap, convenient and non-pollutant sanitation equipment craft.

31. Employees at this layer often conclude problems in companies as impotent implementation of rules for saving the face of fellow villagers, but rarely measure the matching of their competence and occupation.

32. For a time, villagers were very sensitive about outsiders' appropriation of village public rights and interests. For instance, before 1990, many clients would visit the enterprises for cooperation and joint venture. When these enterprises temporarily entertained clients in the dining hall, some villagers still felt sensitive about this and even directly burst in to take away dishes, overthrow tables and criticize clients. Years later, villagers also joke about this.

After all, the action of villagers obviously produces everlasting influences. There is even no restaurant inside the village. When enterprises need to entertain clients, the cook will temporarily prepare distinctive local meals in the factory dining hall (this place is not open in ordinary times). Clients often have meals alone, without the company of village and factory leaders, especially principal leaders. The factory would hold product promotional meetings once a year in Xiaoshan.

33. Since village unitization could not provide identical or superior working, living conditions and social status like the city unit, the village finds it hard to

attract all sorts of high-quality elites required by enterprises. Out of the protection awareness for community public rights and interests, they often impose pressures on those foreign technicians who dwell in this place.

In midsummer 1995, Personnel Bureau and Township Enterprise Bureau in Xiaoshan cooperated with Hubei Province to introduce tens of college and technical secondary school graduates to work in Xiaoshan township enterprises and their registered permanent residence and personnel relation were entrusted to the Personnel Bureau. Through the efforts of principals in village enterprises, one male and female technical secondary school graduate majoring in finances from Huangshi City of Hubei and one junior college graduate majoring in economy and trade from Hubei Economics and Management University were invited to work in village enterprises. The junior college student majoring in economic management worked in the Marketing Department, the girl majoring in accounting worked in the Financial Department, and another graduate worked as the technician in the workshop. The village welcomed three outsiders for the first time and generally referred to them as "college students". I once lived near them for a few days and interviewed them and village enterprise principals and villagers about their work.

As I found, village enterprise principals were faithful in the introduction of "college students". They dealt well with every detail in this aspect from primary investigation to subsequent arrangement of working life, occupation and treatment. The village did not prepare any accommodation for outsiders before and even corporate dining hall occasionally entertained outside clients. Principals in village enterprises arranged three guest rooms of more than 20 square meters in the office building under the lead of "two village committees", and installed new furniture, TV sets, kitchen, liquefied gas and gas appliances in each room. For better settling in the three new graduates, principals even distributed settling-in allowance. When I asked, "Could the three graduates make any contributions in the future? When they grow up and have their own family, they possibly do not find mates here nor build houses here, what will you do then?" The principals answered that "They would make contributions with their learned knowledge all the way. I still expect them to work in our enterprises in the long run. If we want to retain these talents, we have to first retain their heart. Therefore, we have to make efforts to take care of them". It was very hard for them to stay away from home to work in the mountain. I once thought that it was indeed impractical to keep them in the village all the time. I planned to make a new investment in the enterprises of Xiaoshan and moved enterprise Finance Department and Sales Department to Xiaoshan in the next year and the year after next. I supposed that maybe they would be more used to the working environment there.

Villagers had complicated responses to this matter. Most villages were curious and even visited the new college students from time to time. Some villagers, in particular some employees in management post, held hostile attitudes toward these newcomers and thought it a huge waste to give them things and settling-in allowance. According to their speech and act, I considered that villagers could still accept these graduates, but few of them would positively make friends or visit them.

The three college students behaved unsociably in the workplace, but were extremely easy and outgoing in their dormitory. I once asked them why they came here, whether they were used to this place and the factory and about their future plan. The answers given by the three college students were nearly the same. The reason why they came to Xiaoshan was that they felt Hangzhou and Xiaoshan were developed regions. There was no risk to work in village enterprises once the personnel and registered permanent residence were placed in the city. In the worst case, they could still go back to Huangshi according to national policy. When they first came to Xiaoshan, they all chose the most famous enterprises in suburbs, but they never met the general manager. But, business was business. The Personnel Department was not very enthusiastic and did not determine whether they would recruit them. By contrast, since the general manager in Langchao Enterprise of Jianshanxia Village always personally entertained them, took care of them in work and life and gave high income and good treatment, they decided to work here. Few years later, out of language barriers, they could not totally understand the dialect and did not often contact the villagers. At night, they often read books, or chatted with their Hubei fellow townsmen in primary school. They rarely visited villagers. Villagers generally were polite to them, but could not help complaining about their high income, sometimes before them. They could not adapt to the work in the factory for the moment and the benefits of the factory slightly declined.

The manager layer did not deal with the matter seriously and even tolerated such a situation.

In my opinion, it was very difficult for the three college students to integrate into the community. At least, it was more difficult for common college students to work in cities and adapt to city working environment. After half a year, I learned from the interview that the junior college graduate majoring in economics management worked in another enterprise, the girl still worked in the Financial Department and the other graduate was busy with modulating mosquito eradication aerial fog facility.

34. One day, I saw that village committee director asked factory director Yang to help villager Mrs. Li write a "wedding card" with brush. The Village Committee Director took out the notebook to search for the format and content demanded by Li.

The wedding card was to be written on the red paper. When Yang wrote "your daughter" till the end of the line, he thought it impolite and inappropriate to write down the name of the bride in the next line. The quick-witted village committee director advised him to add the letter "woman". I wanted to remind him that "your daughter and woman" should not be used together, but it was too late. Factory director Yang had already written it down on the paper. Later on, he asked what the letter "room" meant. Mrs. Li had excellent classical Chinese knowledge. Village committee director smiled at him, saying that "Mrs. Li specifically reminds to write the letter 'marriage room' here". The wedding card was to be written with high-profile classical Chinese words.

35. See Mao D and He ZY. Rural Value Resources of Funeral and Transformed Village—Brief Analysis on the Funeral in Xiaoshan. *Journal of Zhejiang University.* 1995, 28(6).

36. Compared with the civilian funeral recorded or recommended by Confucian classics in successive generations, the funeral popular in Xiaoshan villages has been simplified, changed or added in many aspects and some links or components are very modern, such as sacrifice food, joss paper (such as foreign

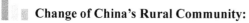
currency) and utensil variety (such as paper-made TV set and other appliances). However, the procedure, size and people's understanding of the funeral nearly totally follow the folk traditions in Xiaoshan before 1949 without substantial difference. In Jianshanxia Village, households who hold funeral should perform the following procedures in general.

Encoffining: In case of any funeral event, family members should first invite a monk, Taoist priest or God and Buddha (also known as sorcerer, a priesthood assumed by peasant) to lead children to send the impermanence. Next, they should dispatch a person to announce the death to relatives, talk with relatives about specific funeral procedures, clean the body and change the clothes for the dead, move the deceased body to the frontcourt and keep vigil beside the coffin for the whole night. On the second day, the monk or Taoist priest should take children to put coins in nearby rivers or ponds, and take out the water with bottle or bowl, known as the "buying water". Till late night, family members should place the favorite things of the dead, shroud and spirit wrapper sent by junior relatives with the dead in the coffin so that the dead could use these objects in the netherworld. Before placing the deceased body in the coffin, children should kneel down to comb for the dead. At night, family members should invite the Taoist priest to perform a religious rite, recite or chant scriptures or classical opera accompanied by musical instrument. There are usually seven religious rites all night long. In some places, family members should invite the Taoist priest to foretell the netherworld and hang the picture of Yama for the worship of dutiful sons. According to the explanation of the funeral presider, this move aims to successfully send the dead to the netherworld.

Sacrifice: On the third day of the funeral, family members should pace the mourning hall and perform the sacrifice rite. Relatives and fellow villagers who join in the funeral should send shroud, wreath and elegiac scroll and singular cash gifts (49 or 51 yuan). After the sacrifice, family members should prepare catering to retain other people.

Burial: One day before sealing the coffin, the "buying water" should be placed on the coffin. Family members should wail at funeral and break the utensil which contains water before carrying the coffin. While carrying the coffin to the cemetery hill, family members should set off firecrackers at each turn or bridge. In some places, the eldest son should walk beneath the coffin and symbolically carry the coffin across the bridge. It means that the family has successfully escorted the spirit of the dead to the abyss bridge and prevents it from falling into the hands of ghosts. On arriving at the cemetery, the Taoist priest leads children to surround the coffin for three rounds in the left and another three rounds in the right. It means that the family has already trampled the way to the netherworld for the dead (but, there is no explanation for three rounds). Before placing the coffin down on the ground, the position of the coffin should be affirmed by the son of the dead. The next move is to conceal the ground and place the monument. After the burial, family members should repay fellow villagers with gifts.

First Seventh Night: Family members should hold the memorial ceremony for the dead on the first seventh day. Many villagers would conduct the religious rite at the same time. The time of the religious rite on the first seventh night is usually five or seven. On the first seventh night, married daughters and other close relatives should also join in the rite. Other possessions of the dead have to be processed, including the burning of some clothes and articles. In the above procedures and on the first seventh night, children should dress in the mourning dress. Some households would also follow city funeral rites to replace mourning dress with crape and white flower.

Other Rites: During the anniversary deathday, Spring Festival, Tomb-Sweeping Day and Spirit Festival (the so-called spirit festival), family members should burn incense, burn joss paper, sacrifice for the dead and pray for the dead to protect the family.

These rites are very complicated. Therefore, villagers have to seek advice from experienced elders or authority persons in the village for funeral rites. The funeral ceremony held in the village also offers experience to other households. The key links in the funeral rite usually conform to ancestral paradigms (before 1949) and strive to comply with norms.

37. The village committee prescribed in October 1995 that "villagers have to adhere to village government rules in tomb building. After receiving the application,

village committee should have field visit and later approve the application. One cave should be built within 25 square meters, while two caves should be built within 35 square meters. Villagers have to pay 50 yuan per square meter foundation fee for every excess square meter" (General Rules of Forestry Management).

38. See Mao D. Village Organization and Village Democracy Study on Jianshanxia Village in Xiaoshan City, Zhejiang Province. *Chinese Social Sciences Quarterly*, 1998(1):35–44; Lang YX. Three Research Topics of Village Election. *Zhejiang Social Sciences*, 2000(1):83–95.

39. After implementing contract responsibility system and villager self-governance system, how to complete national plantation index is always a major concern of the village party. A long time before the improvement of national grain production conditions, party departments at all levels in the province, city or county would dispatch specialist groups to help town cadres preach the importance of national plantation task in the annual spring ploughing season every year. Village cadres also proactively preach and execute national policies. Under the hard efforts of the work group and village party government in Xiaoshan City, the work has been successfully completed. Cadres in subordinate villages have to encounter great difficulties at work because they need to respect the will of households and simultaneously complete the plantation area index. In spite of the arduous nature of the work, village-level organizations and peasants do not cooperate with cadres. The reason is probably that peasants would not obtain lots of benefits by completing national plantation tasks, and even perceive state and government coercive power from government actions. They cannot figure out why the government on the one hand guides peasants to enter the market and on the other hand demands peasants to develop economy according to its policy. During this process, cadres in "two village committees" feel great pressures imposed by the government and villagers. Although the village committees follow the directive of working group and village cadres, they actually do not know how to implement the policy in reality. In the end, after one round of work, there often exist lots of contradictions between village cadres and village-level organizations, village-level organizations and villagers as well as villagers and village cadres.

To be sure, along with the growth of national economy and the settlement of the village, the country gradually loosens the control on developed rural areas. For instance, in grain production, Zhejiang Province does not confront grain output problems, but has to examine how to urge peasants to produce marketable grain variety. Therefore, on February 16, 2000, Zhejiang Province Agricultural Department and Food Bureau cooperated to issue 2000 grain Production and Marketing Information. This was the first time for a provincial government to forsake peasant plantation directive plan. As commented by the front page of Zhejiang Daily, "principals of provincial Agricultural Department and Food Bureau state that the purpose of releasing grain production and marketing information is to notify latest market information to peasants and guide them to produce marketable grain variety and increase income. Meantime, the practice which changes previous" compulsory early season rice plantation area index "respects market law and peasant will" (February 16, 2000).

40. The relation between "two village committees" is a universal institutional problem faced by all administrative villages since the implementation of villager self-governance system. As reported by the first edition of *Zhejiang Daily* titled Consistent Development of the "two village committee" in Huangyan Village on January 7, 2000, "after the change of office term in two village committees, the two committees in Huangyan Village do not cooperate with each other at work. Inconsistent government work has aroused great sensation among peasants and high attention of district leaders. They consider that village grassroots organization construction must be combined with grassroots democracy political construction on the premise of maintaining and respecting the core leading status of village party branch. While legally conducting the work of village committee, it ought to positively accept villager monitoring. Accordingly, this district organizes full policy and statutory training on members in 'two village committees'" and enacts corresponding policies. The district regulates that affairs such as financial expenditures in excess of village committee financial approval limit, village land appropriation and village house building foundation approval, family planning index, distribution of relief fund, village enterprise construction and variation, agricultural scale operation change, construction engineering and other village engineering project bidding and budget, village development plan and annual plan

decision should be discussed by the "two village committees" and signed by village party branch and village committee, while decisions that need to be decided by villager conference or villager representative conference should be legally submitted for approval.

Implementing this system effectively normalizes the power of village cadres and prevents the occurrence of illegal and undisciplined phenomena. One village in Chengguan Town submits a report to village office which demands to grant 400,000 yuan for greening and landscaping projects. It is ascertained that the report should be returned because it does not pass through party member and villager representative conference. Throughout negotiation, the village holds the villager representative conference to listen to the opinions of villagers. The actual expenses have been reduced by 10%. Moreover, according to the statistics of the Petition Department in Huangyan District, since the implementation of this system, village petition volume across the district sharply decreases. Till now, there are simply 31 village petition cases, reducing by 66.7% than 1998".

Excluding journalists' beautification of district news, this report still discloses some general situations about the relation between "two village committees". For instance, how to deal with the relation between "two village committees" lacks trustworthy institutional framework; any problems should be still solved by superior party government; the basic solution is still village government led by the party.

41. What is interesting is that in some villages, some villagers disagree with the layout in which Village Secretary is the primary leader and village committee director is the secondary leader. The possible reason is that after the training of village committee election for few rounds, villagers focus on election. They insist that the secretary should be selected by party members, while village committee director should be selected by overall villagers. In accordance with the majority principle, it seems that the village committee director has more speech rights in village affairs.

42. See Burns JM *et al. Democratic Party*. Trans. Tan JJ. Beijing: China Social Sciences Publishing House, 1993, pp. 6, 34–36 and 42.

Chapter

Risk and Risk Conversion

4.1　The Villagers' Retreat

No matter how much the unit process in the Jianshanxia Village was incomplete, there were already enough reasons to be excited about the institutionalization process and the various town changes it had caused. In the heyday of the village, a senior leader was said to have praised it as a model of a new socialist countryside. Later visitors agreed to this assessment in varying degrees, and they were very willing to attribute some of the unsatisfactory parts of the village to the transitional phenomenon in the village transition. People expressed an expectation or imagination in such an evaluation: The villages have evolved in the form of "progress" to one day, and all these transitional problems will be solved.

People thought maybe it was because the mass transfer of people from the primary industry to the secondary industry and then to the tertiary industry had been considered a modern law, perhaps because China's rural labor force transfer was too difficult. In this context, every time there was a unit process or similar change of a small village type, and rural communities were brought to towns and cities, almost all those who saw or heard about it were really excited about it and gave all kinds of praise and encouragement. If this change was just but also had the characteristic of some kind of "common prosperity", or fit, coincided with the consistent pattern that Chinese socialism has adopted in the city for decades, it was easy to cause some understandable hyperactivity.

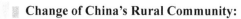

Here is circumstantial evidence: In Hubei Province, Lantian Company, Nanwei Company and so on, with the support of the government, let farmers take the land to buy shares, expand the scale of enterprise operation, etc. The farmers who took part in the operation seemed to feel the same way, almost urban. According to the Yangtze Daily and other media reports, in early February 2000, more than 1,000 households in six administrative villages, such as Yangxin Village, Yuxian Town, Caidian District, and Wuhan, handed over their more than 10,000 acres of land to Wuhan Nanwei Company. According to a formal agreement between the two parties, the company had a "dual mandate" for the farmers and their land, namely, the farmer became the company employee and enjoyed the company's formal worker treatment and the land was also developed and operated by the company. Nanwei Company promised to ensure that the annual net income of farmers would be over 10,000 yuan, and it would increase by a certain percentage every year. All at the same time, the land taxes and fees of farmers should be borne by the company and the township government was no longer involved in the six village farmers' economic activity, only responsible for the family planning, public security and other social affairs management. It was said that the company was a private company in Wuhan City, and since 1997, it has been in Yuxian Town, with the total investment of more than 50 million yuan and has built 1,000 mu of medicinal material base, a high-tech agricultural demonstration park, and 10,000 deer farm project. After signing with Nanwei, these farmers became Nanwei's medicinal plant herbalists, fruit-tree growers, deer workers, etc., and received training from Nanwei Company. Farmers were simply responsible for production, regardless of the sales and claimed to feel relaxed. The general idea was that they were not familiar with the market before, couldn't sell anything and made no money. Now they could be rest assured. It was said that the response to the matter was good, and the town government was particularly relieved. The party secretary of the town said that the biggest headache in the past was the difficulty in collecting the money and the structural adjustment. After the implementation of the dual mandate, they could concentrate on social affairs and cloud.[1]

It seemed that the media, the local government, the company and the villagers were all pleased. The media saw it as a newsworthy story; economists saw it as a new path for rural industrialization and urbanization; the government thought it would reduce the burden of management. The company, of course, thought it may be able to expand its scale and increase its benefits. As for the villagers, they were satisfied with a stable income and could avoid market risks without leaving the village. What was more surprising to the villagers was that the villagers were still engaged in familiar work, but they had become employees of the company. It was a pity that the company did not have to convert the villagers into urban hukou in accordance with the labor law, and there might be a number of ways to relax the company's ties with these new employees in the future. As far as the villagers were concerned, the whole thing would be perfect if they were able to turn their rural hukou into a city hukou in the process.

But, no one seemed to point out the following: This dual mandate was good for the company, but the risks to the local government, especially to the villagers, were obvious. The main problem is that there are always operational risks in the market economy, and enterprises with agricultural products as the main business are not exceptions. Once the enterprise is faced with difficulties, once these difficulties exceed the capacity of the enterprise, and even bankrupt the enterprise, how will the former villagers and the new employees place themselves? This is not to say that these new workers will not survive if the business is stagnant or even bankrupt. Rather, these new workers have actually become a new type of urban and rural employment system. They no longer have the rights of farmers to land in the law, and they do not enjoy the various employment and re-employment paths that the state has arranged for urban residents. As a result, they will not be able to

obtain readily available, legal support channels and conversion methods in the existing employment system once they have a larger problem.

In the context of this book, this actually indicates a problem. It is the difference between the urban unit and the village unit, no matter how the village is institutionalized and achieved. What is particularly intriguing is that the risk and transformation of urban units clearly have some kind of formal and informal mechanism, which is not available in the unit villages.

What does that mean?

This means that there is almost no way out for the unit village!

4.2 The Main Risks of Village Organization

In fact, the whole Chinese unit system was weakening or changing as the Jianshanxia Village struggled to push the unit forward. The city unit began to be non-institutionalized in the market economy, gradually, item by item reduced or removed the unit member's adsorption and protection. In this process, on the one hand, the unit members were gaining new social freedom. On the other hand, the pressure or risk of system transformation was increasingly felt due to the termination of lifetime employment and average benefits.

However, the risks or costs associated with this transformation were far less than the risks faced by the unit villages. At the very least, urban unit members, even if they had to start to face the risk of institutional change, including having to start taking on some sort of unemployment and re-employment risk, could still get a variety of risk compensation or risk conversion methods provided by the government and the unit, including relying on all kinds of safeguard measures or compensations that could be provided by the unit, or relying on the government to provide a transitional mechanism for unemployment and re-employment, or on the unemployment and re-employment mechanism that was being formed in the urban society. They could also rely on other forms of social mobility (such as migration to the countryside, or other cities, or even to the outside world).

The unit villages were obviously different. The basic guarantee for the survival and development of the villagers before the unit organization was the ownership of land resources; but, at the expense of the villagers, there was no equal access to some of the freedom of employment and social mobility enjoyed by members of the urban unit. Therefore, after entering the unit process, the villagers' risk actually increased with the reduction or loss of the land resources. In other words, land used to be a fallback for farmers; when the villagers basically turned to the industrial economy and relied on the village enterprises in the process of village institutionalization, the village enterprise was not only the economic base of the village unit but had replaced the land resources and became the economic pillar of the villagers and villages. But, in the market economy, any economic entity was not likely to be smooth and make progress day by day. With high risk in the operation of enterprises, it was not only difficult for the village enterprises to become a base for farmers to retreat economically but also could make the basis of village organization become rather fragile.

In fact, from around 1992 to around 1995, the village-run enterprises in the Jianshanxia Village had gradually felt more and more pressure or in crisis. The direct cause seemed to be the fierce competition of similar enterprises and similar products in neighboring cities and surrounding areas. The average profit from the competition caused the profit of the enterprise to decline. In order to cope with this situation, the village enterprises tried to expand the scale of the enterprise and tried to diversify their operations, and continuously applied for loans for several investments. The larger investment projects included a joint venture with Italy to invest in a sanitary mattress production line, and the village enterprise invested 10 million yuan; in order to expand the scale of the production of incense, it invested 10 million yuan in the land expropriation, construction of new factories and new production lines; it purchased 17 mu of land in Xinjie, Xiaoshan and a 7,500 square meter old factory building to run a paper box factory to produce packaging boxes for the village-run enterprise with an investment of 1.5 million yuan. All these investments had been demonstrated by experts, each of which seemed reasonable and cost-effective at first, but each investment ultimately did not produce the expected benefits. Among them, the introduction of the sanitary mattress production line from Italy was an underestimation of the consumption market. The project was estimated to have many advantages and conveniences such as this product and the company's main electric mosquito-repellent paper used the same kind of raw materials, it was the first in China, the automation technology level was very high, the products were widely used in hospital beds, families and hotels in China, and some products could be exported to foreign markets. However, no one estimated that the cost and pricing of the product were too high for domestic consumers nor was the difficulty of squeezing products into existing hospital systems and consumer markets sufficiently estimated and of course, there was also a lack of strong restriction on foreign enterprises to fulfill the product resale contract. As a result, after the product was put into operation, although the quality was good, it had been difficult to open the domestic market. A product produced within a working day was often sold after months. As a result, the return of investment funds had been extremely difficult from the start. On the second project, there were also reasonable expectations. At that time, market research showed that the market was good, and the production capacity of enterprises was far behind. In addition, the Japanese businessmen who had cooperated with each other for many years had a definite plan for joint venture with the village enterprise. After several rounds of negotiation, the concrete plan had been determined, and the corresponding conditions of the joint venture factory at the site and the factory were required to be provided by the village enterprises in accordance with the schedule. However, the joint venture was eventually put on hold for some commercial reasons by the Japanese businessmen. As a result, only a quarter of the land that was expropriated and leveled was used to build the factory floor, and the rest remained idle. As for the third project, because it was a low-cost purchase of a bankrupt factory, under normal circumstances it was an extremely cost-effective investment. However, due to the poor investment performance of other projects in the village enterprises, the liquidity gap required for production was too large, and the paper box factory had been unable to start production, thus producing no production benefits. As a result, the village companies had received little from these investments and were paying interest of nearly 4 million yuan a year on these loans. Companies were burdened by this.

A series of adverse reactions were brought about by the bad investment, including the decline in the benefits of the enterprise year after year, the decline in the attractiveness of the enterprise to its employees, and the narrowing of the market coverage of its products and the degree of unit security limited by the reduced economic strength. There had also been subtle changes in the minds of the villagers. Looking back a few years later, some of the parties were surprised that the villagers had changed so much: Once upon a time, people were looking forward to the prosperity of the village enterprises and the income from enterprises. When the business really raised everyone's income and needed everyone to keep working, a lot of people started thinking about their own business. All those who had a little money were beginning to calculate both the money of the village enterprises and the individual economy, for example, to open a factory outside, open a shop in the village, or buy a car to transport. What was particularly frustrating was that villagers who thought so and did so often made more money. The statistics provided by the "two village committees" and village enterprises also indicated that since 1993, the individual and private sectors of the village had maintained steady growth in stability. The benefits accruing to individuals or the private sector were gradually higher than those from the village enterprises. By 1996, the average wage income of employees in village enterprises was

4,438 yuan, while the average net income of the whole village was 4,492 yuan. For the first time, the per capita net income of those employed outside the village enterprises exceeded the per capita wage income of the employees of the village enterprises.[2]

In order to save the decline of village-run enterprises, the "two village committees" and village enterprises took a series of measures. Through various official and private channels, village enterprises actively engaged with businessmen from the United States, France, Japan, Italy and Malaysia to strive for new joint ventures and cooperation projects. At the same time, village enterprises also tried to merge the inefficient, close-to-bankrupt state-owned pharmaceutical factories, in order to find new economic growth. Internally, the management of the village enterprise fully enhanced the update of the old products and the update of the product packaging, and invested a lot of manpower and financial resources in marketing. In addition, the village enterprise also incubated the enterprise internal management mechanism renewal and tried to introduce a shareholding system since 1993. But, to the villagers' regret, all the new foreign joint venture projects had not been implemented for various reasons. Some of the projects were talked about and talked about, there was almost nothing more than signing, but they didn't succeed in the end. Although there was also a return of investment in marketing, it did not really seem to alleviate the debt burden of village enterprises. It seemed even more difficult to increase the efficiency of enterprises by strengthening internal management. It was often just a matter of reason and clarity. In fact, none of them could be carried out to the end. So, to this day, the ordinary villagers, the management backbone of the village enterprises, even the leaders of the village enterprises themselves, as long as they look back on what happened to the business, they still can't help complain or blame themselves for taking care of each other's feelings too much at the time. "The knife in your hand is far from sharp", so that management became harder and harder to manage every day.

With one method after another, the difficulties of the village enterprises became increasingly greater, and the actions of the village collectives gradually became very difficult to oppose or sustain. Finally, inside and outside the village, there were fears that had never been felt before. The township government officials began to tell the visitors that the business reputation of this village is good, the management level is not good. Villagers often worried about what would happen in the future. Village cadres expected enterprises to survive difficult times and often expected the country's macroeconomic situation to improve and economic and credit policies to be relaxed in order to inject new capital into troubled enterprises. Maybe because a variety of ways to solve problems had been tried, gradually no one would believe that solving the difficulties of village enterprises was an easy thing. People from all sides were beginning to feel that the problems facing the enterprises in Jianshanxia Village were, in a direct sense, the specific problems in the operation of the enterprises, but the problems did not seem to be limited to this level. People felt that the mistakes in corporate investment, the debt burden and so on were only visible difficulties. The real trouble was that the whole enterprise and the whole village collective business were starting to look like a fully loaded and broken down car, which was hard to push and pull.

From the observer's point of view, this kind of feeling was actually accurate because the real serious problem encountered by the village enterprises and the whole village might be the weakness of some kind of anti-risk mechanism after the development of the village unit. To be clear, the unit system that the unit villages strived to approach contained a non-market-oriented mechanism, which had made it difficult for the unit villages to cope with the market economy situation which had accelerated since 1992. This could be illustrated in two ways.

On the one hand, communities and enterprises crossed so much that they basically overlapped, and the whole village was like a large unit. However, the principle of community development and the principle of enterprise development in this large unit could not but conflict gradually. In particular, since 1992, the state has tried to promote social access to the market economy, and the society has rapidly departed from the shortage economy. In the case of capital acceleration, a vast majority of consumer goods companies have been squeezed into an era of unprecedented competition and low interest. The business of the Jianshanxia Village was no exception. The company's main products of electric heating and anti-mosquito products were exclusive products in China, and they had adopted the technology from Japan, so it once occupied the absolute advantage of the domestic market. But, with similar products from the United States, Germany, France and Japan in the domestic market at the same time, because the same production technology was widely adopted by domestic manufacturers, the market of mosquito control products had been rapidly divided, and the village enterprises in this village had entered a precipitous competitive environment. In order to cope with the increasingly fierce market competition, enterprises need to operate around the principle of efficiency first in all aspects of the internal management system, including the employment system, the distribution system and so on, even the need to exclude all planned economic rules. On the other hand, the village collectives in this village, in accordance with the characteristics of unit system, still paid attention to the permanent employment of villagers, the increase of average welfare, the construction of community public welfare, and regarded enterprises as blood donors for community development. As long as it was possible, they tended to use the profit of the enterprise without compensation. If the enterprise satisfied this kind of village community request, it would be contrary to the enterprise survival rule. If the village could not get the free blood supply, it could not maintain the process of unit. In this way, village units that were not integrated with market rules and benefit principles were built on enterprises that had to be market-oriented and lacked the government's support for urban units. Both companies and villages in this large unit faced huge risks.

In another aspect, the village enterprises in Jianshanxia Village were also constructed according to the unit system, like small units in large villages. Because of this, enterprises were too restricted by community rules and restrictions, which were difficult to operate according to the modern enterprise system, and could not face the market flexibly effectively. The following points were particularly obvious:

(1) The property rights system of the village enterprise had never been granted to the enterprise operators and employees to clarify the property rights. Therefore, the larger the enterprise scale, the more complex the relationship between the debtor and creditor of the enterprise, the more the enterprise was unable to operate properly. All the people in the village felt that under the name of collective ownership, the assets of the village enterprises could be said to be owned by everyone, but no one had a share, and everyone had the right to control it, but no one could manage it. In the market economy, this is a big taboo to any enterprise.

(2) The property rights system of village enterprises allocated two kinds of contradictory authoritative relations to the management organizations. One authority was based on collective ownership and the other was based on hierarchical management. The former was based on the principle of majority, while the latter was based on rationalization. This had caused insurmountable trouble to the business operation. For example, in the actual process of business operation, employees were actually employed, but the nature of the property rights of the village enterprises and the community relations in their communities all agreed that most of the employees were the ultimate basis for the legitimacy of the enterprise's behavior. Therefore, it was opposed to the integration of employees into a labor system according to the way of employment. As a result, there were a series of overlapping roles and contradictions of behavioral norms within the enterprise. So, observers can see the following: (1) Enterprise employees couldn't

help but feel nervous about their roles from time to time. Employees who worked in an enterprise usually took on a variety of roles, such as employees, one of the masters, managers or leaders, ordinary workers, villagers, neighbors, parents and relatives. Although village-run enterprises had been established for many years, and the products and equipment had been greatly updated, the employees were still used to the family workshop approach in dealing with the relationships between them. Between managers and subordinates and between managers and ordinary employees, they didn't know how to treat themselves and others as working partners or to take into account their relationships with each other in the community. The enterprise management itself, of course, required management and employees to first respect the authority relations on the basis of bureaucracy and obey the authority in the implementation of the system, the implementation of assessment, the implementation of rewards and punishments and so on, dispelling the role of community members and the norms of dealing with the relationship between them. However, most ordinary employees were not accustomed to accepting non-community roles and norms in collective-owned enterprises, and could not coordinate their various roles smoothly. Therefore, once regarded as the employee to be constrained by the company, it was particularly difficult to adapt. Therefore, various measures to eliminate tension had been taken spontaneously, thus forming a variety of unit action strategies to resist the authoritative relations of enterprises. The most common ones were direct confrontation with authority, loafing on the job, sabotage, misappropriation, coalitions, etc. (2) Accordingly, the employment and wages of village-run enterprises were supposed to be a return to employment. Under normal circumstances, whether or not to grant and how to grant employment opportunities and wages are mainly determined by the labor market, the ability of enterprises to pay, the pressure of trade unions and so on. However, it is not so simple in village-run collective enterprises. Since the enterprises were for everyone, it was only natural for employees to enter the factory, and it was natural for them to increase their wages. However, it was almost impossible for the company to lower the wages of some employees and fire some unqualified employees, unless the employees committed gross mistakes that were unanimously considered unforgivable. This was not so different from the urban units of the past; the difference may be that, in urban units and in formal units, promotions usually take seniority as the first standard. In village-run enterprises, even the seniority criteria for staff promotion could not be fully implemented, but the frequency of face-to-face contact, the pressure of interpersonal relationships around them, nepotism and so on needed to be considered.

(3) The distribution of village enterprises as the reward incentive system is in serious conflict with the normal operation of enterprises in the motivation and way: (1) In the three regular parts of income (property income, wage income and redistribution income), the community system tends to highlight the social redistribution income and its average growth; the atmosphere it creates also implicitly supports the average wage income of employees in the enterprise. According to the established practice, there are few wage differences among the decision-making level, management and ordinary employees in the village.[3] This pattern of distribution is clearly incompatible with the values required by conventional enterprises. In terms of the actual effect, the salary income and redistribution income of the villagers and employees do not constitute the appropriate reward stimulus. For those with more corporate responsibility, they especially feel the inconsistency in position, power and interest. (2) Being related to the nature of the village enterprise and the development mode of the loan, the most important wage income in the income structure of villagers is often fluctuating downward or in crisis. As a result, employees' wages are the "surplus" profits after companies pay taxes to the government, pay dividends to banks, and pay collective expenditures to the community. Therefore, the tax and interest seem to be guaranteed. It is precise that the employee's salary is the least guaranteed. This

situation particularly affects the enthusiasm of ordinary employees. (3) After enterprises have to adopt the hierarchical management system in management, it is very important for the staff to provide the necessary stimulation of career prospects. However, because the village-run enterprises adopt a spontaneous unit system and lack state support and organizational connection with the upper-level units and other horizontal units, there is no possibility of further promotion of staff into management, and there are few opportunities for rational lateral mobility and adjustment. (4) Because the village-run enterprises should give priority to the villagers in accordance with the requirements of property rights and the expectations of the villagers, it was difficult for the foreign technicians and labor workers in the enterprises to be rewarded with additional labor contributions or to be satisfied with the same welfare benefits as the villagers. As a result, it was difficult for them to truly integrate into the enterprise. These four kinds of situations work together so that the distribution system of the village-run enterprises could neither provide workers with the property rights and labor pay commensurate with the income incentives nor provide the villagers with vertical upward channels of social mobility. Then there was some sort of stimulus disorder. As people assert, "if these vertical flow channels are lacking, if a lot of people have a strong desire to improve their status, then all they can do is modify their goals or create tensions that threaten social order".[4]

Of all these problems, of course, there is nothing more important than the system of income adjustment in the unit village, which hinders the sustained production or growth of income. From this point of view, of course, enterprises in Jianshanxia Village needed to strive to capture business opportunities outward and strengthen business management inward. But, at the same time, it was especially necessary to solve the problem of reorganizing the enterprise distribution system and the adjustment of the authority relationship; the solution to these problems, of course, needs to start from the adjustment of property rights.

These problems show the common maladies of common units as low-efficiency production organization. Although the unit of Jianshanxia Village belonged to the initiative of the village to learn from the urban unit, rather than being driven by the state administrative power, it still failed to avoid these pitfalls. However, it is precisely because the village unit process was not government-driven that the villages were not as much involved in the process of institutionalization as the reform of the urban units, and the villages had relatively greater degrees of freedom. In fact, the leadership of the local township government, village organization and village enterprises felt these problems in the early 1990s, and they were interested in launching the necessary reforms.

4.3   The End of Enterprise Restructuring and Village Organization

The process of reforming the country's economic system provided such an opportunity for the village. Since 1992, the discussion on the shareholding system of industrial enterprises in China has been booming, with various trials and experiments increasing day by day. Jianshanxia Village seemed to get a glimmer of inspiration from it. The township party government, the "two village committees" and the village enterprise decision-making level all began to feel that it was necessary to carry on the reform to the general enterprise collective ownership; a relatively clear property rights system is the premise of the innovation of enterprise management system and distribution system; a distribution system that is compatible with the property rights system may provide the necessary drive for enterprise development.

The Jianshanxia Village gradually entered the shareholding system transformation of the village-run enterprises. The whole process took nearly four years and consisted of three stages:

The first stage: Approved by the industrial office of the township people's government and the municipal bureau of industry and township industry, from the end of 1993, the village enterprises began to pilot the reform of the joint-stock cooperative system. It mainly focused on relaxing the ties between the collective and the village office, the internal shareholding and internal financing, and clearly highlighted the following:

(1) Attempts were made to clarify the status of the independent legal person and the nature of the shareholding cooperative system and reposition the relationship between the village collective and the enterprise. The revised corporate management system, which was revised between 1991 and 1992, used to define provisions different from village collective management in all aspects of employee management, wage distribution and financial systems. In a direct sense, it showed the distinction between enterprise staff and non-worker villagers, and indirectly expressed the will to bind the relationship between the large village collective and the small village enterprise group. The new shareholding cooperative framework further requires that "the enterprise truly becomes a producer and operator with voluntary association, self-financing, self-management, self-restraint, self-development, self-accumulation, self-responsible for profits and losses". The highest authority of the company was the shareholders' representative body. The village collective was one of the shareholders who held shares in the enterprise, and it is no longer the relationship of former executive leader and the subordinate enterprise.

(2) Corporate collective shares and staff and workers' currency-holding shares took a large share: Village collectives accounted for 10.55%; the company's collective shares accounted for 56.1%. The employees' currency-holding shares accounted for 33.32%.

(3) In order to enhance the attractiveness of enterprises to employees, and to give staff and workers the necessary return, the company set up shadow shares, that is, 30% of the company's own assets for the village factory employees. Among them, 70% were allocated eight shares per

year according to the working age, and 30% were used as bonus shares. The shadow share and currency-holding shares were matched by 1:3. Employees leaving the company would affect the recovery of shares into the company's collective shares.

(4) Proper care was taken of the historical origin of joint-stock enterprises and maintaining friendly relations with the village collectives. Among them, the company's Deputy General Manager and General Manager were still in charge by the principals of "two village committees"; the company gave priority to the allocation of the village collective in the enterprise, and paid 17% of the collective pre-tax profit of the village every year as the collective public expenditure of the village, as well as other expenses such as subsidies for farmers, etc.; the company undertook other expenses in the village (signed by the finance director of the company) and paid the salary of the cadres of the two committees. The company gave village cadres and soldiers who retired after 1975 the share for the years of service, which were converted into shadow shares to be distributed along with retirement benefits.

On January 1, 1994, the company began to formally implement the new articles of association. Because of the reform involved in each household, there was a rush of excitement in the village, the nearly 900,000 yuan of staff and workers' currency-holding shares were in place on time. But, soon after, everyone began to feel that the real effect of the reform was to clarify the relationship between village collectives and enterprises, and to attract some funds in the form of currency-holding stocks. However, the reform had not yet been able to make clear the interests of property rights in the collective part of the enterprise. It was not very clear how workers and staff, as shareholders of the company, exercised all kinds of rights in the enterprise. Although the person in charge of the actual operation of the enterprise enjoyed a small amount of shadow stock reward, it did not seem to have a very direct interest in the risks or profits that the enterprise might encounter in the course of operation. As for the improvement of the ability to repay the debt, the improvement of the operation of the enterprise in the market was not related to the reform.

Therefore, the overall reform in the first stage did not produce the expected results in the enterprise; companies also failed to recover from the decline in efficiency. Local township party and government leaders and the main business leaders were very anxious about this. The Xiaoshan municipal party committee, the municipal government incubation, prepared and launched the transformation of township enterprises in the whole city, and the township party and government leaders and business leaders formed a consensus on further promoting the reform of the enterprise stock system. With their hard work, the village's enterprises moved into the second stage the following year.

The second stage: From October 1995 to May 1996, the focus was mainly on the managers holding large shares, increasing the strength of joint-stock system transformation and trying to thoroughly straighten out the property rights system in enterprises, in order to concentrate on the production and management and deal with the debts of enterprises. Compared with the first stage, this round of restructuring focused on the following key links:

First of all, from the original ownership to the operator holding large shares, the risk, income and property rights of enterprise management were linked. According to the assets assessment, the owner's equity was 5.67 million yuan; through consultation among all the parties in the village, 897,400 yuan worth of currency-holding shares were returned to the staff and 2,772,600 yuan were retained by the village; for the remaining 2 million yuan, 30% (600,000 yuan) was designated as the shadow stock of the enterprise, 70% (1.4 million yuan) was designated as the village collective stock; the sum of the 2 (3.7 million yuan) was 54 % of the total registered capital (yuan 3.7 million) in the new joint-stock company; in addition, the operator personally held

1.7 million yuan or 46% of the total share capital because the agreement stipulated that only those who held a currency share could enjoy the shadow shares (70% of which were paid by cash holders and 30% as employee benefits). The actual equity division of the new company was as follows: personal holdings of 1.7 million yuan, accounting for 55% of the village collective and individual currency-holding shares, and the village group shares of 1.4 million yuan, accounting for 45% of the village collective and individual currency-holding shares.

Second, the new joint-stock company further clarified the relationship between the village collective and the enterprise from the operational feasibility eliminating the fictitious equity of the village collective in the enterprise and at the same time protecting the reasonable rights and interests of the village collective. Upon the joint decision of the "two village committees" and the village economic cooperative, the village economic cooperative came forward and signed an internal agreement with the new company and recognized the owner's rights and interests of the original company, including loan and credit considerations; due to the obvious potential losses of the enterprises and the operating losses of the current year, the sum of the two items had far exceeded the owner's equity, therefore, the village collective agreed to use the 2,772,600 yuan remaining in the village to reduce potential losses in order to support the operation of the new enterprise. On its part, the new company agreed to ensure a balanced administrative income and expenditure at the village level. Even if the company incurred losses in the next year, it would have to pay a full 300,000 yuan to the village collective.

Third, in the process of transformation, the original enterprise staff and workers' currency-holding shares should be dealt with properly. The parties had reached an agreement that the new company would return the full amount of the staff and workers' currency-holding shares. Pending refund, it would take a short-term loan and pay interest at 20% per month. The shadow shares of the original company and the currency-holding shares of the staff and workers were recovered by the company.

In addition, the new joint-stock companies still emphasized the reasonable and lawful dismissal of individuals, collectives and states, and properly took care of village collective and "enterprise collective" under the premise of equitable distribution of profits.[5]

The third stage: After October 1996, the enterprise further turned to the private sector to deal with corporate debt. Since the completion of the second round of system transformation, the enterprise management had not yet produced a fundamental improvement, nor had it reached a new joint venture or a new economic growth point, so the debt risk of the enterprise had been expanded unprecedentedly. Approved by the township people's government and the township industrial office, the "two village committees" and village economic cooperative agreed that the village branch secretary should personally preside over the establishment of the company's transformation leadership team, and decided to transfer and auction the company, so as to "carry out the creditor's rights and liabilities, to make operators and enterprises truly become independent legal persons who take risks, manage themselves, account independently and take responsibility for their own profits and losses". The specific methods included the following: (1) The village collective discounted all the assets (including intangible assets) of the original company at a price of 79,359,500 yuan, which were auctioned to the operator of the original company; the latter bore the original corporate debt of 79,359,500 yuan, which equaled the paid-in assets' value. (2) In addition to the above-mentioned debts, the village collective agreed to undertake and deal with future unpredictable claims and debts arising from bank guarantees in the original company. (3) The village collective emphasized respect for the nature of the farmer's share cooperative system of the original company and the right of everyone to enjoy shares, and stipulated that the transferee should contribute 1.7 million yuan at one time to the withdrawal of the shares of the staff and workers, employ the original staff as best as possible, give all necessary rehousing subsidies to those who were not recruited, protect the basic living standards of the villagers and workers, and "reflect the superiority of socialism".

There was no doubt that once the private enterprise transformation program was put into practice, the unit system of the original village-run enterprises also came to an end; at the same time, the variant leader and subordinate relationship between the village organization and enterprise had been completely decoupled. For most villagers, the gains from equity over the years had been virtually negligible. Therefore, as long as the enterprise was still in operation, and workers continued to work in the enterprise, the enterprise wage base was basically unchanged, and the transformation did not constitute a threat to individual labor and family life. However, to speak from the economic structure formed over the past 20 years of Jianshanxia Village, this certainly meant that the village-level organizations representing the village collectives no longer had the basic departments to promote the unit villages, and even needed to put in place the necessary financial resources for their existence from then on. The cadres of the "two village committees" were particularly worried about this. Fortunately, the unit village process over the years had left behind some tradition of solving problems. With regard to the financial security of village collectives following the restructuring of enterprises, the parties involved in the restructuring soon reached an agreement: In order to ensure the administrative expenses of the village collectives, the transferee paid the village collective more than 350,000 yuan in the form of land lease fees every year, which increased year by year. Through this link, the resistance from the two committees of the village and the economic cooperatives basically disappeared.

The transformation of the village-run enterprise finally reached its limit in a formal auction. After this, other follow-up work also appeared to be more normal and smooth. With the joint effort of local government and business operators, more than a year later, the company cleaned up its debts with the bank and related parties in the form of assets, bonds and debt; at the same time, through coordination, the company leased premises and land from banks and related parties in the form of payment of rent, and continued production and basically provided the residents of the village with employment and wages as usual. The village community fully considered and understood the difficulties of the enterprise, reducing administrative expenses and agreeing that the lease of land be reduced by about half for the company. As a result, over the years, the turmoil, anxiety and trouble caused by the debt pressure of the enterprise, the transformation, gradually subdued. The small mountain village seemed to have regained its composure. The village's two committees operated as usual, and most of the villagers still got paid for work at the factory. The production line in the workshop was still ticking at a fixed pace. When it was hot, the villagers gathered together every evening in the flowing stream to chat.

But, all the people who had gone through the process felt that some of the most important things in the village had changed: Look at the city, the city people's units were suddenly out of fashion; look at the village, the village also had no strength to learn from the city people's unit. Suddenly, people didn't seem to feel that this was a satisfactory way to end. Even more importantly, it seemed that no one really could predict exactly how and where the disintegrated villages would go.

Nevertheless, observers can still be almost ruthless, claiming that the village has finally gone through the most meaningful phase of the village community's transition in more than 20 years and that over 20 years of unit-building process in Jianshanxia Village, it is still full of inexhaustible meaning. Of course, it's not an unreasonable claim. At the very least, Chinese social researchers should pay attention to this kind of case when discussing rural social structure and community type; researchers in contemporary Chinese history might feel the need to reinterpret the social team framework of the People's Commune. For those concerned about farmers and farmers' theories, the case may yet again remind us that the relationship between countryside, farmers and modernization is inevitable. Compared with the study of the system of units, when the system gradually fades out of the Chinese urban society, people who regard the system of units as the ideal model of socialism may be somewhat regretful and even willing to attribute the failure of the system in contemporary China to various human errors. However, this is not the case. In this regard, the unit system building that the village has experienced in the process of spontaneous learning and approach to urban society provides a special confirmation.

Endnotes

1. See *City Express* of Hangzhou, February 11, 2000, p. 4.

2. See Overview of *Yunshi Township Jianshanxia Village*, 1993, pp. 9–10; 1994, pp. 11; 1995, pp. 11–14; 1996, p. 12, 14–15 and 17.

3. For example, before and after 1995, the monthly salary of employees was about 500–700 yuan (depending on the type of work), the monthly salary of workshop managers and above was 600–800 yuan, the salary of the Deputy General Manager and cadres of the "two village committees" was about 1,000 yuan and the General Manager about 1,500 yuan.

4. Saunders. *On the Community*, p. 373. In addition, as described in the previous chapter, villages had to remain non-open to the unit boundaries, thus blocking new resources into the village exchange and the enterprise exchange, which undoubtedly also blocked the enterprise's blood vessels.

5. For example, the company's articles of association emphasize that 15% of the provident fund and 5% of the public welfare fund shall be reserved from the net profit of the company. It is stipulated that in the future, the national tax reduction and exemption shall be collectively owned by the enterprise and shall not be distributed.

Bibliography

Alford RR. Paradigm of Relations between State and Society. *Stress and Contradictions in Modern Capitalism*. 1975: 145–160.

Baker HDR. *Chinese Family and Kinship*. New York: Columbia University Press, 1979.

Bell C and Newby H. *Community Studies: An Introduction to the Sociology of the Local Community*. New York: Praeger Publishers, 1972.

Bo YB. *A Review of Some Major Decisions and Events*, Vol. 1. Beijing: CPC Central School Press, 1991.

Brow P. *Exchange and Power in Social Life*. Trans. Sun F and Zhang LQ. Beijing: Huaxia Press, 1988.

Charles L. *Politics and Markets: The Political and Economic System of the World*. Trans. Wang YZ. Shanghai: SDX Joint Publishing Company, 1992.

Chen JY and Hu BL. *Village Economy and Village Culture in Contemporary China*. Taiyuan: Shanxi Economic Press, 1996.

CPC Central Party School. *Selected Documents of the CPC Central Committee*. Beijing: CPC Central Party School Press, 1992.

Friedman E, Pickowicz PG, Selden M *et al. Chinese Village, Socialist State*. New Haven, CT: Yale University Press, 1991.

Hu RY. *Inefficient Economics: Rethinking the Theory of Centralization*. Shanghai: Sanlian Bookstore, 1992.

Hu S. *Seventy Years of the Communist Party of China*. Beijing: CPC History Press, 1991.

Hu YS and Lu XY. *China's Economic opening and Social Structure Change*. Beijing: Social Sciences Literature Press, 1998.

Jing J. *The Temple of Memories: History, Power, and Morality in a Chinese Village*. Stanford: Stanford University Press, 1996.

Kornai J. *Shortage Economics*, Vols. 1 and 2. Trans. Zhang XG, *et al*. Beijing: Economic Science Press, 1986.

Li SJ and Qiu X. *A study on the Social Organization System at the Grass-roots Level in Rural China*. Beijing: China Agricultural Publishing House, 1994.

Lu F. Unit: A Special Form of Social Organization. *China Social Science*. 1989(1):71–80.

Madsen R. *Morality and Power in a Chinese Village*. California: University of California Press, 1984.

Nee V and Su SJ. Institutional Change and Economic Growth in China: The View from the Village. *The Journal of Asian Studies*. 1990, 49(1):3–25.

Oi JC. *State and Peasant in Contemporary China*. California: University of California Press, 1989.

Olson M. *Logic of Collective Action*. Trans. Chen Y *et al*. Shanghai: SDX Joint Publishing Company, 1995.

Parsons. *Structure and process of Modern Society*. Trans. Liang XY. Beijing: Guangming Daily Press, 1988.

Parsons T. *The Structure of Social Action*. New York: McGraw-Hill, 1937.

Pfeffer J. *Power in Organizations*. Marshfield, Mass: Pitman Publishing, 1981.

Pollinger K and Poplin DE. Communities: A Survey of Theories and Methods of Research. *Contemporary Sociology*. 1973, 2(6):616–618.

Rozelle S and Li JG. *Economic Behavior of Village Cadres in China's Economic Reform*. Beijing: Economic Management Press, 1992.

Shi JT. *Historical Materials of China's Agricultural Cooperative Movement*, Vol. 1. Beijing: SDX Joint Publishing Company, 1957.

Suttles GD. *The Social Construction of Communities*. Chicago: University of Chicago Press, 1972.

The General Office of the Communist Party of China (the CPC Central Committee). *Socialist Climax in Rural China*. Beijing: People's Press, 1956.

Walder AG. *Communist Neo-traditionalism: Word and Authority in Chinese Industry*. California: University of California Press, 1986.

Wang CG. *Social Changes in Rural China*. Kunming: Yunnan People's Publishing House, 1996.

Xu Y. *Chinese Rural Villager Autonomy*. Wuhan: Central China Normal University Press, 1997.

Xu Z. *Community and Social Development*. Taipei: Zhong Zheng Bookstore, 1970.

Yan YX. *The Flow of Gifts: Reciprocity and Social Networks in a Chinese Village*. Stanford: Stanford University Press, 1996.

Zhang HA. *China's Rural Grass-roots Regime Construction*. Chengdu: Sichuan people's Publishing House, 1982.

Zhang ZY, Huang FZ and Li GA. *Review and Prospect of Economic Reform in 20 Years*. Beijing: China Planning Press, 1998.

Zhe XY. Village: Pluralistic Border—Conflicts and Symbiosis between Economic Boundary Opening and Social Boundary Closure. *Chinese Social Science*. 1996(3):66–78.